A Multi-Intentioned View of the Extent of the Atonement

A Multi-Intentioned View of the Extent of the Atonement

GARY L. SHULTZ JR.

WIPF & STOCK · Eugene, Oregon

A MULTI-INTENTIONED VIEW OF THE EXTENT OF THE ATONEMENT

Copyright © 2013 Gary L. Shultz Jr. All rights reserved. Except for brief quotations in critical publications or reviews, no part of this book may be reproduced in any manner without prior written permission from the publisher. Write: Permissions. Wipf and Stock Publishers, 199 W. 8th Ave., Suite 3, Eugene, OR 97401.

"Scripture quotations taken from the New American Standard Bible®, Copyright © 1960, 1962, 1963, 1968, 1971, 1972, 1973, 1975, 1977, 1995 by The Lockman Foundation Used by permission." (www.Lockman.org)

Wipf & Stock
An Imprint of Wipf and Stock Publishers
199 W. 8th Ave., Suite 3
Eugene, OR 97401

www.wipfandstock.com

ISBN 13: 978-1-62032-846-0

Manufactured in the U.S.A.

To Kristin, my wife, my love, and my best friend

Contents

Foreword by Bruce Ware | ix
Acknowledgments | xiii

CHAPTER 1 Introduction | 1

CHAPTER 2 Historical Background for a Multi-Intentioned View | 12

CHAPTER 3 Jesus Christ's Payment for the Sins of All People in the Atonement | 54

CHAPTER 4 The General Intentions of the Atonement | 89

CHAPTER 5 The Particular Intentions of the Atonement | 122

CHAPTER 6 Conclusion | 153

Bibliography | 161
Name Index | 177
Scripture Index | 183

Foreword
by Bruce Ware

ONE MARVELS AT THE difficulty evangelical Christians have had in answering what appears to be a very simple and straight-forward question: "For whom did Christ die?" At one level, we all agree – Christ died for sinners. Amen and amen! But when we probe a bit further and inquire, "Do you mean that he died for all sinners or just those sinners who believe and are saved in the end?" the answers reveal fundamental differences of understanding that exist among committed, Bible-believing, evangelically minded, gospel embracing Christians.

A significant complicating factor that has contributed both to the level of confusion and disagreement among us is the simple observation that most Christians, indeed most theologians, since the time of the Reformation have sought to give a single answer to the question, "For whom did Christ die?" Calvinists in the line of Theodore Beza and the dominant camp of Reformed theology have answered this question in clear and simple – and singular — terms: "Christ died for the elect." That is, they have understood the extent of the atonement, as taught in Scripture, to encompass all of those, but only those, who will be eternally saved through Christ's atoning death (e.g., John 10:11, 15; Acts 20:28; Eph 5:25). In understanding the extent of the atonement, then, as encompassing only the elect, they have seen this doctrine of particular redemption (or limited atonement, as it is named in the famous acrostic TULIP) to exhibit a beautiful symmetry with the doctrines of unconditional election, irresistible grace, and perseverance of the saints – all of which, then, focus on those whom God, in his mercy and kindness, has ordained from eternity past to save. Those whom God has chosen from before the foundation of the world to be saved (unconditional election), those to whom he provides grace that unfailingly brings them to saving faith (irresistible grace), and those whom he will not fail to save in the end (perseverance of the saints), are also those for whom Christ has died certainly and efficaciously to save (limited atonement). This line of Five-point Calvinists, then, understands limited atonement or particular redemption as cut from the same cloth, as it were, as these other doctrines of grace, showing God's unmerited favor and eternal love for the grouping of sinners whom he has ordained from eternity past to save.

But Five-point Calvinists are not the only group to offer a simple and single answer to the question, "For whom did Christ die?" Arminians in the line of Jacob Arminius and John Wesley offer an answer to this question also in clear and simple – and singular – terms: "Christ died for all people, at all times, everywhere." That is, they have understood the extent of the atonement, as taught in Scripture, to encompass all of the human race, descended from Adam (e.g., John 3:16; Rom 5:8, 15; 1 Tim 2:6; 1 John 2:2). In understanding the extent of the atonement, then, as encompassing all sinful humans without exception, they have seen this doctrine of unlimited atonement to exhibit the universality and impartiality of God's love for all people everywhere. Since God loves all the people in the world (John 3:16a), he sent his Son to die for all these sinful human beings (John 3:16b), that whoever believes in the Christ who died for them might be saved (John 3:16c). Even though only those who believe in Christ will receive the forgiveness of sin that Christ purchased for all when he died on the cross, nevertheless, Christ's death is no more for some than it is for others. In God's love for all, he sent his Son who "died for all" (2 Cor 5:14, 15), so that those who believe may be saved. The universal love of God for all, then, stands behind the death of Christ which is for all.

What these two major theological positions have in common on this issue is this: both believe that the death of Christ is fundamentally for a single intended purpose. Calvinist advocates of particular redemption argue that since God has elected only some to be saved, Christ therefore died for the single intention of saving those elect persons; Arminian advocates of unlimited atonement argue that since God equally and impartially loves all people in all of the world throughout all of time, Christ therefore died for the single intention of paying for the sin of all those people whom God loves so that any and all who believe in Christ may be saved. With these very different understandings of both the extent of the atoning work of Christ and what divine intention stands behind each of these respective views of that atoning death, there seems to be no middle ground, no mediating position that might seek to incorporate both sets of biblical teachings and insights from the truth of God's word that each side may have.

The beauty of a multi-intentioned model of the extent of the atonement can be seen exactly at this point. Might it not be the case that God's intentions in the atoning death of Christ are multiple, not single? Might it not be that in the cross of Christ God intends both to demonstrate his universal love for all of sinful humanity (John 3:16) while also intending by this death surely and certainly to save those whom he has chosen as his own from before the foundation of the world (Eph 1:3–8)? In other words, might there not be multiple intentions that God designs in the death of Christ, not just one single intention? And if so, might there be a way forward to incorporate more naturally all that Scripture teaches concerning Christ's death, some of which teaching shows God's broader intentions and some of which shows his narrower intentions?

A multiple intentions view of the extent of the atonement captured my own imagination during the earliest years of my teaching theology, even before I had completed my doctoral work. Over many years now of teaching theology, I continue to be drawn to this both/and model, and find it a compelling way to understand even more of the greatness of God's purposes in the death of Christ than either of the single intention models are able to show. For this reason, I am grateful for the excellent treatment and defense of a multi-intentioned view of the extent of the atonement that Dr. Gary Shultz has provided for us here. It was my great delight to have Gary as my doctoral student at Southern Seminary, and now it is my joy to commend to readers this informative and insightful study. May God be honored through this work, as the cross of Christ is examined to understand more fully the glorious intentions of God in the death of his dear Son.

Bruce A. Ware
Professor of Christian Theology
The Southern Baptist Theological Seminary
Louisville, Kentucky

Acknowledgments

MANY PEOPLE CONTRIBUTED TO the completion of this book. As a revision of my doctoral dissertation, I am thankful for my professors and fellow students at the Southern Baptist Theological Seminary who sharpened my thinking concerning the extent of the atonement and continually encouraged me in my work on this topic. I am particularly thankful for the guidance of my dissertation committee, including Chad Brand, David Puckett, and my supervisor and doctoral mentor Bruce Ware, who also graciously provided the foreword for this work. I am grateful for the prayers and support of my church, First Baptist Church in Fulton, MO, a wonderful group of believers whom I have the privilege of pastoring. My understanding and appreciation of Christ's work on the cross has only increased as we have worshipped him together. I have taught the content of this book to several classes of students at Baptist Bible Theological Seminary, and I am grateful for their feedback, as well as the prayers and interaction of my fellow professors. My family, especially my parents and in-laws, Gary and Susan Shultz and Tim and Joy Gray, has always encouraged this work, and I am thankful for their support.

The person who has contributed the most to this project, however, is my wife, Kristin. Without her love, support, encouragement, and sacrifice, I would have never finished this book. I started writing on the extent of the atonement in 2005, two years after we were married, and from that time until now we have experienced many significant life changes together, from finishing our educations to having two little girls. Throughout it all she has truly been the personification of God's grace in my life (Prov 18:22), a living reminder of the gifts that Jesus Christ died to provide for me. I dedicate this book to her.

Finally, all praise, glory, and honor to my God and Savior, Jesus Christ. It has truly been a privilege to spend so much of my life studying and reflecting upon the atonement, and what God has done for humanity through the sacrifice of his Son. I hope this book leads others to see the glory of Christ's cross and to embrace the salvation he has accomplished for us.

CHAPTER 1

Introduction

THE DEBATE OVER THE EXTENT OF THE ATONEMENT

AT ISSUE IN THE extent of the atonement is the question: for whom did Jesus Christ die? Evangelicals have debated the answer to that question since the Reformation with no consensus, though the issue can be traced back to the earliest days of church history. The recent revival of Calvinist theology within evangelicalism has only intensified the debate, as the extent of the atonement is the most disputed of the "five points of Calvinism."[1] As Calvinists and Arminians continue to contrast their respective systems of theology, the extent of the atonement continues to be a point of contention.[2] Other reasons contribute to the ongoing nature of this debate as well. Scripture refers to it often, but almost always indirectly, and in the context of other doctrinal or practical matters, which makes it open to different interpretations. Those on both sides of the debate often talk past each other, using the same vocabulary but defining their terms differently, which produces unnecessary confusion. Uncharitable and arrogant rhetoric often drives those

---

1. This revival has been chronicled in many places, most notably in Hansen, *Young, Restless*.

2. Dozens of books have been published since the turn of the century, describing the merits of either the Calvinist or the Arminian theological system and the demerits of the other, including discussions of the corresponding positions on the extent of the atonement. Two recent books are representative: Horton, *For Calvinism* and Olson, *Against Calvinism*.

on both sides of the issue to accentuate their differences, preventing healthy discussion and circumventing consensus.[3]

Traditionally there have been two primary evangelical positions regarding the extent of the atonement.[4] Either Jesus died only for those who experience the saving benefits of his atonement, or he died for all people regardless of their salvific destiny. The former position is most commonly referred to as "limited atonement," but is also called "definite atonement" or "particular redemption."[5] Particular redemption asserts that God offered his Son, Jesus Christ, as an atoning sacrifice in order to save a particular group of people, his elect, and therefore Christ only paid for the sins of the elect. Christ's death did not make salvation possible for all people, though there is some disagreement concerning the sufficiency of the atonement for all of humanity.[6] Supporters of particular redemption base their position in part upon verses of Scripture that seem to restrict the atonement to those who are saved, such as Matthew 1:21; John 6:37–40; 10:11, 15; Acts 20:28; Romans 8:31–39; 2 Corinthians 5:15; Ephesians 5:25; Titus 2:14; and Revelation 5:9. They also appeal to several biblical and theological arguments to make their case. Supporters of particular redemption assert:

1. Since God is completely sovereign, and his will can never be thwarted, all people would be saved if Christ died for all people, because Christ would desire to save everyone for whom he died, and therefore unlimited atonement logically results in universalism.

---

[3]. Andrew Naselli gives ten suggestions for avoiding schism on this issue in "John Owen's Argument," 60–82.

[4]. Throughout this book, when we speak of Christ's atonement, or his atoning sacrifice, we are referring to what Christ accomplished to make salvation possible, or penal substitution, in which God gave himself in the person of Jesus Christ to suffer the punishment of death rightly due to fallen sinners as the consequence of sin. Christ suffered the wrath of God against sin in the place of humanity, satisfying God's justice and holiness and manifesting his love, so that anyone who believes in Christ by faith is saved from his sin and has an eternal relationship with God. Penal substitution is the foundation of all the other dimensions of the atonement, such as the conquering of evil and the display of God's love toward humanity and hatred toward sin.

[5]. Throughout this book we will refer to this position as "particular redemption" instead of "limited atonement." Many who hold to this position dislike the term "limited atonement" because they believe that the name has put the position at a disadvantage, for who wants to believe in an atonement that is limited in some way? See Letham, *The Work of Christ*, 228–29; and Nicole, "Particular Redemption," 168–69.

[6]. Berkhof, *Systematic Theology* 393–94; Grudem, *Systematic Theology*, 597; and Nicole, "Particular Redemption," 166. Advocates of particular redemption who deny the sufficiency of Christ's atonement for all people include Theodore Beza and John Gill, but this is a minority position and one rejected by Reformed creeds such as the Canons of Dort (1619) and the Westminster Confession (1646). For a contemporary representative of this position, see Nettles, *By His Grace and For His Glory*, 305–22.

2. If Christ paid for every person's sins, then God would be unjust to send anyone to hell, because he would then be making them pay for sins that had already been paid for by Christ. If even the sin of unbelief is paid for, then God would be unjust to punish sinners for their unbelief.

3. Since Christ died to actually secure salvation for his people (Rom 5:10; Gal 1:4, 3:13; Eph 1:7), he could not have died for all people because not all people are saved.

4. Scripture seems to present Christ's atonement and intercession as coextensive (John 17), which means that Christ only died for those for whom he also intercedes, the elect.

5. Unlimited atonement creates conflict within the Trinity because it has the Son working to save all people while the Father and the Spirit work to save only the elect.

6. Unlimited atonement undermines union with Christ, for if believers are presently united with Christ, they were certainly united with him in his death and resurrection.

Many consider particular redemption to be the traditional Calvinist position, though it has never been a consensus view within Calvinism.[7]

The second answer given to the question of whom Jesus died for is that Jesus died for every single person who has ever lived and who ever will live. This position is most popularly known as "unlimited atonement," but is also called "general atonement," "general redemption," or "universal atonement."[8] Unlimited atonement asserts that God offered his Son as an atoning sacrifice in order to pay for the sins of everyone in the entire world. This atonement then makes salvation possible for all people, without exception, and becomes effective when accepted by the individual through faith. Unlimited atonement appeals to Scriptures such as Isaiah 53:6; John 3:16; Romans 5:6-8; 2 Corinthians 5:14-15, 19; 1 Timothy 2:4-6; 4:10; 2 Peter 2:1; 3:9; 1 John 2:2; and 4:14. Like advocates of particular redemption,

---

7. For a representative argument of particular redemption, see Owen, *Death of Death* along with the introductory essay in that book by J. I. Packer. Other representative evangelical explanations of the position include Berkhof, *Systematic Theology*, 392-99; Grudem, *Systematic Theology*, 594-603; Hodge, *Systematic Theology*, 2:544-62; Kuiper, *For Whom Did Christ Die*; Letham, *Work of Christ*, 225-47; Long, *Definite Atonement;*, 57-74; Murray, *Redemption Accomplished and Applied*, 59-75; and Nicole, "Definite Atonement," 199-207.

8. We will refer to this position throughout this book as "unlimited atonement." It should not be confused with universalism, or the idea that all people will be saved, which is not part of this position.

supporters of unlimited atonement also use several biblical and theological arguments to advance their position. They assert:

1. Since God loves all people, it is inconceivable that he would send Christ to die for only part of the human race.
2. God's desire for the salvation of all people demands an unlimited atonement (1 Tim 2:4; 2 Pet 3:9).
3. The universal gospel offer demands an unlimited atonement.
4. The atonement does not automatically save the elect; Christians must put their faith in Christ's atonement for it to save them, therefore unlimited atonement does not necessarily result in universalism.
5. God is not unfair in sending those whom Christ died for to hell as long as they are not in Christ through faith.
6. Passages of Scripture that describe the atonement as being for believers do not necessarily rule out other passages of Scripture that speak of it being for all people.

Unlimited atonement is the traditional Arminian, Lutheran, and Catholic position, and some Calvinists hold to it as well.

Many consider the Calvinist understanding of unlimited atonement to be different enough from the non-Calvinist understanding so as to be considered on its own. Disagreement between the Calvinist and non-Calvinist positions has to do with the intent, or purpose, of the atonement. The majority of those in the unlimited atonement camp, Arminians and non-Calvinists, believe Christ's intent in the atonement was to pay for the sins of all humanity equally.[9] Calvinists who hold to unlimited atonement, however, believe that Christ paid for the sins of all humanity, but he did so with different intentions for the elect and nonelect.[10] Labels such as Amyraldianism, hypothetical universalism, limited/unlimited atonement, four-point Calvinism, and moderate Calvinism all have been used of this position. Many evangelicals use one of these terms as a blanket term for all Calvinistic proposals of the extent of the atonement, but there are significant differences in some of these proposals.[11] While none of the Calvinistic

---

9. E.g., Marshall, "For All," 322–46; and Picirilli, *Grace, Faith, Free Will*, 85–138.

10. E.g., Demarest, *Cross and Salvation*, 189–93; and Lightner, *Death Christ Died*, 46–37. Allen refers to this position as "dualism." Allen, "The Atonement," 63.

11. As we will see in chapter 2, blanket labels such as Amyraldianism and hypothetical universalism are therefore unhelpful because they cover up these differences. Each of these labels refers to a particular position. The labels of moderate Calvinism or four-point Calvinism are also open to misinterpretation, but are more helpful in that they are broader. Therefore we will refer to unlimited atonement from a Calvinist

positions on the atonement have created widespread consensus, this recognition of more than one purpose in the atonement offers us a promising way forward in the debate.

THE NEED FOR A MULTI-INTENTIONED APPROACH

The debate over the extent of the atonement centers on the intent or purpose of the atonement. Louis Berkhof puts it this way: "On the other hand, the question does relate to the design of the atonement. Did the Father in sending Christ, and did Christ in coming into the world, to make atonement for sin, do this with the design or for the purpose of only saving the elect or all men? That is the question and that only is the question."[12] In seeking to ascertain whom Christ died for on the cross, both particular redemption and unlimited atonement attempt to explain the purpose or intent that God had in the atonement. Particular redemption holds that God's intention was effectually to bring about salvation for a specific group of people, and therefore Christ died only for those people. Unlimited atonement holds that God's intention in the atonement was to provide a payment for the sins of all people, a payment that becomes effective at the moment of saving faith, and therefore there is no one for whom Christ did not die.

The way the issue is normally framed, however, leads one to assume that there is only one purpose, or at least only one predominate purpose, in the atonement, and therefore the answer to the question of the extent of the atonement lies in discovering that one, right purpose. The traditional positions lead us to ask if the atonement is absolutely efficacious, or is it merely provisional? Either Christ only died for the salvation of the elect, or he only died to pay for the sins of humanity. This is problematic, however, for two reasons. First, both purposes stress clear biblical truths. Particular redemption emphasizes God's sovereignty in salvation, the objective nature of the atonement, and God's special love for the elect. On the other hand,

---

perspective as "moderate Calvinism" or "four-point Calvinism."

12. Berkhof, *Systematic Theology*, 394. Advocates of both unlimited atonement and particular redemption agree with this statement. See Demarest, *Cross and Salvation*, 193; Letham, *Work of Christ*, 225–26; Lightner, *Death Christ Died*, 33; Nicole, "Definite Atonement," 200; Picirilli, *Grace, Faith, and Free Will*, 103–04; and Wells, *Cross Words*, 236–39. Grudem, however, disagrees with this approach. He believes that it is just another form of the larger dispute between Calvinists and Arminians. Instead, he focuses on the question of whether or not Christ paid for the sins of those who are eternally condemned, and he answers no. Grudem, *Systematic Theology*, 601. This is an important question to ask, and one that we will deal with in this book, but it is also a question that can only be answered by considering the purpose(s) of the atonement.

unlimited atonement emphasizes God's love for all people and God's desire for all people to be saved.

Even more importantly, focusing on only one purpose leads one to contradict other aspects of biblical teaching. Particular redemption has historically had a difficult time explaining the meaning of words such as "world" and "all" that the Scripture uses in relation to the saving work of Christ (e.g., Isa 53:6; 2 Cor 5:14–15, 19; 1 Tim 2:4–6; 4:10; 1 John 2:2).[13] Particular redemption seems to contradict verses in Scripture that speak of the atonement as being for unbelievers (2 Pet 2:1) or that speak of its universal implications (Col 1:19–20), though many supporters of particular redemption recognize at least some of the atonement's universal benefits.[14] Some have argued that particular redemption has a difficult time explaining why the universal gospel call is necessary.[15] Many proponents of unlimited atonement also find it difficult to understand why the atonement would be sufficient for all, as most advocates of particular redemption claim, if Christ only died for the sins of the elect.[16]

Unlimited atonement seems to avoid the difficulties of particular redemption but has other problems of its own. It is difficult in the unlimited view to account for numerous Scriptures that seem to emphasize the definite and special relationship between Christ's atonement and believers (e.g., Matt 1:21; John 6:37–40; 10:11, 15; 15:13; Acts 20:28; Rom 8:31–39; Eph 5:25; and Titus 2:14), though advocates of unlimited atonement usually respond to this argument by remarking that if Christ died for all, then in certain situations there is no problem with stating that he died for a particular group of people.[17] It is difficult to reconcile the doctrines of unlimited atonement and unconditional election.[18] Unlimited atonement seems to diminish or at least

---

13. This is not to say that advocates of particular redemption have not attempted to explain what these verses mean. For example, John Owen went to great lengths to explain why verses that employed such seemingly universal terms as "world" and "all" were not speaking in universal terms. Owen, *Death of Death*, 190–204.

14. E.g., Kuiper, *For Whom Did Christ Die?*, 78–100.

15. E.g., Chafer, "For Whom Did Christ Die?," 315; Shultz, Jr., "Why a Genuine," 111–23.

16. E.g., Erickson, *Christian Theology*, 852.

17. Sailer is typical when he writes "If Christ died for *all* men, then it is certainly permissible to say that he died for some men when a more intimate group is in the purview of the writer." Sailer, "Wesleyan View," 191. This position is correct as far as it goes, but it does not account for the special relationship between Christ's atonement and believers that these verses seem to emphasize.

18. For now we will assume the truth of unconditional election, which can be defined as "God's gracious choice, made in eternity past, of those whom he would save by faith through the atoning death of his Son, a choice based not upon anything that

call into question God's sovereignty in salvation, as God's plan to provide salvation to all people is rejected by so many.[19] Arminians also assert that the atonement provided prevenient grace for all people, and that the atonement cleanses all people from the guilt of Adam's original sin.[20] The biblical validity of an Arminian view of prevenient grace, however, seems dubious.[21]

The primary problem with both of these positions is that they seem unnecessarily to restrict God's intentions in sending his Son to die on the cross to a single intention, either dying to specifically save the elect or dying to make salvation available for all people. In doing so neither position is able to account, as we will argue, for all of the relevant biblical texts or the theological factors that impact the debate. Moderate Calvinist answers to the extent of the atonement have rightly recognized that the solution to this quandary is to recognize that both purposes are biblical, but these proposals have normally highlighted one intention over another and failed to explain how the multiple purposes of the atonement fit together. Neither have these proposals consistently distinguished themselves from the two traditional positions and called for a third position as viable alternative. There is a need for a position that highlights the multiple intentions of the atonement, preserves the strengths of both traditional positions, and overcomes their weaknesses. I have labeled this position the "multi-intentioned view." Some evangelicals have begun to call for a view of the extent of the atonement that moves beyond particular redemption and unlimited atonement by explicitly recognizing the multiple intentions of the atonement.[22] There has yet to be,

---

those so chosen would do, or any choice that they would make, or on how good or bad they might be, or on anything else specifically true about them (i.e., their qualities, characters, decisions, or actions) in contrast to others, but rather based only upon God's own good pleasure and will." Ware, "Divine Election," 4. We will defend the truth of unconditional election in chapter 5.

19. Boettner, *Reformed Doctrine*, 156.

20. Dunning, *Grace, Faith, and Holiness*: 339; Langford, *Practical Divinity*, 34; Olson, *Arminian Theology*, 158–78; and Wiley, *Christian Theology*, 2:353.

21. Combs, "Does the Bible," 3–17; Demarest, *Cross and Salvation*, 83–84; Erickson, *Christian Theology*, 938; and Schreiner, "Does Scripture Teach Prevenient Grace," 229–46.

22. E.g., Carson, *The Difficult Doctrine of the Love of God*, 73–79; Culver, *Systematic Theology*, 572–91; Demarest, *Cross and Salvation*, 189–95; Driscoll and Breshears, *Death by Love*, 163–81; Hansen, "Two Aspects," 85–98; Lewis and Demarest, *Integrative Theology*, 2:409–10; Nelson, "Design, Nature, and Extent of the Atonement," 115–38; and Ware, "Extent of the Atonement," 1–5. G. Michael Thomas's historical study of the debate over the extent of the atonement in Reformed theology from 1536–1675 points toward the validity of this view as well, although Thomas's brief conclusion seems to favor Karl Barth's understanding of the extent of the atonement, which ends up in a universal election of all of humanity in the atonement. Thomas, *The Extent of the Atonement*.

however, a full-length book explaining and defending a multi-intentioned view. This book intends to fill that void.

A MULTI-INTENTIONED VIEW OF THE EXTENT OF THE ATONEMENT

Therefore the purpose of this study is to develop, explain, and defend, both biblically and theologically, a multi-intentioned view of the extent of the atonement. In the course of this explanation and defense we will see that a multi-intentioned view is more consistent with all of the relevant biblical texts concerning the extent of the atonement and that it fits more smoothly into an overall theological framework then either particular redemption or unlimited atonement. A multi-intentioned view holds that God the Father, in sending his Son to die on the cross, had both particular and general intentions for the atonement. In accordance with the Father's will, the Son then died to fulfill these multiple intentions. Based upon the Son's atoning death on the cross, the Spirit then works to apply the atonement in both particular and in general ways. God's multiple intentions in the atonement indicate that the atonement is in some ways for all people, but that it is for the elect in certain ways in which it is not for all people. God's particular intention in the atonement was to secure the salvation of the elect.[23] The Son fulfills this intention by sending the Holy Spirit to apply salvation to the elect on the basis of his atoning work. The Father's general intention in the atonement was for the Son to pay the penalty for the sins of all people.[24] He did this in order to make the universal gospel call possible, to make common grace (and not only salvific grace) possible, to provide an additional basis of condemnation for those who reject the gospel, to serve as the supreme example of God's character, and to make the reconciliation of all things possible.

Our study will be primarily constructive, that is, we intend to put forth a multi-intentioned view as a viable theological understanding of the extent of the atonement. Our purposes are only secondarily polemical, in that as the multi-intentioned view is constructed, we will demonstrate its advantages both biblically and theologically to the alternative positions. As a constructive theological assertion, we will establish the validity of the multi-intentioned view by demonstrating its coherence, comprehensiveness, adequacy, and consistency.

23. We will call this purpose "particular" in that it only applies to a particular group of people, the elect.

24. We will call this purpose "general" in that it applies to people in general, both the elect and the nonelect.

We will express the coherence of the multi-intentioned view by demonstrating how it coheres with Scripture. We assume the truth of *Sola Scriptura*, that the Bible is inspired, inerrant, and absolutely authoritative in all matters of faith and practice. As Richard Lints states, "The biblical revelation is the final court of appeals for the theologian."[25] Therefore it is necessary to establish the multi-intentioned view from Scripture by carefully determining what Scripture says on the subject. While there are those who claim that biblical exegesis cannot resolve the debate over contentious doctrines such as the extent of the atonement, the most likely interpretations of the biblical texts must be allowed to affect and even change one's theological framework.[26] To assert otherwise is to contradict the evangelical position on the authority of Scripture. For this reason the third, fourth, and fifth chapters of this book will support the multi-intentioned view biblically by examining the passages of Scripture that speak to this issue and showing what they contribute to the doctrine. The exegesis of the relevant biblical texts will also establish the comprehensiveness of the multi-intentioned view, as the entire Bible's teaching on the extent of the atonement is taken into account.

In addition to establishing the coherency and comprehensiveness of the multi-intentioned view, chapters 3 through 5 will also establish the consistency of the multi-intentioned view. The consistency of a doctrine is established by showing how it fits within an entire theological system. Since God is the author of the Bible, doctrines will always be consistent with other doctrines. If a doctrine is not consistent with other clearly established biblical doctrines, this is a good indication that it is not a viable doctrine. We will see that the multi-intentioned view is internally consistent as well as more consistent with other important Christian doctrines then the alternative views and, therefore, a more viable theological option.

Chapter 3 will establish the biblical and theological basis for understanding Christ's atonement as a payment for the sins of all people, elect and nonelect. The Scriptures that express this truth are Isaiah 53:4–6; John 1:29; 3:16–17; 4:42; 6:51; 12:46–47; 2 Corinthians 5:14–15, 18–21; 1 Timothy 2:4–6, 4:10; Titus 2:11; Hebrews 2:9; 2 Peter 2:1; 1 John 2:2; and 4:14. Chapter 3 will exegete and explain what these passages teach concerning the extent of the atonement in four sections: Isaiah 53:4–6, the Johannine literature, the Pauline literature, and the General Epistles. A section that explains

---

25. Lints, *The Fabric of Theology*, 66.

26. E.g., Strange, *An Analysis of Inclusivism*, 23. Marshall responds to Strange's assertion by stressing the importance of establishing any theological position from Scripture and explaining what one should do when both sides of a debate claim that they are being more "biblical" then the other. Marshall, "For All," 323–25.

why a complete and unlimited payment for sin does not entail universalism will follow the biblical defense of Christ's payment for the sins of all people.

Chapter 4 will focus on the biblical and theological explanation of God's general intentions in the atonement. God the Father sent God the Son to the cross in order to pay for the sin of all people so that he could make the universal gospel call possible, so that he could provide an additional basis of condemnation for those who hear the gospel and reject it, so that he could provide common grace to all of his creation, so that he could provide the supreme example of his character, and so that he could reconcile all things to himself. This biblical and theological explanation will establish the atonement's general intentions.

Chapter 5 will focus on the biblical explanation of God's particular intention in the atonement: securing the salvation of the elect. In this chapter we will first seek to biblically establish God's intention of securing the salvation of the elect in the atonement. This intention is evident because of God's sovereignty throughout salvation, his special love for the elect, and the unity of the Father and the Son in salvation. We will then biblically and theologically establish Christ's accomplishment of this particular intention. Christ accomplished the securing of the salvation of the elect by sending the Spirit to apply salvation to the elect on the basis of his atonement. This chapter will also explain how the particular aspects of the atonement cohere with the universal aspects.

The fourth criterion of validity for a theological assertion is adequacy. Using this criterion, we will establish that the multi-intentioned view is a more viable description of the biblical texts then competing views. We will do this in two ways. First, the chapters of biblical and theological explanation will demonstrate how the multi-intentioned view makes the best sense of all the relevant biblical information. Before we can do this, however, we will need to explain how others throughout church history have made sense of the biblical teaching and theological arguments concerning the extent of the atonement. Therefore chapter 2 of this book will offer an historical survey of the extent of the atonement. While Scripture is the primary, normative source for theology, historical considerations help us see how the Holy Spirit has illuminated others and keep us from being blinded by contemporary concerns. Chapter 2 will not only help us see the validity of the multi-intentioned view, but place it in its context. This historical background will show the development of the doctrine throughout church history and will include representative explanations of particular redemption, unlimited atonement, and moderate Calvinist views.

Following the historical considerations and the biblical and theological support for the multi-intentioned view, chapter 6 will serve as a conclusion to our study. Chapter 6 will recapitulate and review our findings, offer some practical and theological implications, and lay out a view of where we might go from here in the debate over the extent of the atonement. I believe at the conclusion of this study you will see that a multi-intentioned view does the best job of incorporating all of what the Bible says about the extent of the atonement, is more theologically comprehensive than other views of the extent of the atonement, and has the best potential for consensus on who exactly Jesus Christ died for when he was crucified for our sins.

CHAPTER 2

Historical Background for a Multi-Intentioned View

INTRODUCTION

DOCTRINAL DEBATE DOES NOT form in a vacuum, and that is certainly evident in the doctrine of the extent of the atonement. The evangelical debate between particular redemption and unlimited atonement traces its roots back to the debate over the doctrine during the Reformation, which in turn goes back to Augustine. In order to set the multi-intentioned view of the extent of the atonement in its proper context, we will therefore trace the development of the doctrine of the extent of the atonement from the time of Augustine to the present, investigating important explanations and eras in the doctrine's history. The historical context of the debate demonstrates that while unlimited atonement has always been the majority view of the church, particular redemption has been a persistent minority view. There have also been a number of moderate Calvinist attempts to explain this doctrine. The continuing disagreement in the debate and the persistence of both particular redemption and moderate Calvinist views lend credence to the multi-intentioned view, as it attempts to emphasize the strengths of both views and provide a more comprehensive explanation of the doctrine. Historical considerations also help us see that despite views that have come close to it, there has yet to be a detailed explanation of a multi-intentioned view.

AUGUSTINE

Before Augustine (354–430) there was no debate over the extent of the atonement. The early church fathers before Augustine held to unlimited atonement. The dominant understanding of the atonement in the early church was Irenaeus's recapitulation theory, which holds that just as all people were somehow present in Adam, so were they somehow present in Christ, which of course demands an unlimited atonement.[1] It was not until the doctrinal debate between Augustine and Pelagius that dispute arose over the issue.[2] At the heart of their debate were opposite understandings of human nature, which resulted in opposite understandings of God's grace, salvation, and sin. This point is so accepted among scholars on both sides of the issue that almost all historical works on the extent of the atonement begin their discussion with Augustine.[3]

Pelagius taught that human beings had an unconditional free will and therefore the ability by nature to act rightly or wrongly. God has given human beings the power to act, and it is completely up to them how they act. Human beings have the ability to obey God completely and to eschew sin, and they are obliged to do so. Based on his notion of human nature, Pelagius rejected the doctrine of original sin and taught that humans' wills have no bias toward sin as a result of the Fall; Adam's sin is merely propagated by example. These conceptions of human nature and sin led Pelagius to assert that grace was universal and merely God's demonstration to humanity of how to act in order to receive salvation.[4]

Believing that Pelagianism was not only unbiblical, but compromised the gospel, Augustine voiced his opposition to Pelagius and asserted the doctrines of original sin and God's sovereign grace. Augustine taught that humanity was created free, with the ability not to sin (*posse non peccare*), but that because of its fall into sin the human race is now without the ability not to sin (*non posse non peccare*).[5] The entire human race was in Adam when he sinned, and therefore the entire human race is a mass of damnation

---

1. Kelly, *Early Christian Doctrines*, 376–77.

2. Bavinck, *Sin and Salvation*, 456; Davenant, *Dissertation*, 318–19; Thomas, *The Extent of the Atonement*, 4; Turretin, *Institutes*, 2:455.

3. Bavinck, *Sin and Salvation*, 456; Blacketer, "Definite Atonement in Historical Perspective," 307–08; Davenant, *Dissertation*, 317–39; Elwell, "Atonement, Extent of," 115. Jarvis Williams has recently attempted to demonstrate that several patristic theologians held to particular redemption, but this is unconvincing, as all of his references can be easily be understood within an unlimited atonement framework. Williams, *For Whom Did Christ Die?*, 2–11.

4. Pelikan, *The Emergence of the Catholic Tradition*, 315.

5. Augustine, *The Perfection of Human Righteousness*, 292.

(*massa damnationis*).⁶ Each human being still has a free will, but one's free will is in bondage to sin and can only choose to sin.⁷ Therefore the will of a person must be transformed if he or she is to desire salvation. God imparts to some the ability to choose him, and this is his grace; he makes unwilling people willing to choose him.⁸ This view of grace led Augustine to assert that God has predestined all who will be saved, the elect, by an act of his sovereign will and according to his own good pleasure; all others are left justly condemned in their sins.⁹

Augustine's attempts to protect and preserve God's sovereign grace in salvation led him to touch on the extent of the atonement. For if the Father has predestined the elect to salvation and the Spirit only redeems the elect, then it seems that Christ's intention on the cross would be in harmony with the Father's and the Spirit's intentions in the salvation. Therefore his atonement would only be for the elect. Although Augustine never explicitly stated this view, he made some statements that point strongly in this direction. For example, he equated those who were predestined to those whom Jesus had come to redeem by the shedding of his blood.¹⁰ Augustine indicated that those who were not elect were not bought by the blood of Christ's atonement.¹¹ Augustine also stressed that the blood of Christ was a special gift for the elect and that Christ's death actually saved those people for whom it was intended.¹²

More indicative of Augustine's view on the extent of the atonement, however, are several statements that he makes in regard to many of the texts normally used to defend unlimited atonement. Augustine understands the term "world" in John 3:16–17 and 2 Corinthians 5:19 not in universal terms, but as referring to the "world of the elect."¹³ He interprets 1 John 2:2 as stating that Christ is the propitiation for the "whole world" in the

---

6. Augustine, *On the Gift of Perseverance*, 302–04.

7. Augustine, *Answer to the Two Letters of the Pelagians*, 117–18.

8. Augustine, *Enchiridion*, 62–63.

9. Augustine, *On the Predestination of the Saints*, 241–42.

10. Augustine, "Sermon 138," 388.

11. Augustine, "*Tractatus in Joannis Evangelium*," vol. 35, column 1742. Concerning this statement, Jonathan Rainbow notes "The apposition of the phrases *ad sempiternam interitum praedestinatos* and *non ad vitam aeternam sui sanguinis praetio comparatos* was theologically significant; it showed that in Augustine's mind predestination to destruction and not having been won to eternal life by the blood of Christ were parallel concepts, for both concepts describes those who are not 'sheep.' And the sheep in this context were the elect." Rainbow, *The Will of God and the Cross*, 12.

12. Augustine, in *Corpus Christianorum, Series Latina*, 36:404, 498.

13. Augustine, "Sermon 121," 234.

sense that he is the propitiation for the "Church in all nations, the Church throughout the whole world."[14] Augustine also understands the universalism of John 1:9 and 1 Timothy 2:4-6 in a restricted manner.[15] All of the verses that Augustine could have used to argue for an unlimited atonement he instead interpreted in a way that restricts the atonement to the elect only. These interpretations indicate that Augustine believed the extent of Christ's atonement was limited to the elect.[16]

The church generally affirmed Augustine's views on grace, sin, and salvation at the Council of Carthage (418), whereas the church deemed Pelagianism as heresy. Several of the subsequent followers of Augustine and his theology also seemed to limit Christ's death on the cross to the elect alone.[17] For the most part, however, the Catholic Church never accepted some of Augustine's more controversial doctrines, such as his doctrine of double predestination[18] and his understanding of Christ's atonement as being only for the predestined elect. As Rainbow states, "Augustine bequeathed a problem to his successors in the middle ages: they all wanted to be 'Augustinian,' but very few of them wanted to believe that God did not really will the salvation of every human, had predestined some to life and some to damnation (what Isidore of Seville, writing some two hundred years later, would call 'double predestination'), and had sent Christ only for those predestined to eternal life."[19] The Synod of Orange (529) affirmed a moderate form of Augustine's

14. Augustine, *Ten Homilies*, 8:266.

15. Augustine, *Enchiridion*, 103.

16. Others who understand Augustine as teaching that the atonement was for the elect only include Bavinck, *Sin and Salvation*, 456–58; Blacketer, "Definite Atonement," 308–10; Garrett, *Systematic Theology*, 61–62; Geisler, *Systematic Theology*, 379–81; Godfrey, "Tensions within International Calvinism," 72–74; Letham, *The Work of Christ*, 226; Rainbow, *The Will of God*, 9–23; and Thomas, *The Extent of the Atonement*, 4–5.

17. Among these would be Prosper of Aquitaine, Lucid, and Fulgentius of Ruspe. See Bavinck, *Sin and Salvation*, 456–57; Blacketer, "Definite Atonement," 310; Godfrey, "Tensions within International Calvinism," 135–36; Rainbow, *The Will of God*, 23–24; and Turretin, *Institutes*, 455.

18. There is a disagreement as to whether or not Augustine held to double predestination. Those who believe that Augustine held to double predestination include Berkhof, *Systematic Theology*, 109–10; Mozley, *The Augustinian Doctrine of Predestination*; Jewett, *Election and Predestination*, 6; Pelikan, *Emergence of the Catholic Tradition*, 298; and Rainbow, *The Will of God*, 9. Those who believe that he did not hold to double predestination include Karl Barth, *The Doctrine of God*, 16; Fesko, *Diversity within the Reformed Tradition*, 18–19; Hodge, *Systematic Theology*, 2:316; Rist, "Augustine on Free Will and Predestination," 2:420–24; and Sharp, "The Doctrines of Grace," 89. Augustine rarely addressed this question, but he makes several statements that seem to suggest that he believes in double predestination, and it certainly fits within his theology.

19. Rainbow, *The Will of God*, 21.

theology (though it said nothing about the extent of the atonement), and its decrees constituted orthodoxy in the Western Church for the following centuries.[20] Unwilling to follow Augustine on the extent of the atonement, the Western Church generally taught that Christ's atonement was for all people. This was also the accepted doctrine in the Eastern Church, which never accepted Augustinianism, and had a much more optimistic view of the human condition regarding sin and humanity's free will.[21]

THE NINTH CENTURY

After Augustine's elaboration of the doctrine, the next significant episode in church history concerning the extent of the atonement took place in the ninth century, revolving around a monk named Gottschalk (c.804–c.869).[22] Gottschalk studied Augustine in depth and began to proclaim his teachings, including the doctrines of double predestination and particular redemption. Gottschalk based his doctrine of particular redemption upon the absolute sovereignty and omnipotence of God in all things, the fact that some are saved and some are lost, the immutability of God's will, and the idea that if Christ died to save any who were not saved then the blood of Christ is wasted and God's will is ineffectual.[23] He believed there was one intention in the atonement: God only desires to be the redeemer of the elect, and only redeems the elect.[24] While the church at the time was generally Augustinian, it understood Augustine through the findings of the Synod of Orange, and thus Gottschalk's views were considered novel and controversial. Gottschalk was most likely faithful to Augustine's theology and did not shy away from its implications, but he went further than Augustine and made no attempt to accommodate the universalistic thrust of certain New Testament passages such as John 12:32 or 1 Timothy 2:4. Instead, he simply interpreted them as supporting his position. His opponents, most famously Hincmar of Reims, understood Gottschalk as teaching that God willed sin and that God was arbitrary and unjust; they also believed that his view contradicted Scriptures such as 1 Timothy 2:4–6. Gottschalk was accused of heresy for his views,

---

20. Ibid., 25.

21. Kelly, *Early Christian Doctrines*, 372–74.

22. For an explanation of Gottschalk's theology and the controversy that surrounded it, see Archibald, "A Comparative Study," 20–33; Freeman, "The Doctrine of Predestination," 648–60; Nineham, "Gottschalk of Orbais," 1–18; Pelikan, *Growth of Medieval Theology*, 80–95; and Rainbow, *The Will of God*, 25–32.

23. Freeman, "The Doctrine of Predestination," 651–55.

24. Archibald, "A Comparative Study," 25, 32.

including his understanding of the extent of the atonement, which resulted in his imprisonment for the last twenty years of his life.[25] He did have some support in the church, but not enough to avoid censure.[26]

Gottschalk and his opponents have an important place in the history of the debate over the extent of the atonement because it was during this ninth century controversy that the two prevailing views and their corresponding arguments fully developed. Gottschalk drew his arguments for particular redemption from Augustine, and future advocates of particular redemption reiterated his arguments.[27] Likewise, the arguments that Gottschalk's opponents advanced against his understanding of particular redemption and in support of an unlimited atonement would later become standard. These arguments included the claim that particular redemption contradicted the incarnation of Christ (based on the idea that Christ's was a universal human nature), that verses such as 1 Corinthians 8:11 imply that some of those whom Christ died for are lost, that verses such as 1 Timothy 2:4–6 and 1 John 2:2 demand a universal understanding of the atonement, that particular redemption implied God was evil towards his creation, and that if particular redemption was true then God was deceptive in regards to the free offer of the gospel.[28] One argument that was to have lasting influence was Hincmar's idea that there were two redemptions: one that was efficient for the salvation of the elect only, and one that applied both to the elect and the reprobate.[29] During the ninth century four councils pronounced against Gottschalk and particular redemption, and unlimited atonement was the dominant view in the church. There were, however, three councils that did pronounce for particular redemption.[30] The debate was never resolved, simply postponed.

25. Freeman, "The Doctrine of Predestination," 656–60; and Rainbow, *The Will of God*, 29–32.

26. Those who supported Gottschalk included Ratramnus of Corbie, Prudentius of Troyes, Lupes of Ferrieres, Deacon Florus, and Remigius of Lyons. Archibald, "A Comparative Study," 20.

27. I agree with Archibald's observation that "the details concerning the Ninth Century Predestinarians demonstrate that well before Calvin or Beza made up their minds about the extent of the atonement, the two basic alternatives were well established. . . . In addition to these basic alternatives, one finds in the ninth century controversy many of the detailed arguments that would resurface in the sixteenth century, for and against particular redemption." Ibid., 29.

28. Archibald, "A Comparative Study," 28; and Pelikan, *Growth of Medieval Theology*, 90–92.

29. Schaff, *History of the Christian Church*, 4:531–32.

30. The councils of Quiercy (849), second Quiercy (853), Toul (859), and Toucy (860) all pronounced against particular redemption. The councils of Paris (849), Sens

18   A Multi-Intentioned View of the Extent of the Atonement

MEDIEVAL SCHOLASTICISM

Peter Lombard

The next significant contribution to the doctrine of the extent of the atonement came from Peter Lombard (1095–1169). Lombard made a fundamental distinction in the extent of the atonement that has had lasting impact. Echoing previous statements, he introduced the distinction between the "sufficiency" of the atonement made for all people and the "efficiency" of the atonement made for the elect only.[31] Lombard seems to be echoing the sentiments of Hincmar and his two redemptions, one for the elect and one for all people. He might also have drawn from Ambrose, who stated, "If Christ has died for all, nevertheless he suffered especially for us."[32] Whatever his source, he was clearly trying to protect both the universality and the particularity of the atonement, but he did not elaborate further on how they fit together.

Lombard's lack of explanation has led to some confusion over whether or not he affirmed particular redemption or unlimited atonement. Even though unlimited atonement was the majority view at this point in church history, strict Augustinians such as Gregory of Rimini and John Wycliffe held to particular redemption, so it is possible that the Augustinian Lombard may have held this position as well. This confusion over Lombard's position reflects the ambiguity inherent in the "sufficient/efficient" schema, despite its popularity even in the present day as a statement of one's view concerning the extent of the atonement.[33] Instead of explaining God's intentions in the atonement, Lombard simply described the effects of the atonement. Despite this ambiguity, Lombard's emphasis on the universality of the atonement and his rejection of double predestination mean he most likely

---

(853), and Valence (855), all pronounced for particular redemption. Rainbow, *The Will of God*, 31–32.

31. Lombard, *Sentences*, vol. 192, column 799.

32. Ambrose, *Exposition of Luke's Gospel*, V.7, quoted in Godfrey, "Tensions within International Calvinism," 72.

33. As we will see later in this chapter, both Thomas Aquinas and John Wycliffe employed the "sufficient for all, efficient for some" schema, even though Thomas held to an unlimited atonement and Wycliffe held to particular redemption. During the Synod of Dort all of the disputants affirmed this formula, despite their differing views on the extent of the atonement. Advocates of both positions in the present day still employ the formula with its different meanings, although it brings no additional clarity to the dispute. As Archibald states, "The common solution in its medieval form is ambiguous. It does not distinguish between an efficiency based upon a limited intention and efficiency based upon a limited appropriation." Archibald, "A Comparative Study," 366.

held to an unlimited atonement.[34] Lombard's dependence upon Anselm's satisfaction view of the atonement strengths this conclusion, as Anselm asserted that sin is an infinite offence against God, and therefore it requires an infinite satisfaction, and only Jesus Christ as God and man could offer such an infinite satisfaction.[35]

Thomas Aquinas

There is no question concerning what position Thomas Aquinas (1225–1274) took on the extent of the atonement. Like Lombard, Thomas departed from the strict Augustinian view of particular redemption by advocating an unlimited atonement. In agreement with Augustine, Thomas believed in the absolute sovereignty and omnipotence of God in all things.[36] Unlike Augustine, however, Thomas believed that in some sense God's saving will and desire are intended for all people, even though all people are not saved. Thomas held these two beliefs together by making a distinction in the will of God. "God wills all men to be saved by his antecedent will, which is to will not simply but relatively; and not by his consequent will, which is to will simply."[37] Thomas believed that 1 Timothy 2:4 describes God's universal saving will, but that this will in no way abrogates God's will concerning the predestination of the elect.[38] Thomas held together the two aspects of God's saving will in his doctrine of the extent of the atonement by using Lombard's "sufficient for all, efficient for some" formula. Thomas used the "sufficient for all" aspect of this formula to assert that God really and truly wills to save all of humanity through the death of Christ.[39] He believed that Christ on the cross made satisfaction for the sin of all individuals.[40] Thomas stated, "Christ's passion was a sufficient and superabundant satisfaction for the sins of the whole human race; but when sufficient satisfaction has

---

34. Rainbow sees Lombard as a consistent Augustinian, and therefore a limited redemptionist. Rainbow, *The Will of God*, 34. Blacketer concurs with this assessment, although he believes that Lombard's view is ambiguous. Blacketer, "Definite Atonement," 311. Others, however, maintain that Lombard held to an unlimited atonement. Freeman, "The Doctrine of Predestination," 666; Strehle, "Theological Systems," 22–23; and Thomas, *the Extent of the Atonement*, 5.

35. Anselm, *Why God Became Man*, 260–356.

36. Thomas Aquinas, *Summa Theologica*, 1.25.5.

37. Ibid., 1.23.4.

38. Ibid.

39. Ibid., 3.79.7.

40. Ibid., 3.46.1, 3.50.1.

been paid, then the debt of punishment is abolished."[41] Unlike Augustine and Gottschalk, Thomas consistently interpreted universal passages such as John 12:32 and 1 John 2:2 as statements concerning Christ's death for all individuals.[42] He believed this unlimited satisfaction brought all people, including the reprobate, under Christ's feet, and that even the reprobate were potentially united to Christ's body.[43]

Thomas certainly did not believe, however, that all people are saved by Christ's atonement. He used the "efficient for some" part of Lombard's formula to make the distinction between the benefits of the atonement for believers and unbelievers. In order for the atonement to be efficient for a person, he must be united to Christ.[44] Only the elect are saved, and they are saved as Christ's death is applied to them through the means of grace, or the sacraments.[45] Christ's objective atonement had to be subjectively applied in order to benefit the believer.[46] Thomas wrote that "Christ's passion sufficed for all, while as to its efficacy it was profitable to many."[47] Thomas believed that there were many for whom Christ died that would never experience the saving benefits of his death, therefore there was no necessary connection between the extent of Christ's death and its application.

Thomas's view is significant in that he did not believe God's absolute sovereignty in salvation demanded a limited atonement. He strongly maintained that the atonement was sufficient for every individual and covered every sin. He was the first to explain in detail the "sufficient for all, efficient for some" formula, and he used it to affirm a universal atonement and a limited application of that atonement unto salvation. Thomas's view has been highly influential. The Council of Trent followed him in affirming the universality of Christ's sacrifice and the limited application of its benefits.[48] Some assert, however, that Thomas's explanation of the extent of the atonement and his strong stress on God's sovereignty and omnipotent will provided a strong foundation for future explanations of particular redemption, although it is clear that Thomas never draws this conclusion.[49]

41. Ibid., 3.49.3.
42. Ibid., 3.48.2.
43. Ibid., 3.8.3.
44. Ibid., 3.49.3.
45. Ibid.
46. Ibid., 3.78.3.
47. Ibid.
48. "But though he died for all, all do not receive the benefit of his death, but only those to whom the merit of his passion is communicated." *Council of Trent*, Sixth Session, Article 4, in *Tracts and Treatises on the Reformation of the Church*, 93.
49. Strehle believes that Thomas's Aristotelian interpretation of Christ's work led

John Wycliffe

Thomas's unlimited view of the extent of the atonement, although broadly Augustinian, was rejected by those in the church who considered themselves completely faithful to Augustine. Men such as Thomas Bradwardine, Gregory of Rimini, John Wycliffe, and John Hus all followed Gottschalk and defended particular redemption as the true Augustinian (and biblical) view of the extent of the atonement. John Wycliffe (c.1329–1384) in particular is worth mentioning here because of the unique element he contributed to the debate. Wycliffe held to particular redemption, believing that the doctrine of predestination meant that Christ loved the church from all of eternity, and gave himself only for her.[50] Wycliffe followed Thomas, however, in using the sufficient/efficient schema, but instead of using it to defend an atonement that was unlimited in its extent he used the formula to defend his view of particular redemption. Wycliffe employed the formula to affirm that Christ's atonement considered in and of itself was theoretically sufficient for an infinite number of people, although in reality it only bought salvation for the elect (and was therefore efficient only for them). Wycliffe based his use of the formula, and the sufficiency of Christ's atonement for the entire human race, on 1 John 2:2.[51]

In employing the formula, Wycliffe asserted that the atonement's theoretical sufficiency for all people brought non-saving benefits of the atonement to the nonelect.[52] The elect receive salvation because of the atonement, but the nonelect also receive nonsalvific blessings because of the atonement. These blessings include the alleviation of punishment for the reprobate, both

---

to Duns Scotus's view of particular redemption. "For if the cross of Christ becomes the means by which God accomplishes a particular end, and if the end of Christ's sufferings is deliverance from sin, those who are finally delivered from sin can only be the object for which Christ suffered. It will be left to Duns Scotus to draw this inevitable conclusion." Strehle, "Theological Systems," 38. Duns Scotus was a Nominalist who believed that God's will was primary in his dealings with his creation. He did not believe that Christ's satisfaction on the cross was sufficient within itself, as Anselm and Thomas did, but that it was only sufficient insofar as God accepted it. Duns believed that God willed all people to be saved, and that Christ's death could have been sufficient for all of humanity if God willed it, but since God only intends to save some Christ's death could have only been for them. Not only that, but since only Christ's humanity merited satisfaction for sin, it is necessarily limited, and must be understood as finite. For Duns's view, see Strehle, "Theological Systems," 39–52. Duns's argument that the application of the atonement must determine its extent has become a common one among advocates of particular redemption.

50. Wycliffe, *Wycliffe's Latin Works*, 10:439–40.
51. Ibid., 10:60.
52. Ibid., 10:57.

temporal and eternal, and the presence of righteousness in the reprobate (although this righteousness is never saving). Wycliffe based these blessings not only on the sufficiency of the atonement for all people, but also on the fact that Christ shares the same human nature as the reprobate. Wycliffe used the idea of nonredemptive benefits of the atonement to explain John 12:32, where Jesus says that he will draw all men unto himself.[53] Rainbow calls these nonredemptive benefits of the atonement "scholastic accretions" that found their way into Wycliffe's particular redemption,[54] but the idea of nonredemptive benefits of the atonement from a particular redemption viewpoint has been a popular one since Wycliffe, and remains so in contemporary evangelicalism.[55]

JOHN CALVIN

With the exception of Martin Luther, John Calvin (1509–1564) is the most influential theologian of the Reformation.[56] Despite the infamous "L" of the

53. Ibid., 10:468.
54. Rainbow, *The Will of God*, 44.
55. E.g., R. B. Kuiper's last chapter in his book on the extent of the atonement, *For Whom Did Christ Die?* (in which he defends particular redemption) is on the universal benefits of the atonement. John Murray is another example of a prominent advocate of particular redemption who saw benefits in the atonement for the nonelect, and pointed out these benefits in *Redemption Accomplished and Applied*. Whether or not there are grounds within the particular redemption view for these nonredemptive benefits will be examined in chapters 3 and 4.
56. Luther's views on the extent of the atonement are not as relevant to the evangelical debate over the subject, however, and will not be surveyed here, for two reasons. First, it is extremely difficult to tell what Luther's views on the subject were. It is possible that he held to particular redemption, as Luther was clearly Augustinian and held to double predestination, as particularly seen in his *Bondage of the Will*. Concerning the extent of the atonement, Luther rejects the universalistic interpretations of 1 Tim 2:4 and states "For in an absolute sense Christ did not die for all, because he says: 'This is my blood which is poured out for you' and 'for many'—he does not say: for all—'for the forgiveness of sins (Mark 14:24; Matt 26:28)." Luther, *Lectures on Romans*, 232. Luther does make some statements, however, that can be taken as supporting unlimited atonement (see Douty, *Did Christ Die*, 139 for a list of several quotations). Strehle believes that Luther's Christocentric soteriology and strong *Christus Victor* overtones in his doctrine of the atonement indicate that he held to an unlimited atonement. Strehle, "Theological Systems," 63–84. As Thomas points out, Luther never formulated a clear doctrine of particular redemption, although it certainly fits with his views of election. Thomas, *The Extent of the Atonement*, 7. In my opinion Luther saw both particularity and universality in the atonement and was never clear on how they fit together.

Second, the issue did not become a debate in Lutheran theology like it did in subsequent Reformed theology, because no matter what Luther's position may have been, Lutherans who followed Luther held to unlimited atonement. Lutheranism rejected

Calvinist TULIP, however, Calvin's position on the extent of the atonement is less then clear. For whatever reason, Calvin never systematically explained his view on the extent of the atonement. He was certainly aware of the issue, having spent time with Martin Bucer in Strasbourg during the time when Bucer was debating the issue with the Anabaptists.[57] He also addressed the extent of the atonement in a polemical context.[58] Calvin wrote many statements that seem to indicate that he believed in particular redemption, but he also wrote many statements that seem to indicate that he believed in unlimited atonement.

Calvin's vagueness on the issue has led to numerous explanations of what his view of the extent of the atonement was. Many scholars believe that he held to unlimited atonement, and that subsequent followers of his theology such as Moïse Amyraut correctly interpreted his views on the subject.[59] Many other scholars, however, believe that Calvin held to particular redemption, as tradition has normally understood him to believe, and that followers of his theology such as Theodore Beza were the accurate interpret-

---

particular redemption in the Formula of Concord (1580). The Formula affirmed both unlimited atonement and unconditional election without attempting to reconcile the two doctrines (in fact teaching that attempts to reconcile them always fail), thus taking a middle road between Calvinism and Arminianism. Archibald, "A Comparative Study," 40–46; and Strehle, "Theological Systems," 96–120. Contemporary Lutheranism agrees with the Formula of Concord, believing the relationship between the two doctrines to be similar to the mystery of the Trinity. For contemporary expressions of the Lutheran view, see Pieper, *Christian Dogmatics*, 32; and Scaer, "Nature and Extent," 179–87.

57. Bucer believed that Christ died only for the elect, but that the gospel should be preached to all people. He reconciled these two views by calling all people to believe in their election, since all who would believe would be elect. Bucer, *Common Places*, 98–100. Many Anabaptists, who held to unlimited atonement, resided in Strasbourg, and public debates concerning the issue took place between Bucer and Hans Denck in 1526. Denck was expelled from Strasbourg, as was Melchior Hoffman in 1533. For further explanations of these debates, see Archibald, "A Comparative Study," 37–39; Beachy, *The Concept of Grace*, 16–20; Rainbow, *The Will of God*, 49–63; and Thomas, *The Extent of the Atonement*, 7–8.

58. Calvin, *Concerning the Eternal Predestination of God*, 148. This point rebuts the claim that Calvin would have put forth particular redemption much more clearly as his view if it had been a contested point, found in Helm, *Calvin and the Calvinists*, 18; and Leahy, "Calvin and the Extent of the Atonement," 54–64.

59. Armstrong, *Calvinism and the Amyraut Heresy*, 265–66; Bell, "Calvin and the Extent of the Atonement," 115–23; Daniel, "Hyper-Calvinism and John Gill," 777–828; Douty, *Did Christ Die*, 141; Hall, "Calvin against the Calvinists," 19–37; Hartog, *A Word for the World*; Kendall, *Calvinism and English Calvinism*, 13–28; Kennedy, *Union with Christ*; Lane, "The Quest for the Historical Calvin," 95–113; Ponter, "Review Essay," 139–59; idem, "Review Essay (Part Two)," 253–71; Strehle, "Theological Systems," 84–95; and Torrance, "The Incarnation and 'Limited Atonement,'" 83–94.

ers of his thoughts on the subject.[60] Some scholars have also proposed that it is simply impossible in light of Calvin's ambiguity on the issue to know his position.[61] While it is impossible for us to survey the whole of Calvin's thought on the subject and the various interpretations of it, it is clear that Calvin took special care to emphasize both the particular and the general aspects of the atonement.

No one can deny that Calvin repeatedly referred to redemption and the atonement in universal terms and sometimes spoke of the atonement in relation to unbelievers.[62] He often referred to Christ's dying for "all"[63] or for the "world."[64] On several occasions Calvin interprets passages that use the word "many" to mean "all," universalizing them instead of using them to support particular redemption.[65] He stated that unbelievers are doubly culpable for rejecting Jesus Christ because he died for their sins.[66] He strongly affirmed a universal offer of God's grace in the gospel call.[67] He emphasized

---

60. Archibald, "A Comparative Study," 69–384; Blacketer, "Definite Atonement," 313–15; Godfrey, "Reformed Thought," 137–39; Helm, *Calvin and the Calvinists*, 13–50; Leahy, "Calvin and the Extent of the Atonement," 54–64; Muller, *Christ and the Decree*, 33–35; Murray, "Calvin on the Extent of the Atonement," 20–22; Nettles, "John Calvin's Understanding," 293–315; Nicole, "John Calvin's View," 197–225; and Rainbow, *The Will of God*, 64–185.

61. Boersma, "Calvin and the Extent of the Atonement," 333–55; Peterson, *Calvin and the Atonement*; and Thomas, *The Extent of the Atonement*, 12–35, all conclude that Calvin was ambiguous on the topic and a definitive decision on the matter is not possible, but that particular redemption is more likely than not his view.

62. It is clear that Calvin's use of the words "all," "every," or "world" are not always used to indiscriminately refer to all individuals. Sometimes they do, however. As always, these words must be understood in their respective contexts.

63. Calvin, *Philippians, Colossians, and Thessalonians*, 148; and idem, *New Testament Commentaries*, 3:343.

64. Calvin, *Catholic Epistles*, 52; idem, *The Deity of Christ*, 55; and idem, *Galatians and Ephesians*, 157.

65. Speaking of Matt 10:28, Calvin states, "'Many' is used, not for a definite number, but for a large number, in that he sets himself over against all others. And this is the meaning also in Rom. 5:15, where Paul is not talking about a part of mankind but of the whole human race." Calvin, *New Testament Commentaries*, 2:181. Speaking of Mark 14:24, Calvin states, "The word 'many' does not mean a part of the world only, but the whole human race: he contrasts 'many' with 'one,' as if to say that he would not be the Redeemer of one man, but would meet death to deliver many of their cursed guilt. No doubt that in speaking to a few Christ wished to make his teaching available to a larger number." Ibid., 2:311. Calvin made similar remarks concerning Isa 53:12; Rom 5:15; and Heb 9:27. See Kennedy, *Union with Christ*, 32–35. These interpretations are in marked contrast to advocates of particular redemption such as Murray, *Redemption Accomplished and Applied*, 62–63; and Owen, *Death of Death*, 45–46.

66. Calvin, *Sermons on Isaiah's Prophecy*, 141.

67. Calvin, *New Testament Commentaries*, 5:78; and idem, *Sermons on Isaiah's*

the need for believers to be in Christ through the power of the Holy Spirit in order to avail themselves of Christ's death for them.[68] It is also significant that Calvin did not respond to the Council of Trent's assertion of unlimited atonement, as he normally addressed points of disagreement with Roman Catholic doctrine.[69]

For all the evidence that points toward an unlimited atonement in Calvin's writings however, there is at least as much evidence that supports the idea that he held to particular redemption. As undeniable as it is that Calvin often referred to redemption and the atonement in universal terms, he just as often described Christ as redeeming a particular group of people, such as his elect,[70] his church,[71] his people,[72] and his sheep.[73] Calvin criticized the "sufficient for all, efficient for some" formula because it did not explicitly recognize God's sovereign will in the application of salvation.[74] He also interpreted several of the most crucial passages supporting unlimited atonement (1 John 2:2; 1 Tim 2:4–6; John 12:32) in a way that seems to rule out unlimited atonement.[75] In these interpretations, Calvin followed Augustine's understanding of these texts, and the strong Augustinian influence

---

Prophecy, 41.

68. Calvin, *Galatians and Ephesians*, 76; and idem, *Sermons on Galatians*, 106.

69. John Calvin, *Tracts and Treatises*, 3:109. As Kennedy states "It has been widely recognized that in Calvin's refutation of the decrees from the Council of Trent, Calvin did not disagree with the statement on universal atonement. Indeed, he specifically mentions the decree dealing with the extent of the atonement and states that he is not in disagreement with it. . . . Had Calvin held to particular redemption, it is difficult to believe that he would not have taken the opportunity to dispute the Council of Trent on this point." Kennedy, *Union With Christ*, 38. See also Daniel, "Hyper-Calvinism," 790; Kendall, *English Calvinism*, 12; and Thomas, *The Extent of the Atonement*, 28.

70. Calvin, *Matthew, Mark, and Luke*, 68; and idem, *Sermons on the Epistles to Timothy and Titus*, 403.

71. Calvin, *Harmony of the Evangelists*, 162.

72. Calvin, *Institutes of the Christian Religion*, 3.24.2.

73. Calvin, *Gospel of John*, 402.

74. Calvin, *Eternal Predestination*, 149. Calvin did say in one place, however, that he allowed the truth of the sufficient/efficient schema, although he did not think that it was applicable in 1 John 2:1–2. Idem, *Catholic Epistles*, 173.

75. E.g., Calvin understood the "world" in 1 John 2:2 to refer only to those who would believe throughout the various regions of the earth, not to all individuals. Calvin, *Catholic Epistles*, 173. He also understood the term "all" in 1 Tim 2:4–6 to refer to "classes of men but never to individuals." Idem, *Timothy, Titus, and Philemon*, 57. In in his sermon on this passage, Calvin struggled to hold together his interpretation of "all" as "all classes" and the offer of salvation to all, where "all" includes those who reject the gospel, and thus unbelievers. Idem, *Sermons on the Epistles to Timothy and Titus*, 145–85.

upon Calvin supports the view that he held to particular redemption.[76] In at least one place, Calvin also seemed strongly to deny that Christ's atonement was for unbelievers. Speaking of the presence of Christ in the Lord's Supper and how only believers truly partake of Christ in the Lord's Supper, Calvin states, "But the first thing to be explained is how Christ is present with unbelievers, to be the spiritual food of souls, and in short the life and salvation of the world. And he [Heshusius, Calvin's adversary in this debate] adheres so doggedly to his words, I should like to know how the wicked can eat the flesh which was not crucified for them, and how they can drink the blood which was not shed to expiate their sins?"[77] Finally, in light of the strong opinions of many other Reformers in favor of particular redemption (such as Bucer and Theodore Beza), it is difficult to imagine that Calvin would not have challenged their views if he disagreed.[78]

After accounting for all of the evidence, those who resolutely describe Calvin as holding to one view or the other seem to be overstepping their bounds. Instead, Calvin seems to hold to both universality and particularity in the atonement. He held to universality in regards to the universal gospel offer and particularity in regards to election. Depending upon the context of his remarks, he stressed either the particularity or the universality of the atonement. He never fully resolved this tension. Several elements of Calvin's theology, however, suggest that if the tension were to be resolved, it would be resolved in the direction of particular redemption.[79] Many of Calvin's

---

76. One of the main theses of Rainbow's book is that Calvin stands in the line of strict Augustinians and therefore it would be extraordinary if he were an advocate of unlimited atonement. Rainbow, *The Will of God*, 47, 134. Archibald also advances this idea. Archibald, "A Comparative Study," 354–55.

77. Calvin, *Theological Treatises*, 285. There are some, however, who try to explain how this statement can fit into an unlimited atonement perspective. See Bell, "Calvin and the Extent of the Atonement," 120; Daniel, "Hyper-Calvinism and John Gill," 821–22; and Kennedy, *Union with Christ*, 54–56.

78. Concerning Beza's straightforward explanation of particular redemption in his *Tabula Praedestinationis*, Michael Jinkins writes, "Published in 1555 as a clear statement of Reformed doctrine, indeed as a defense of the Calvinist position on predestination, we find no indication that Beza's summary was rejected by Calvin. And, since Calvin did not seem to hesitate to criticize those with whom he did disagree, we may assume that Calvin did not see Beza's early statement on predestination as being essentially at variance with his own views, at least not at this critical point." Jinkins, "Theodore Beza," 135.

79. Thomas points out four elements in Calvin's theology where he clearly seemed to favor the particular over the universal. Thomas, *The Extent of the Atonement*, 34–35. (1) Predestination and providence are closely related, and God's will can be seen from the result of both predestination and providence. Therefore if all do not hear the gospel and believe, this is because God had particular intentions for the gospel. (2) Of God's two wills, the absolute/particular and the revealed/universal, Calvin believed the

followers (down to the present day) held to strict positions of particular redemption, and they fully believed that they were adhering to Calvin's own position in doing so. No matter which view Calvin held, the ambiguity in his theology is significant for three reasons. First, it leaves open the possibility that particular redemption is not the only way to account for the God's sovereignty in salvation and particularity in the atonement. Second, Calvin's lack of clarity may indicate his own intuition that some kind of position such as the multi-intentioned view is needed. Third, it would result in heated debate in the future, as Reformed theologians struggled with how to articulate the extent of the atonement during the Synod of Dort and the Amyraldian controversy.

THEODORE BEZA

Theodore Beza (1519–1605), Calvin's friend and successor in Geneva, perhaps did more than anyone else to solidify particular redemption as the "Reformed" view on the extent of the atonement. Beza held strongly to the view, and he was influential to the point that some scholars claim him as the source of particular redemption within Reformed theology.[80] As Calvin's successor, Beza spent much of his time defending Calvin's teachings against Roman Catholics, Lutherans, and Socinians, and his writings on the extent of the atonement reflect this. In these polemical contexts Beza stressed the particular aspects of Calvin's theology because they were the ones most often in dispute.[81] Beza's view is noteworthy not only because of his relationship with Calvin, but because of the supralapsarian structure of his theology and the logical precision he brought to the doctrine.

Beza's views on the extent of the atonement are evident from the time of his early writings. In 1551 Beza wrote to Heinrich Bullinger and asked him for his support of Calvin's views concerning predestination and reprobation. In this letter Beza had already outlined his supralapsarianism, convinced that the logic of unconditional election demanded that reprobation

---

former was more basic. (3) Election for Calvin is always eternal, while God's promise in the gospel has its place in the temporal dealings of God with his creation. (4) While election and promise are both tied to Christ, Christ is not the whole meaning of election as he is of the promise of the gospel. In election, therefore, we deal with the hidden God. Thomas ends this section by stating, "In the scope thus given for speculation and logical deduction, a theology more consistently particularistic than Calvin's own was almost bound to emerge." Thomas, *The Extent of the Atonement*, 35.

80. Armstrong, *Calvinism and the Amyraut Heresy*, 41–42, 137–38; and Hall, "Calvin against the Calvinists," 27.

81. Thomas, *The Extent of the Atonement*, 42.

be based solely on the decree of God, and not the foreseen sin of humanity.[82] Beza published his famous *Tabula Praedestinationis* in 1555 in which he fully explains his supralapsarian theology and its implications.[83] In Beza's double predestination, Christ's atonement is subordinated to election, demanding particular redemption. As Thomas states, "The rigorous application of the decree-execution, or primary-secondary causality, framework is apparent in the way Christ is seen as a means, albeit chief among other means, for the execution of the decree of God to glorify himself by saving an elect portion of mankind. This subordination of Christ to the decree pointed the way to a doctrine of limited atonement."[84]

Beza's mature view on the subject can be seen in his participation in the Colloquy of Montbéliard in 1586, and it is the same as his view in 1551. The main controversy at Montbéliard was between the Reformed and the Lutherans over the Lord's Supper, but in the context of this debate issues concerning predestination were also discussed. Beza was the main representative of the Reformed contingent, and Jakob Andreae was the representative of the Lutherans. The colloquy did not go well, and afterwards a Calvinist, Eusebius Schonbergius, published a tract attacking the Lutheran positions presented there. The Lutherans responded to this by publishing their own tract in 1587. Beza in turn responded to this Lutheran tract and presented a detailed explanation of his view of the extent of the atonement in *Ad Acta Collquii Montisbelgardensis Tubingae Edita, Theodori Bezae Responsio*.

Beza believed that the benefits of the atonement must be confined to the elect alone. He interpreted verses such as John 3:16, 1 Timothy 2:4–6, and 1 John 2:2 as referring only to the elect, and denied that they should be understood universally. The atonement was entirely efficacious; salvation was not made possible in Christ, but was made actual for the elect. In no way did Christ die for those who were damned, for if he had, his death would have failed. For Beza the atonement guaranteed the salvation of the elect, because if sin is expiated, then salvation must follow. He believed that Andreae's position of unlimited atonement implied that people were not condemned for their sins, but only for their unbelief in Christ. Andreae denied this, but Beza was unwilling to consider that any might perish for whom Christ had died.[85] Andreae's main response to Beza's arguments was to invoke the sufficient/efficient formula, insisting that Christ's death is suf-

---

82. Beza, *Correspondance de Théodore De Bèze*, 71–73.

83. A reproduction of this table can be found in Thomas, *The Extent of the Atonement*, 46.

84. Ibid., 47.

85. Godfrey, "Tensions within International Calvinism," 85–86; and Thomas, *The Extent of the Atonement*, 57–58.

ficient for all individuals.[86] Beza granted the general truth of this statement, but disagreed with Andrae's interpretation, which had been the classical understanding since Thomas Aquinas. Beza believed the statement as commonly understood was ambiguous and failed to explain God's intention in the atonement, as he saw no universality in the atonement whatsoever.[87] He followed Duns Scotus in redefining the formula to mean that it was sufficient only in its intrinsic nature, and meant for the elect alone.[88]

Beza's views on the extent of the atonement were influential, and by the end of the sixteenth century particular redemption was increasingly popular in Reformed theology, with men such Olevianus, Pareus, Vermigli, Zanchi, and Perkins all holding to particular redemption.[89] It was by no means the consensus view, however. Theologians such as Bullinger, Musculus, Kimedoncius, Tossanus, Ward, Ussher, Davenant, and Martinus all held to unlimited atonement before the Amyraldian controversy.[90] The diversity among the Reformers concerning the extent of the atonement in the sixteenth century would surface amidst the controversy over Arminianism at the Synod of Dort in 1619, and it was the primary reason the Synod adopted the sufficient/efficient formula, as we will see below.

JACOB ARMINIUS AND THE SYNOD OF DORT

Jacob Arminius (1559–1609) was a student of Theodore Beza, but his differences with the accepted tenants of Reformed theology resulted in the movement that bears his name, Arminianism. Arminius considered himself part of the Reformed community and never wished to leave it, but his different positions concerning predestination, providence, the will and grace of God, human freedom, and the extent of the atonement resulted in great controversy that eventually led to the condemnation and exclusion of his views. In 1602 Arminius wrote his most comprehensive treatment of predestination and its related subjects, entitled *An Examination of a Treatise, Concerning*

---

86. Andreae stated, "He has satisfied sufficiently for the sins of all individuals, so that there would be no need for a new or additional sacrifice if a thousand worlds, so to speak, remained to be reconciled to God. One drop of the blood of the Son of God would suffice for them." Quoted in Thomas, *The Extent of the Atonement*, 57.

87. Godfrey, "Tensions within International Calvinism," 86–87; and Thomas, *The Extent of the Atonement*, 57.

88. Strehle, "The Extent of the Atonement," 17.

89. Godfrey, "Reformed Thought," 139–52; Letham, *The Work of Christ*, 226–27; Nicole, "Heidelberg Catechism," 138–45; and Thomas, *The Extent of the Atonement*, 96–97, 109–16.

90. Ibid., 248–51.

the *Order and Mode of Predestination and Amplitude of Divine Grace*, by Rev. William Perkins, D.D., A Theological Writer of England, in response to the supralapsarian doctrine of William Perkins, whose views concerning predestination and the atonement were similar to Beza's.[91] Arminius's view of unlimited atonement is the view that the Remonstrants believed in, the Synod of Dort rejected, and many evangelicals hold today.[92]

Arminius's conception of election was fundamentally different than the accepted Reformed view. He believed that predestination relates to people as sinners, whereas supralapsarianism considers people before they have even been created.[93] He asserted that predestination must be understood as having its grounds only in Christ, and on the basis of his sacrificial death.[94] For Arminius this meant that election could not be understood as a decree that Christ executes on the cross or as an ordination of God in which the believer plays no part; election is only on the basis of a person's being in Christ through faith.[95] This conception of election led Arminius to reverse the traditional order of decrees. For Arminius, the decree to elect did not precede the decree to send Christ to make atonement for sin, as in traditional Reformed theology. Since election is only on the basis of Christ's death, the decree to send the Son to pay for the sins of the world must have preceded the decree to elect those who would believe in the Son's atonement. Arminius essentially equates election with the application of Christ's death. He states, "What else, indeed, is predestination than the preparation of the grace, obtained and provided for us by the death of Christ, and a preparation pertaining to the application, not to the acquisition or provision of grace, not yet existing? For the decree of God, by which he determined to give Christ as a Redeemer to the world, and to appoint him the head only of believers, is prior to the decree, by which he determined to really apply to some, by faith, the grace obtained by the death of Christ."[96]

By reversing the order of the decrees, Arminius was able to assert that Christ's death was not intended only for the elect, and was therefore unlimited in scope. Out of his universal love for humanity, God sent Christ as the substitutionary sacrifice for the sins of all people.[97] Arminius avoided uni-

---

91. For an overview of Perkins's views, see Malone, "The Doctrine of Predestination," 103–17; and Moore, *English Hypothetical Universalism*, 27–68.

92. E.g., Picirilli, *Grace, Faith, Free Will*, 85–138.

93. Arminius, *Order and Mode of Predestination*, 291.

94. Ibid., 295.

95. Ibid., 311.

96. Ibid., 346–47.

97. Arminius held to a penal substitutionary atonement; he did not hold to the governmental theory. H. D. McDonald writes that for Arminius Christ's death was not a

versalism by appealing to the sufficient/efficient formula: Christ's death was universally sufficient, but efficacious only for those who believe in it.[98] Arminius believed that the only way to avail oneself of Christ's atonement was through faith. He stated that God requires faith from all people, as seen in the universal gospel offer, and this also demands that the atonement was for all.[99] Arminius also believed that Christ's sacrifice on the cross and Christ's present intercession in heaven should be carefully distinguished.[100] There is a clear difference between the accomplishment of salvation and the application of salvation. Christ's work brought about potential reconciliation for all, and it is through faith that the potential reconciliation becomes actual for believers.[101] This faith is a work of the Holy Spirit through prevenient grace, which frees the human will in order to accept or reject the message of the gospel.[102] Prevenient grace itself is a result of Christ's universal atonement.

Arminius died in 1609, but by the time of his death his theology had already gained a strong following. In 1610 forty-three of his followers met in the Netherlands, where they wrote a statement of their convictions, their "Remonstrance." The second article of the Remonstrance described the Arminian position on the extent of the atonement: "That in agreement with this Jesus Christ the Savior of the world died for all men and for every man, so that he merited reconciliation and forgiveness of sins for all through the death of the cross; yet so that no one actually enjoys this forgiveness of sins

---

payment of a debt or an equivalent for the punishment due to sin (*Atonement*, 200–1). Arminius seems to explicitly contradict this assertion. He believed that sin must be punished, and it can be punished either in the individual sinner or in a substitute. God provided the equivalent punishment due to the sins of humanity in the substitutionary death of Jesus Christ, and in Christ's death mercy and justice coincide. This sacrifice was for all sinners, and therefore for all people. Arminius states, "The justice of God may be displayed in the exaction of punishment from the individuals who have sinned; the same justice may also be displayed in the exaction of the same punishment from him, who has, according to the will of God, offered himself as a pledge and surety for those sinners." Arminius, *Writings*, 3:214. For a defense of the view that Arminius held to a penal substitutionary view of the atonement, see Clarke, *The Ground of Election*, 88–89; and Hicks, "The Theology of Grace," 70–79.

98. Arminius, *Order and Mode of Predestination*, 345.
99. Ibid., 327–28.
100. Ibid., 347.
101. Ibid.
102. Ibid., 470–71. Concerning Arminius's thought, Carl Bangs states, "The part man plays in salvation is believing. Evangelical belief is the free choice to receive offered grace, which offered grace makes the free choice possible. In all this man does nothing apart from grace: he earns nothing; he contributes nothing; but he chooses freely, and it is a choice which can refuse to make, for grace is not an irresistible force." Bangs, *Arminius*, 216.

except the believer—also, according to the word of the gospel of John 3:16, 'God so loved the world that he gave his only-begotten Son that whosoever believeth in him shall not perish but have everlasting life.' And in the first epistle of John 2:2, 'He is the propitiation for our sins; and not only for ours, but also for the sins of the world.'"[103] The majority of Reformed theologians during this time reacted strongly against Arminianism., and this negative reaction led to the Synod of Dort in 1618–19, which decisively rejected Arminianism and put forth a comprehensive statement of Reformed theology.

Synod of Dort

The purpose of the Synod of Dort was to resolve the controversy over Arminian theology, including the extent of the atonement. Deputations from all of the Reformed nations commented upon the Remonstrant positions, and the final articles of the Synod, the Canons of Dort, were based upon their reports. The Remonstrants did not make any contributions to the debates, and were not present when their views were condemned.[104] The details of this Synod have been presented in several other places,[105] but due to the importance of this Synod for Reformed theology, we will take a brief look at its findings concerning the extent of the atonement.

The Synod unanimously rejected the Arminian concept of unlimited atonement, and the delegates all used virtually the same arguments against the Arminian position: the implications of the substitutionary nature of the atonement, the unity of Christ's work, the perfection of Christ's work, and the connection of the extent of the atonement with the doctrine of predestination.[106] There was, however, much disagreement among the deputations as to how the extent of the atonement should be explained. Two problems impacted the Synod's explanation of the extent of the atonement. The first problem concerned the language used to express the extent of the atonement. Most of the delegates were comfortable using the common solution, but there was strong disagreement on what the common solution meant. The second problem was that almost all of the discussion concerning the extent of the atonement had emerged in a polemical context. The Synod

---

103. Godfrey, "Tensions within International Calvinism," 106.

104. Strehle, "Extent of the Atonement," 4–7.

105. Archibald, "A Comparative Study," 390–95; Godfrey, "Tensions within International Calvinism," 132–269; Nicole, "Moyse Amyraut," 21–29; Pelikan, *Reformation of Church and Dogma*, 237–45; Strehle, "Theological Systems," 204–50; and Thomas, *The Extent of the Atonement*, 128–59.

106. Archibald, "A Comparative Study," 392.

would have to decide whether their explanation would be polemical or a more balanced, constructive statement.[107] Views at the Synod ranged from the strict supralapsarian particularism of Geneva to the "hypothetical universalism" of Great Britain.[108] Geneva did not want to use the sufficient/efficient formula because it was too ambiguous, while Great Britain based their position upon the distinction, believing that it was absolutely necessary to assert both the atonement's universal sufficiency and its limited efficacy.[109] In order to accommodate these differences, the Synod compromised by using the sufficient/efficient formula, but left the interpretation of that statement open enough for all of the delegates to be comfortable with it.[110]

Despite the Synod's moderate position on the extent of the atonement, several statements paved the way for particular redemption to be solidified as the "Reformed" position. As Strehle states, "Although there is not a specific statement which categorically denies a universal intent, there are certain statements which explicitly contend that the work of Christ is a product of God's everlasting love for the elect and is specifically ordained to save them."[111] These statements include Article 8 in the Second Head of the Canons of Dort, which focuses on the efficacy of Christ's death. Halfway through this article it states, "God willed that Christ through the blood of the cross (by which he confirmed the new covenant) should effectually redeem out of every people, tribe, nation, and tongue all those and only those who were from eternity chosen to salvation and were given to him by the Father."[112] Article 9 then grounds God's will in this matter in his eternal love for the elect.[113] While the Canons do affirm the infinite value and suf-

---

107. Godfrey, "Tensions within International Calvinism," 130–31.

108. Godfrey describes the different camps at the Synod: "The various Theses presented to the Synod on the Second Article revealed a considerable diversity of expression and thought among the Orthodox. . . . A careful examination indicates three broad divisions into which the various *Judicia* fall. The largest group is composed of those delegations which expressed a simple, strict Calvinist point of view. All the provincial Dutch delegations, as well as the Palatine, the Helvetian, the Genevan, and Emden delegations belonged to this group. The Theses of Martinius represented the second, moderate group although the sympathies of Davenant and Ward were also with Martinius. The third group, which might be called the mediating group, placed themselves between the strict Calvinists and the moderates. This aggregation included the Dutch professors, Lubbertus, the English, Crocius, and Pareus. The Theses of Isselburg, Hesse, Nassau, and DuMoulin may also belong with the mediating group, although they reflect a more rigorous approach than others of this group." Ibid., 225–26.

109. Thomas, *The Extent of the Atonement*, 134–36.

110. Strehle, "The Extent of the Atonement," 17–19.

111. Ibid., 19–20.

112. This translation is from Hoekema, *Canons of Dort*, 145.

113. Ibid., 145–46.

ficiency of Christ's death, they do not explain if this universal sufficiency of the atonement is because of its intrinsic nature or because the atonement has a universal saving intention.[114] As Thomas points out, no explanation is offered as to how the universal sufficiency of the atonement relates to the nonelect.[115] The Canons do emphasize the universal gospel offer, and also acknowledge that people perish because of their own sin and not because of any defect in Christ's death.[116] They represent a more moderate view of particular redemption than that of supralapsarianism, as they do stress some universality in the atonement, but still emphasize the particularity of God's sovereignty in the atonement.[117]

The Synod of Dort's explanation of the extent of the atonement became the accepted explanation for the Reformed church. The Canons of Dort unambiguously reject the Arminian view, and carefully use language that allows for particular redemption or a Moderate Calvinist view of unlimited atonement. Due to its nature as a compromise, however, the Synod's statement on the extent of the atonement was not the final word in the debate. The debate over the extent of the atonement would resurface thirty years later in the controversy over Amyraldianism, when Amyraut and his followers would insist that their views were in line with the Synod's conclusions, despite the efforts of their opponents who claimed that they were contradicting the Synod.[118]

MOÏSE AMYRAUT

Moïse Amyraut (1596–1664) developed the theological system now referred to as Amyraldianism, known especially for its unique views of predestination and the extent of the atonement. While he was not the first to make an attempt at combining unconditional election and unlimited atonement, his views came under fire due to the recent Canons of Dort. Amyraut first explained his views in a 1634 publication that was intended for a popular audience, the *Brief Traitté de la Predestination et de ses principales Dependances*.[119] This treatise was controversial, especially as it clearly espoused an unlimited atonement as well as a conditional will of God by which he

---

114. Ibid., 143.

115. Thomas, *The Extent of the Atonement*, 133.

116. Hoekema, *Canons of Dort*, 144.

117. Godfrey understands the Synod as a "victory of a moderate form of contemporary Calvinism." Godfrey, "Tensions within International Calvinism," 268.

118. Strehle, "Synod of Dort," 22–23.

119. Armstrong, *Calvinism and the Amyraut Heresy*, 80–81.

desires the salvation of all people.[120] Amyraut responded to this controversy by publishing six sermons meant to clarify his position in 1636,[121] as well as a work where he attempted to demonstrate the compatibility of his doctrine with John Calvin's.[122] These writings led to a heresy trial at the National Synod of Alençon in 1637, where Amyraut was pronounced orthodox but also warned to stop using certain language that was causing offense.[123] The remainder of Amyraut's life would be consumed with the controversy over his doctrine of universal grace, and shortly after his death his views would be decisively condemned at the Swiss Formula Consensus Helvetica in 1675.[124]

Amyraut believed that in the atonement Christ paid for the sins of all individuals; not only is the atonement sufficient for all sin but Christ actually intended to die for all individuals. He states, "The sacrifice that he has offered for the propitiation of their offenses has been offered equally for all. And the salvation that he has received from his Father in order to communicate it to men in the sanctification of the spirit and the glorification of the body is destined equally to all, provided, I say, that the disposition necessary in order to receive it is also equally present."[125] The atonement is only hypothetically or conditionally universal, however, for the salvation that the atonement provides is only effectual when the condition of faith is fulfilled. Amyraut believed that only the elect would fulfill the condition of faith, and the Holy Spirit is the one who applies the atonement to the elect through

---

120. "Its most debated teaching was the affirmation that God sent his Son into the world to redeem all men provided that they believe. That is, as we have seen in Cameron, there is an antecedent will of God which extends salvation to all men but which becomes effective only as it is appropriated by faith." Armstrong, *Calvinism and the Amyraut Heresy*, 82.

121. These sermons were entitled *Six Sermons de la Nature, Estendue, Necessité, Dispensation, et Efficace de l'Evangile*. An explanation of their contents can be found in Nicole, "Moyse Amyraut," 67–75.

122. This work was entitled *Eschantillon de la Doctrinede Calvin touchant la Predestination*, and was prefaced to the six sermons. An explanation of its contents can be found in Nicole, "Moyse Amyraut," 75–84.

123. Armstrong, *Calvinism and the Amyraut Heresy*, 88–96; and Nicole, "Moyse Amyraut," 119–32.

124. For an explanation of this opposition up to and including the 1675 formula, see Thomas, *The Extent of the Atonement*, 224–44. Those who opposed Amyraut the most vehemently during this time included Pierre du Moulin, Friedrich Spanheim, John Owen (who wrote *Death of Death* as a response to Amyraldian and Arminian views of the extent of the atonement), and Francis Turretin.

125. Amyraut, *Brief Traitté*, 78; trans. and quoted in Armstrong, *Calvinism and the Amyraut Heresy*, 211. The word "equally" was dropped in each case from the 1658 edition of the *Brief Traitté*.

faith, according to the absolute will of the Father.[126] This hypothetical aspect of the atonement has led many to refer to Amyraut's view as "hypothetical universalism."[127] We should note, however, that Amyraut's hypothetical universalism is not the same as the hypothetical universalism present at the Synod of Dort, and was developed independently of that view.[128]

Amyraut based his position upon a distinction he saw in the will of God: God has a conditional will and an absolute will. This idea of God's two wills (hidden and revealed, commanding and decreeing, permissive and absolute) is a familiar one in Reformed theology, but Amyraut uses it in a unique way by reversing the traditional emphasis. Like other Reformers, Amyraut believed that God's absolute will includes his unconditional election and irresistible grace, and that it is always infallibly effective.[129] Whereas this absolute will was the primary object of theology for a traditional Reformed theologian such as John Calvin or Theodore Beza, Amyraut believed that God's absolute will was incomprehensible and therefore not a proper object of theological study. For Amyraut this means that God's conditional will is paramount, and it is therefore the focus of his theology.[130] In addition to an absolute election of some to salvation according to his absolute will, God conditionally elected all people to be saved according to his conditional will.[131] Christ's atonement fulfilled God's conditional will, and since God desires the salvation of all people on the condition that they believe, Christ died for all people provided that they believe.[132] Amyraut also taught that Christ died especially for the elect, because only the elect believe, but for him the particularity of the atonement was always subordinate to its universality, just as the absolute will was always subordinate to the conditional will.[133]

---

126. Armstrong, *Calvinism and the Amyraut Heresy*, 212–15.

127. "Amyraldianism" and "hypothetical universalism" are often used synonymously to refer to the moderate Calvinist understanding of the extent of the atonement. This was the practice in the seventeenth century, as can be seen in Richard Baxter, *Plain Scripture Proof*, 289, 332, and it continues to be practiced in the present day.

128. Amyraldianism places the decree of election after the decree to send Christ to redeem the world, making the object of predestination redeemed humanity, while hypothetical universalism was generally infralapsarian. Therefore, while both views see the atonement as unlimited they should properly be distinguished. Moore also makes this point in *English Hypothetical Universalism*, 217–20.

129. Thomas, *The Extent of the Atonement*, 194.

130. Armstrong, *Calvinism and the Amyraut Heresy*, 201.

131. Thomas, *The Extent of the Atonement*, 190.

132. Strehle, "Universal Grace," 348.

133. Thomas, *The Extent of the Atonement*, 203.

Amyraut's conception of God's will matched his understanding of God's covenants with humanity. Amyraut believed that the universal, conditional love of God was displayed in a universal, conditional covenant, and that this universal covenant was based upon Christ's atonement.[134] This universal, conditional covenant also revealed God's universal, conditional will for the salvation of all people, which in turn revealed his love, mercy, and goodness. The atonement must be unlimited in light of God's nature as one who is loving and merciful. Because the covenant was universal, the gospel call was meant for all people, and Amyraut argued that it was therefore only possible because of Christ's unlimited atonement.[135] Alongside this universal, conditional covenant of grace was an absolute covenant of grace, but this absolute covenant was not the work of the Son; it was the work of the Spirit.[136] For Amyraut, the atonement was only universal, and the particularity of God's saving work was appropriated to the Spirit. Amyraut also expressed this difference in the Son and the Spirit's work by making a distinction between objective grace (the universal work of the Son in the atonement) and subjective grace (the particular work of the Spirit in applying salvation to believers).[137]

---

134. Amyraut, following his mentor John Cameron, believed that the concept of covenant was at the center of theology. Amyraut believed that there were three covenants: the covenant of nature, the covenant of law, and the covenant of grace. These covenants build upon one another, so the covenant of grace is superior to the covenants of nature and law. They also succeed one another in history, so that now the covenant of grace is the preeminent manifestation of God's mercy and goodness. Amyraut believed that each covenant was appropriately attributed to one of the members of the Trinity. The covenants of nature and law pertain chiefly to the Father, the covenant of grace relates to the Son, and the application of the covenant of grace is the Spirit's work. For an explanation of Amyraut's covenantal theology, see Armstrong, *Calvinism and the Amyraut Heresy*, 140–57, 203–21; and Thomas, *The Extent of the Atonement*, 194–97.

135. Thomas, *The Extent of the Atonement*, 201.

136. Armstrong, *Calvinism and the Amyraut Heresy*, 209.

137. Armstrong explains, "And as the sun was designed to give light to all men, so the objective grace procured by Christ is designed for all men. However this sufficient objective grace must be desired, must be willingly received. If a man does not open his eyes the light of the sun is of no avail to him. The analogy holds in relation to grace as well, for although Jesus is the light of the world, he is of no avail to the one the eyes of whose understanding have not been illuminated, who does not participate in this light through faith." Amyraut used this distinction to keep the provision of salvation by Christ and the application of salvation by the Spirit as two separate activities. For Amyraut, there is no necessary connection between the atonement of salvation by Christ and the application of salvation by the Spirit. Strictly speaking, while salvation is only possible because of the atonement, the atonement in and of itself does not save anyone. Ibid., 210–11.

Amyraut's view of the extent of the atonement was driven somewhat by apologetic, pastoral, and homiletic concerns.[138] Ultimately, however, Amyraut's unlimited atonement was demanded by his unique system of theology, as it was a necessary corollary to his universal, conditional covenant and the universal, conditional saving will and love of God. Reformed theologians brought a multitude of charges against this unique theological system, and attacked it as vehemently as they did Arminianism. They frequently labeled Amyraut's views as illogical, absurd, rationalistic, and novel.[139] Most saw Amyraldianism as functionally equivalent to Arminianism, and many of the same arguments used against the Arminian view of unlimited atonement were used to argue against Amyraut's view as well.[140] Despite their censure in the Swiss Consensus of 1675, however, a number of Christians held Amyraldian views general during the seventeenth and eighteenth centuries. Once again, the Reformed Community could not reach a firm resolution regarding the extent of the atonement. As Michael Thomas states, "It seems fair to conclude that the question of the extent of the atonement, already handled ambiguously by the Synod of Dort, was never satisfactorily answered by the Reformed churches throughout their early and classical period."[141]

138. Thomas, *The Extent of the Atonement*, 200–03.

139. Francis Turretin leveled four absurdities against Amyraldianism. First, it requires that Christ died for multitudes that have never heard and will never hear the gospel. Second, it requires that Christ died for those whom the Father has eternally decreed would never receive salvation (those he predestined to reprobation). Third, it requires that he died for those who are already in hell, and that he suffered the punishment for those who are already suffering the punishment for their sins. Fourth, this view requires that Christ be the Savior and Redeemer of those who are never saved, and therefore he would be an imperfect and impartial Savior; the author of the acquisition of salvation but not its application. Turretin, *Institutes*, 471–72. Amyraut's position was not necessarily absurd, however, if Amyraut's theological presuppositions, which were quite different from those of the orthodox Reformed, were granted.

140. These arguments can all be found in Owen's work. (1) It was argued that the atonement could not have been for all since many were already in hell when Christ died; to suffer for them would have been useless. Owen, *Death of Death*, 61, 135–36. (2) The sacrifice, intercession, and resurrection of Christ, and the giving of the Spirit, are all apart of one work, and cannot be divided. Ibid., 110–24. Owen, however, divorced Christ's universal lordship from his death, probably because he saw the implications of this universal lordship at least suggested an unlimited atonement. Ibid., 92. (3) If Christ died for all sins, then he died for unbelief, therefore unbelief cannot be why some people are not saved by the atonement. Ibid., 61–62. (4) God cannot require a double payment for sin. Ibid., 157–58. (5) Biblical texts require particular redemption. Ibid., 124–309. Owen essentially saw the atonement as an accomplished fact, and in his mind to separate the procurement of salvation from its application or to introduce conditionality into the atonement was to make it an empty atonement.

141. Thomas, *The Extent of the Atonement*, 241.

RICHARD BAXTER

Richard Baxter's (1615–1691) view on the extent of the atonement is noteworthy both for its uniqueness and because of the way that Baxter's theology has impacted evangelicalism.[142] Baxter's view, even more so than Amyraut's, is truly a "middle way" between Calvinism and Arminianism. Baxter saw the Arminian view as an extreme reaction against particular redemption and the popularization of the Calvinist view as an extreme reaction against Arminianism, and attempted to mediate between the extremes of the two positions. He wrote *Universal Redemption of Mankind by the Lord Jesus Christ*, his book defending this view, by 1650, although it was not published until 1694. J. I. Packer, an advocate of particular redemption, goes so far as to state that "Baxter made the best of 'hypothetical universalism' that can ever be made of it."[143] His is a way that few have followed, however, for reasons explained below.

Baxter believed that the atonement was unlimited, and that Christ died for the sins of every individual.[144] He also believed in God's sovereignty throughout redemption, holding to unconditional election and irresistible grace. Baxter believed that God has done all that the Arminians affirm (universal grace), and more, and this more is God's particular grace in election and the application of salvation.[145] What set Baxter's view apart from previous explanations of the extent of the atonement, however, is his use of the "political method."[146] This theological emphasis made Baxter's position unique in two ways. First, it led him to assert a governmental theory of the atonement instead of penal substitution, similar to that of Hugo Grotius and many Arminians after Arminius.[147] For Baxter this meant that Christ did not satisfy the law in the place of sinners through substitution, but instead satisfied the justice of the Lawgiver (God) so that all people could

---

142. Baxter's theology represented a *via media* between Arminianism and strict Calvinism. This middle way greatly influenced English theology, both Anglican and Dissenting, in his own day and into the next two centuries. Baxter also influenced the development of American evangelical theology as can be seen through his impact upon the New England School via Samuel Hopkins. See McGonigle, *Sufficient Saving Grace*, 66–67; and Sell, *The Great Debate*, 31–32, 109–10.

143. Packer, *Redemption and Restoration*, 400.

144. Baxter, *Universal Redemption*, 286–87.

145. Baxter, *Practical Works*, 8:529.

146. For more on Baxter's political method see Beougher, *Richard Baxter*, 38; and Packer, *Redemption and Restoration*, 213.

147. Baxter, *Universal Redemption*, 390. For an explanation of Grotius's governmental theory of the atonement, see McDonald, *Atonement of the Death of Christ*, 203–7.

now be accepted on account of their faith rather than through the law.[148] Baxter did not follow Grotius's view completely, however, but maintained some Anselmic and Reformed emphases in contradiction to Grotius and the Arminians.[149]

The second way that Baxter's political method impacted his view of the extent of the atonement is through his idea that the universal government of God in the covenant of grace demands a universal atonement.[150] God's work as governor is for all people. Through Christ's unlimited atonement, God provides common grace and the universal gospel call, meaning that all those who perish apart from Christ do so because of their rejection of him, not because they were ordained by God to do so.[151] In this way, universal redemption also protected the justice of God and preserved the horrors of hell.[152] Baxter insisted that all people had a chance to be saved; any notion of particular redemption harmed evangelism.[153] Baxter also insisted, however, that only the elect would be saved. Christ's death provided everyone an opportunity to be saved if they would choose Christ, but only the elect choose Christ through the power of the Spirit. For Baxter Christ's work on the cross is wholly universal and his redemption includes all people; it is only the Spirit's regenerating work that is confined to the elect.[154] Baxter carefully distinguished the absolute promises of God for the elect from the moral government of God which was for all people because of Christ's unlimited atonement.[155]

Baxter's hypothetical universalism is unique in that he attempted to unite the Governmental view of the atonement with a Calvinistic understanding of God's sovereignty in redemption. Packer believes that in doing

---

148. Beougher, *Richard Baxter*, 49–50.
149. Ibid., 50.
150. Baxter, *Universal Redemption*, 446–47.
151. Ibid., 104.
152. Packer, *Redemption and Restoration*, 233–35.
153. Baxter, *Universal Redemption*, 223.
154. Ibid., 347.
155. Ibid., 305, 430–31. Packer elaborates, "His [Christ's] infallible drawing of the elect, by which he brings them to faith, the covenant condition, is no part of moral government, as such, but the act of a Divine Proprietor 'as absolute Lord above Laws.' Nor is Christ's statement about his intention thus to draw them any part of the law of his kingdom, the covenant of grace. Those who included absolute promises to the elect in their definition of the covenant, Baxter held, were confusing the exercise of *imperium* and *dominium*, which must be held apart. In fact, Christ bestows varying degrees of grace and opportunity upon different individuals, according to the dictates of infinite wisdom. But this is something quite distinct from his legislation, by which he offers salvation on equal terms to all." Packer, *Redemption and Restoration*, 223.

so, Baxter avoids what he sees as the glaring inconsistencies of other versions of hypothetical universalism.[156] Despite this assertion, evangelicals today do not appeal to Baxter's view of the extent of the atonement. This seems to be the case for two reasons. First, Baxter's political method is clearly a product of his time, and is no longer used.[157] Second, Calvinists generally reject the governmental theory of the atonement, with the result that Moderate Calvinists generally do not appeal to the governmental nature of the atonement as support for their view. From both sides of the debate, Baxter's mediating position on the extent of the atonement seems to concede too much truth.

JOHN OWEN

John Owen's (1616–1683) seventeenth century work on the extent of the atonement, *The Death of Death in the Death of Christ* (1648), is a polemical work directed against the Arminian, Amyraldian, and hypothetical universalism views of unlimited atonement. Many reformed theologians consider it to be the definitive work defending particular redemption.[158] Owen's defense of particular redemption is not substantially different from prior explanations of the doctrine, but the thoroughness of his arguments, both for particular redemption and against unlimited atonement, make his work perhaps the most exhaustive treatment of particular redemption ever written. Owen's view of particular redemption is also noteworthy due to the influence he has had upon the evangelical debate concerning the extent of the atonement, as all who deal seriously with the subject must interact with his arguments.

The Death of Death in the Death of Christ is divided into four "books." The first two books attempt to demonstrate the truth of particular redemption by explaining the intentions behind Christ's atonement and the atonement's actual accomplishments. For Owen, the intentions and

---

156. Packer believes that hypothetical universalism makes God unwise because Christ's death for the nonelect was pointless, and it makes God unjust because God is bound to save those for whom Christ has died. According to Packer, Baxter avoids these inconsistencies by accepting a Governmental view of the nature of the atonement and by denying that one can inquire into the relationship between God's general love for the world and his special love for the elect. Ibid., 399–400.

157. As Packer states, "His assumption that seventeenth–century political ideas were the key to Biblical theology appears today absurdly naïve." Ibid., 402.

158. E.g., Packer states, "It is safe to say that no comparable exposition of the work of redemption as planned and executed by the Triune Jehovah has ever been done since Owen published his. None has ever been needed." Packer, "Introductory Essay," 12–13. See also Thomas, *Extent of the Atonement*, 225.

accomplishments of the atonement demanded particular redemption, because he understood all of the intentions and the accomplishments of the atonement as salvific.[159] This means that the applications of the atonement are only salvific; all for whom the Father intended the atonement will be saved by the atonement.[160] Owen argued that because God's intention in the atonement was to save all for whom Christ died, unlimited atonement either resulted in God's failure to achieve his intention, which was blasphemous, or it resulted in universalism, which was unscriptural.[161] In order to demonstrate that God's intentions in the atonement were only for the elect, and that therefore Christ died only for the elect, Owen spends the first half of his book setting forth the agent of salvation (the Triune God), the means of salvation (the atonement and intercession of Jesus Christ), and the end of salvation (the glory of God through the salvation of the elect).[162]

Owen begins his defense of particular redemption by explaining the unity of the Triune God in redemption, both in intention and means. The Father has two intentions in his plan of redemption. First, he sends the Son into the world in order to save the world, with the world referring to believers. Owen distinguishes three acts of the Father in sending the Son into the world. First, the Father appointed Christ to the office of Mediator, and in doing so promises Christ that he will give him his people and certainly apply the saving benefits of the atonement to them. Second, the Father furnished the Son with all of the gifts and graces that would be necessary for his saving work. Third, the Father entered into a covenant with the Son, promising him that his atonement would certainly accomplish the salvation of the elect. All of these actions of the Father require particular redemption.[163] The Father's second intention in the atonement is to lay the punishment of the sins of the elect upon the Son. Owen understood the atonement to be an identical, penal, and substitutionary payment for the sins of the elect. This meant that Christ fully satisfied the wrath of God against the sins of the elect, and therefore that the elect are actually saved by the atonement. For Owen, the nature of the atonement was such that if the atonement was for all people than all people had to be saved.[164]

---

159. Owen, *Death of Death*, 46.
160. Ibid., 47.
161. Ibid., 47–48.
162. Ibid., 51.
163. Ibid., 51–59.
164. Ibid., 59–62, 157–58.

In response to the Father's intentions the Son submits through his incarnation, oblation, and intercession.[165] The Holy Spirit then assists the Son throughout the Son's incarnation, oblation, and resurrection.[166] Owen includes no mention of the Spirit's work in applying the atonement to the elect, instead describing the application of the atonement as a work of the Son throughout the book. As the Father and the Spirit's work in redemption concentrates in Christ, Owen then explains the means of redemption, or the Son's atonement and intercession. Owen maintains that the atonement and intercession of Christ are inseparably connected and are for the exact same people, which demands particular redemption.[167] After expounding the agent and means of redemption, Owen then explains the goal of redemption. The supreme goal of redemption is the glory of God, and this is achieved through the intermediate goal of redemption, or the actual salvation of God's elect people.[168] Throughout the first two books of *The Death of Death in the Death of Christ* Owen explicitly denies that there are multiple intentions in the atonement. He states, "That there is any other end of the death of Christ, besides the fruit of his ransom and propitiation, directly intended, and not by accident attending it, is utterly false. Yea, what other end the ransom paid by Christ and the atonement made by him can have but the fruits of them, is not imaginable."[169] The sole purpose of the atonement is to save the elect, for the elect alone are the objects of God's love.[170]

In the last two books Owen brings forth sixteen arguments against unlimited atonement and responds to all of the biblical and theological arguments brought against particular redemption. Some of the most significant arguments that Owens uses to refute unlimited atonement are that the gospel does not go out to all people, meaning that if Christ did die for all people than God is either unwise, unloving, or frustrated; Christ's satisfaction for the sin of the people for whom he died ensured their salvation, meaning he could not have died for all; Christ is the mediator for all for whom he died; Christ procured sanctification and the gift of faith for all for whom he died; and Christ actually redeemed, reconciled, and satisfied the sins of those for whom he died.[171] In responding to the arguments used for unlimited atonement, Owen first goes through all of the texts typically used to argue for

---

165. Ibid., 62–65.
166. Ibid., 66–67.
167. Ibid., 67–88.
168. Ibid., 89–91.
169. Ibid., 104. See also 79–80, 87–88, 99, 105, 118.
170. Ibid., 115, 119.
171. Ibid., 126–74.

unlimited atonement and explains why they do not support that doctrine.[172] He then specifically responds to several arguments of Thomas More, who had written a book entitled *The Universality of God's Free Grace in Christ to Mankind* (1646) defending unlimited atonement.[173] Owen ends his book by briefly responding to several theological arguments used to support unlimited atonement and by including several quotes from the early church fathers that seem to indicate their support for particular redemption.[174]

Owen's work on the extent of the atonement is a model of Reformed, supralapsarian theology. Everything that God wills to happen will happen, which means that if God desires the salvation of someone he or she will be saved. Therefore Christ could only have died for the elect, because it is clear that all people are not saved. Due to the atonement's nature as an exact substitution for the sins of the elect, the atonement was an objective fact that actually accomplished the salvation of the elect, and it was in no way conditional.[175] Owen did allow for the universal sufficiency of the atonement, following the Canons of Dort, but he maintained that this sufficiency was empty apart from intention, and that the atonement was in no way for the nonelect.[176] Owen's view of particular redemption continues to be influential in contemporary evangelicalism, and many of his arguments are still used in the debate today.

JOHN WESLEY

John Wesley (1703–1791) has greatly impacted evangelicalism, as his views, perhaps even more so than Jacob Arminius's, have significantly influenced

---

172. Ibid., 182–256. Many of these exegetical arguments will be examined or noted in chapters 3 and 4.

173. Ibid., 256–91. Concerning More's book, Packer notes, "More's exposition seems to be of little intrinsic importance; Owen, however, selects it as the fullest statement of the case for universal redemption that had yet appeared in English and uses it unmercifully as a chopping-block." Packer, "Introductory Essay," 24.

174. *Death of Death*, 292–312. Owen includes quotes from several of the early church fathers, such as Athanasius and Ambrose, but it is likely that the only two men whom Owen quotes that actually believed in particular redemption were Augustine and Prosper, as we saw at the beginning of this chapter.

175. Ibid., 123.

176. Owen believed that the universal sufficiency of the atonement grounded the universal gospel call, but that this sufficiency in no way meant that the atonement was for the nonelect. The intention of the atonement determines who it was for, not its intrinsic nature, and for Owen the atonement was only intended for the elect because it only saves the elect. Ibid., 264, 271–72.

Arminian theology.[177] Wesley's view of unlimited atonement is not substantially different from Arminius's view, but it does have several particular emphases that are common in Arminian evangelical theology today. Whereas Arminius's view was more academic, Wesley's was more popular and practical. His first major exposition opposing predestination and particular redemption was a sermon he preached on April 29, 1739 entitled *Free Grace*, which he subsequently published.[178] This sermon was based upon Romans 8:32 and its thesis was that the grace of God which brings salvation is free in all and free for all.

In this sermon Wesley advances his notion of free grace by challenging the doctrine of unconditional election. He asserts that any unconditional decree of only some to salvation entails a corresponding decree to damnation for the rest.[179] He then proceeds to list the consequences of this doctrine. Predestination makes preaching void because the destiny of all men is already irresistibly decreed, it undermines the call to holy living because it tends to destroy the pursuit after godliness, it takes away the comfort of Christianity because people will always fear that they might be reprobate, it takes away the zeal for good works, and it makes the gospel unnecessary because the gospel can add nothing to the already certain salvation of the elect or change the fate of the nonelect.[180] Wesley rebuts predestination exegetically by appealing to verses such as 1 Timothy 2:6; Hebrews 2:9; and 1 John 2:2, insisting that such verses teach God's universal love for humanity and rule out any notion of an absolute decree of predestination.[181] Wesley made no attempt to ground free grace in Romans 8, but instead insisted that free grace was a result of Christ's unlimited atonement.[182] This sermon facilitated the division of the burgeoning Methodist movement into two camps: an Arminian one led by Wesley and a Calvinist one led by George Whitefield.[183]

Although there is no evidence that he ever preached this sermon again, Wesley published it nine times during his lifetime, and his views on the subject of predestination or the extent of the atonement never changed.[184] In 1741, Wesley published another sermon where he focused more on the ex-

---

177. Olson, *Arminian Theology*, 24–25.
178. The text of this sermon can be found in Wesley, *Works*, 3:542–63.
179. Ibid., 3:547.
180. Ibid., 3:547–53.
181. Ibid., 3:553–54.
182. Ibid., 3:559–63.
183. McGonigle, *Sufficient Saving Grace*, 119–29.
184. Ibid., 120.

tent of the atonement entitled *Scripture Doctrine Concerning Predestination, Election, and Reprobation*.[185] In considering the question of whose sins Christ died for, Wesley presented all of the texts that speak of Christ dying for the "world," "all," "whosoever," etc. as teaching that Christ died for the sins of every person. He presents seven arguments that demand Christ's unlimited atonement: the prophets, Christ, and the apostles all teach it, there is not one Scripture that says he did not die for all or affirms that he only died for some, God commands the gospel to be preached to every person, he calls all people to repent (Acts 17:30), those who are lost are damned for not believing in Christ and so he must have died for them or they would be damned for not believing a lie, and Scripture speaks of those whom Christ bought by his death who do not believe in him (2 Pet 2:1). There are also dreadful absurdities that follow from believing limited atonement: if Christ did not die for all, then unbelief is not a sin because the lost have nothing to believe in; it would be a sin for the lost to believe in Christ because they would have to believe a lie; those who preach the gospel to all people are lying; and the view makes God unjust when he declares that he is not willing that any should perish (2 Pet 3:9), because he is willing that many should perish.[186] People are not lost because Christ did not die for them; rather, they are lost because of unbelief, and all people are not saved because all people do not believe.

Wesley also believed that an unlimited atonement was necessary for prevenient grace. Prevenient grace is one of the key doctrines of Arminianism, and it was extremely important for Wesley.[187] According to Wesley, prevenient grace is God's initial work in salvation,[188] and this grace is available to all people, including the unregenerate, because it is freely offered in Christ's atonement.[189] Wesley based this view on his understanding of Romans 5:18.[190] Like Arminius, Wesley believed that through prevenient grace God restored every human being's free will, allowing each person to accept or reject the gospel. Prevenient grace does not in and of itself save, but as a person responds to this grace God gives him more grace that leads to his salvation. For Wesley, justification is by grace alone through faith alone.

---

185. Wesley included this sermon in his 1758 apologetic work *A Preservative against Unsettled Notions of Religion*. It was published six times during Wesley's lifetime.

186. McGonigle, *Sufficient Saving Grace*, 140–43.

187. Renshaw, "Atonement," 151.

188. Wesley, *Works* [CD-ROM], 6:509.

189. Ibid., 8:277.

190. Ibid.

Wesley followed in the footsteps of Arminius and the Remonstrants, shunned the liberal excesses of Arminianism in the eighteenth century, and affirmed the central Reformed doctrines of original sin and justification by faith alone. Like Arminius, Wesley believed in a penal substitutionary atonement and believed that the entire ground of justification by faith is Christ's penal substitutionary atonement, but rejected the strict Calvinist notion that a substitutionary atonement demanded the salvation of all for whom Christ was the substitute.[191] His understanding of unlimited atonement and the arguments he used to counter particular redemption continue to have influence today.

NINETEENTH CENTURY EVANGELICALISM TO TODAY

The contemporary evangelical movement is a descendant of the great eighteenth-century evangelical revivals led by men such as John Wesley, George Whitefield, and Jonathan Edwards.[192] Just as Wesley and Whitefield did, today's evangelicals unite around key theological issues such as biblical inspiration, the importance of evangelism, the need for a conversion experience, and the importance of living a life of discipleship,[193] but they continue to divide over the extent of the atonement. As has been true throughout church history, the majority view in evangelicalism today (and of Christianity outside of evangelicalism) is unlimited atonement, though particular redemption is still a strong minority view.[194]

Particular Redemption

In the nineteenth and early twentieth centuries the "Princeton" theologians such as A. A. Hodge, Charles Hodge, and B. B. Warfield provided a strong biblical and theological basis for particular redemption within evangelicalism.[195] These men were Reformed theologians who followed the theol-

---

191. Wesley, *Works*, 1:186. Many of Wesley's followers would deviate from him by affirming the governmental theory of the atonement as opposed to penal substitution, but not all of them did.

192. For an account of this movement from the revivals to today, see Brand, "Defining Evangelicalism," 284–87.

193. Ibid., 304.

194. Advocates on either side of the debate recognize this. Bloesch, *Jesus Christ*, 168; and Nicole, "Particular Redemption," 165.

195. Hodge, *The Atonement*, 347–429; idem, *Outlines of Theology*, 401–25; Hodge, *Systematic Theology*, 2:544–62; Warfield, *Person and Work*, 325–530; and idem, *Plan*

ogy of Augustine, John Calvin and the Westminster Confession of Faith. Regarding the atonement, they taught a strict penal substitutionary view in which Christ satisfied the demands of God's law in the sinner's place.[196] Particular redemption was for them a necessary doctrine not only because they believed that Scripture taught it, but because it was consistent with the covenant of grace, the doctrine of election, the special love of God for the elect, and the nature of the atonement. All three men restated and affirmed the sufficient/efficient formula, following the Canons of Dort.[197] Particular redemption was also understood to be the classical Reformed position, and seen as a necessary part of Calvinist theology. As Warfield states, "Calvinism insists that the saving operations of God are directed in every case immediately to the individuals who are saved. Particularism in the processes of salvation becomes thus the mark of Calvinism. As supernaturalism is the mark of Christianity at large, and evangelicalism the mark of Protestantism, so particularism is the mark of Calvinism. The Calvinist is he who holds with full consciousness that the Lord, in his saving operations, deals not generally with mankind at large, but particularly with the individuals who are actually saved."[198]

Following the Princetonians, there have been several other notable evangelical works defending the doctrine of particular redemption in the twentieth century. Loraine Boettner[199] and Louis Berkhof[200] both articulated and defended a Calvinistic theology in which particular redemption was seen as a necessary and significant doctrine. John Murray's classic book on Reformed soteriology, *Redemption Accomplished and Applied*, includes a chapter on particular redemption that ties the extent of the atonement to the nature of Christ's atonement as a penal substitutionary sacrifice.[201] R. B. Kuiper's work on the subject is noteworthy in contrasting particular redemption with other views of the extent of the atonement and because it in-

---

of Salvation, 89–106. James A. Boyce, one of the earliest Southern Baptist theologians, following his mentor Charles Hodge, also affirmed particular redemption. Boyce, *Abstract*, 336–40. Other significant defenses of particular redemption in the nineteenth century include Cunningham, *Historical Theology*, 2:323–70; Dabney, *Systematic Theology*, 513–35; Shedd, *Dogmatic Theology*, 2:464–89; Smeaton, *Apostle's Doctrine*; and Symington, *Atonement*, 184–234.

196. Hodge, *Outlines of Theology*, 401–15; Hodge, *Systematic Theology*, 2:480–543; and Warfield, *Person and Work*, 325–530.

197. Hodge, *Outlines of Theology*, 418–21; Hodge, *Systematic Theology*, 2:544–46; and Warfield, *Plan of Salvation*, 100–06.

198. Warfield, *Plan of Salvation*, 89.

199. Boettner, *Reformed Doctrine*, 150–61.

200. Berkhof, *Systematic Theology*, 392–99.

201. Murray, *Redemption Accomplished and Applied*, 59–75.

cludes a chapter on the general intentions in the atonement.[202] Gary Long's book is a theological defense of particular redemption that emphasizes the unity of the triune God's saving works and purposes.[203] Roger Nicole[204] and J. I. Packer[205] have written several articles and essays expounding the classic articulation of particular redemption, and several systematic theologies of the twentieth century have also defended the doctrine.[206] More recent explanations of particular redemption typically build upon and reiterate most of the biblical and theological work done by the above theologians and their predecessors such as Augustine, Calvin, Beza, and Owen.[207] Many recent theologians continue to defend particular redemption because they believe it is the only view of the extent of the atonement that is consistent with the biblical nature of the atonement as penal substitution or with God's gracious sovereignty throughout salvation.[208]

Unlimited Atonement

The Arminian understanding of unlimited atonement entered evangelicalism through the works of Jacob Arminius and the John Wesley. Nineteenth century Arminian theologians were divided on the nature of the atonement, but were united in their view of unlimited atonement. Men such as Richard Watson, William Burton Pope, and Thomas Summers defended unlimited atonement along with penal substitutionary atonement, just as Arminius and Wesley did.[209] Other nineteenth century Arminian theologians, however, such as Charles Finney and John Miley, advocated a governmental

202. Kuiper, *For Whom Did Christ Die?*

203. Long, *Definite Atonement*.

204. E.g., Nicole, "Definite Atonement," 199–207; idem, "Covenant, Universal Call," 403–11; idem, "Heidelberg Catechism," 138–45; idem, "John Calvin's View," 197–225; and idem, "Particular Redemption," 168–69.

205. E.g., Packer, "Introductory Essay," 1–25; idem, "The Love of God," 277–91; idem, "To All Who Will Come," 179–89; and idem, "What Did the Cross Achieve," 3–45.

206. E.g., Buswell, *Systematic Theology*, 2:70–133; Grudem, *Systematic Theology*, 594–603; and Reymond, *New Systematic Theology*, 671–702.

207. E.g., Barnes, *Atonement Matters*; Dunham, "Limited Atonement"; Elliott, "A Biblical Defense"; Reisinger, *Limited Atonement*; and Wells, *A Price for a People*.

208. E.g., Hill and James III, *The Glory of the Atonement*; Jeffery, Ovey, and Sach, *Pierced for Our Transgressions*, 268–78; Letham, *Work of Christ*, 225–47; Morey, *Studies in the Atonement*, 57–74; Peterson and Williams, *Why I Am Not an Arminian*; Piper, *Fifty Reasons*; Sproul, *The Truth of the Cross*; and Wells, *Cross Words*, 233–46.

209. Pope, *Compendium*, 2:263–316; Summers, *Systematic Theology*, 2:35–44; and Watson, *Theological Institutes*, 2:102–37.

theory of the atonement along with unlimited atonement.[210] This division over the nature of the atonement among Arminians has sometimes resulted in the mistaken charge that the governmental theory of the atonement is the standard Arminian view, and that unlimited atonement is incompatible with a penal substitutionary atonement.[211]

Division among Arminians concerning the nature of the atonement has continued into the twentieth and twenty-first centuries, but so has a consensus concerning the extent of the atonement. Some, such as F. Leroy Forlines, Thomas Oden, and Robert Picirilli hold to penal substitution,[212] while others such as H. Orton Wiley, R. Larry Shelton, and H. Ray Dunning hold to the governmental theory of the atonement.[213] Recent work articulating and defending unlimited atonement has included several articles and essays as well as some popular-level books.[214] The most common arguments for unlimited atonement from an Arminian perspective continue to be the numerous universal texts of Scripture describing God's salvific work and desire, the universal nature of God's love, the consistency of unlimited atonement with other Arminian doctrines such as conditional election and prevenient grace, and the necessity of the universal gospel call.

Although there were some Calvinists who defended unlimited atonement in the nineteenth century,[215] moderate Calvinism has persisted within evangelical theology due primarily to the work of the Dispensationalist movement and Baptists. Dispensationalist theologians such as Lewis Sperry Chafer, Henry C. Thiessen, Emery H. Bancroft, John Walvoord, Charles Ryrie, and Robert Lightner, have all held to unlimited atonement within a generally Calvinistic soteriology.[216] They hold to doctrines such as penal

---

210. Finney, *Finney's Lectures*, 258–82; and Miley, *Systematic Theology*, 2:65–240.

211. Letham, *Work of Christ*, 230–31; Nicole, "Definite Atonement," 202; Palmer, *Five Points of Calvinism*, 47–48; Peterson and Williams, *Why I Am Not an Arminian*, 198–99; and Reymond, "Consistent Supralapsarian," 165–68.

212. Forlines, *The Quest for Truth*, 187–203; Oden, *The Word of Life*, 344–425; and Picirilli, *Grace, Faith, Free Will*, 85–138.

213. Dunning, *Grace, Faith, and Holiness*, 331–93; Shelton, "Initial Salvation," 485–505; and Wiley, *Christian Theology*, 2:279–300.

214. E.g., Hunt, *What Love is This*, 293–308; Lake, "He Died for All," 31–50; Marshall, "For All," 322–46; idem, "Universal Grace," 51–69; Miethe, "The Universal Power of the Atonement," 78–85; Sailer, "A Wesleyan View," 189–98; and Walls and Dongell, *Why I Am Not a Calvinist*.

215. More notable ones include Campbell, *The Nature of the Atonement*; and Wardlaw, *Discourses*.

216. Bancroft, *Christian Theology*, 118, 154; Chafer, *Systematic Theology*, 3:183–205; Lightner, *Death Christ Died*; Ryrie, *Basic Theology*, 318–23; Thiessen, *Lectures*, 240–42; Walvoord, *Jesus Christ Our Lord*; and idem, "Reconciliation," 3–12.

substitutionary atonement, effectual calling, total depravity, and unconditional election, but do not believe that these doctrines demand particular redemption. On the contrary, they argue that the biblical teaching demands unlimited atonement. In order to differentiate between the ways that the atonement affects the elect and the nonelect, the provision of salvation in the atonement and the application of salvation are carefully distinguished.[217] These theologians do share some affinities with Arminians, however, as at least some believe that an unlimited atonement paid for sin to such an extent that those who do not personally commit sin (such as infants) are never guilty of sin and therefore saved on the basis of the atonement.[218] Some also agree with Arminians that the only basis for condemnation is unbelief, as people are no longer culpable for their other sins because every other sin has been paid for in the atonement.[219]

Baptists have been divided over the extent of the atonement almost since their beginning.[220] Unlike many denominations, Baptists have always included Calvinists, moderate Calvinists, and Arminians in their ranks, and many have attempted to mediate between the two systems. Twentieth century evangelical Baptists such as Augustus Strong, E. Y. Mullins, Norman Douty, Gordon Lewis, Bruce Demarest, Millard Erickson, and James Leo Garrett, have all argued for a moderate Calvinist understanding of unlimited atonement.[221] These arguments are normally exegetically and practically based. Erickson is typical when he states, "We conclude that the hypothesis of universal atonement is able to account for a larger segment of the biblical witness with less distortion than is the hypothesis of limited atonement."[222] Like Dispensationalists, these Baptists also emphasize the difference between the provision and application of salvation.[223] Much debate has recently

217. Bancroft, *Christian Theology*, 118; Chafer, *Systematic Theology*, 193–94; Lightner, *Death Christ Died*, 90–91; Ryrie, *Basic Theology*, 322–23; and Thiessen, *Lectures*, 242.

218. Bancroft, *Christian Theology*, 154; and Thiessen, *Lectures*, 241–42.

219. Bancroft, *Christian Theology*, 154; Chafer, *Systematic Theology*, 195–99; Lightner, *Death Christ Died*, 94, 100–02; Thiessen, *Lectures*, 241; and Walvoord, "Reconciliation," 11.

220. For a discussion of the differences between Particular and General Baptists as they relate to the extent of the atonement, see Garrett, *Systematic Theology*, 65–66. For the history of the debate over soteriology among Baptists see Nettles, *By His Grace and for His Glory*.

221. Douty, *Did Christ Die*; Erickson, *Christian Theology*, 842–52; Garrett, *Systematic Theology*, 59–69; Lewis and Demarest, *Integrative Theology*, 2:409–10; Strong, *Systematic Theology*, 771–73; and Mullins, *The Christian Religion*, 336.

222. Erickson, *Christian Theology*, 851.

223. Ibid., 851–52; Garrett, *Systematic Theology*, 69; Lewis and Demarest, *Integrative Theology*, 2:409–10; and Strong, *Systematic Theology*, 772–73.

taken place within the Southern Baptist Convention concerning Calvinism and Arminianism, including the extent of the atonement, with advocates for both particular redemption and unlimited atonement making their cases.[224] These debates mirror those in evangelicalism as a whole, as the extent of the atonement continues to be a point of contention among Bible–believing Christians.

CONCLUSION

Augustine was the first theologian to challenge the consensus of unlimited atonement in the early church, proposing that Christ died for the elect alone. His desire to preserve the sovereignty of God throughout salvation led him to this view. The Catholic Church generally accepted Augustine's views on God's sovereignty in salvation, albeit in a modified form, but for the most part rejected his view of the extent of atonement. The Gottschalk controversy in the ninth century revolved around a revival of Augustine's views on the extent of the atonement. This controversy clarified the two primary positions in the debate as well as the majority of their respective exegetical and theological arguments. Some theologians, such as Peter Lombard and Thomas Aquinas, did their best to explain how unlimited atonement fit with God's sovereignty in salvation, while others, such as John Wycliffe, followed Augustine in maintaining particular redemption. John Calvin incorporated Augustinian theology into Protestantism, leading many of his Reformed contemporaries and disciples, such as Theodore Beza and John Owen, to argue for particular redemption. Jacob Arminius, Moïse Amyraut, Richard Baxter, and John Wesley all rejected particular redemption and offered their own variations of unlimited atonement. Arminius and Wesley rejected Calvinistic soteriology and proposed views of unlimited atonement that were consistent with their understanding of God's sovereignty, while Amyraut and Baxter both accepted Calvinistic soteriology and attempted to offer mediating positions on the extent of the atonement. The debate over the extent of the atonement has continued among evangelicals to the present day.

The multi-intentioned view offers a way forward. In attempting to hold together the particular and the general aspects of the atonement, the multi-intentioned view follows in the footsteps of moderate Calvinistic attempts to explain how an unlimited view of Christ's atonement fits with a strong view of God's sovereignty in salvation. In this way the multi-intentioned view is similar to the views of theologians such as Thomas Aquinas, John

---

224. For examples of this recent debate, see Allen and Lemke, *Whosoever Will*; and Waggoner and Clendenen, *Calvinism*.

Historical Background for a Multi-Intentioned View

Davenant, Moïse Amyraut, Richard Baxter, and moderate Calvinists such as Lewis Sperry Chafer or Millard Erickson. What makes the multi-intentioned view unique, however, is the way that it draws together and explains four important aspects of the atonement. First, as we will see in chapter 3, Christ actually paid for the sins of all people in order to accomplish his general purposes; he did not hypothetically or conditionally pay for the sins of the nonelect. Second, as we will explore in chapter 4, God's work of general redemption on the cross is for specific purposes that go beyond the revealed will of God for the salvation of all. In other words, Christ intended to die on the cross to pay for the sins of all people in order to accomplish the universal aspects of God's plan for creation. There is therefore nothing "conditional" or "hypothetical" about the atonement; it accomplishes exactly what God wants it to accomplish. Third, as we will demonstrate in chapter 5, Christ's atonement secured the salvation of the elect. Moderate Calvinist views of the extent of the atonement typically understand the atonement in and of itself to be only universal, and only the application of the atonement to be particular. In the multi-intentioned view the atonement is for all, but it is not for all people in the same way. It does some things for all people, and some things that are just for the elect. Fourth, the general payment for sin in the atonement does not absolve people from their responsibility for their sin. Unlike the common assertions of moderate Calvinism, the multi-intentioned view does not hold that people are only condemned for their lack of faith or that the general payment for sin guaranteed the salvation of anyone. It is only the particular intentions of the atonement that save the elect.

The multi-intentioned view is not an attempt to find a "middle way" between Calvinism and Arminianism. Nor is it an attempt to incorporate Arminian elements into a Calvinistic soteriology. Instead, it is an attempt to highlight the truths of both particular redemption and unlimited atonement while avoiding their weaknesses. The multi-intentioned view agrees with particular redemption because it argues that Christ on the cross intended to certainly secure salvation for the elect and the elect alone. On the other hand, it agrees with unlimited atonement because it argues that Christ paid for the sins of every single person, elect and nonelect. It disagrees with both views, however, because it holds to what each view rejects. Christ intended both to secure the salvation of the elect and to pay for the sins of all people in his redemption. The goal of the multi-intentioned view is to properly emphasize and understand all of the Bible's teaching on the extent of the atonement.

CHAPTER 3

Jesus Christ's Payment for the Sins of All People in the Atonement

INTRODUCTION

JESUS CHRIST'S PAYMENT FOR the sins of the elect and the nonelect through his penal substitutionary atonement is necessary in order to account for the multiple intentions that God had in the atonement. Not only does the atonement ground God's particular, salvific intentions for the elect, but it grounds his general intentions for all of humanity and creation as well. Advocates of particular redemption, however, dispute the idea that a universal payment for sin was necessary in order for the atonement to affect the nonelect and the creation. While most advocates of particular redemption freely admit that there are universal implications or benefits of the atonement, they see no need to ground these benefits in a universal payment for sin.[1] Instead, they understand these universal benefits as a result of the universal sufficiency of Christ's atonement,[2] a result of the universal mediatorial

---

1. Bavinck, *Sin and Salvation*, 470–75; Berkhof, *Systematic Theology*, 438; Boettner, *The Reformed Doctrine of Grace*, 160–61; Kuiper, *For Whom Did Christ Die?*, 78–81; Murray, *Redemption Accomplished and Applied*, 61–62; and Nicole, "Definite Atonement," 199.

2. Kuiper, *For Whom Did Christ Die?*, 79–81.

dominion of Christ,[3] or indirect blessings that come through the blessings bestowed upon the elect in the atonement.[4]

Problems exist, however, with these understandings of the basis of the atonement's general intentions. As we will see in this chapter and the next, the general benefits of the atonement can only be grounded in the atonement's universal sufficiency if this sufficiency refers to an atonement that sufficiently pays for the sins of all people. Particular redemption does not understand sufficiency in this way, but instead understands the universal sufficiency of the atonement to refer to its intrinsic merit as the sacrifice of the infinite God-man.[5] Therefore, particular redemption, despite holding to the universal sufficiency of the atonement, is unable to account for the universal intentions of the atonement, as it is difficult to see how an atonement designed to be only for the elect has designed benefits for the nonelect. As Robert Lightner states, "The very admission of limited redemptionists that some benefits extend to the non-elect means they make the design of God twofold, applying some benefits directly to the elect and others indirectly to the non-elect. Thus, there is inconsistency in the limited view when some of Calvary's achievements are made to extend to all men while others are restricted to the elect. Consistency would restrict all the benefits to the one for whom Christ died; and since in the limited concept Christ died only for the elect, it is illogical to include the non-elect in any sense."[6] The idea that the general benefits of the atonement are indirect benefits of an atonement that was only for the elect seems to be more consistent, but is also unable to recognize any specific intentions in the atonement for the nonelect. The view that these benefits accrue to the nonelect because of Christ's universal dominion (cf. Phil 2:5–11; Col 1:19–20) is true as far as it goes, but it seems difficult to uphold the unity of Christ's work if his kingly work is universal while his priestly work is limited.

The idea that Christ paid for the sins of the elect and the nonelect is necessary in order to account of the general intentions that God had in the atonement, and is therefore central to the multi-intentioned view. In light of this importance, this chapter will biblically and theologically demonstrate Christ's payment for the sins of all people. The Scriptures that express this

3. Murray, *Redemption Accomplished and Applied*, 61–62.

4. Bavinck, *Sin and Salvation*, 471; and Berkhof, *Systematic Theology*, 438.

5. Commenting on the sufficient for all/efficient for some formula adopted by the Synod of Dort, Hans Boersma states, "Christ's death is sufficient for the whole world simply because of who Christ is and because of what he suffered. Dort does not add that his death is sufficient for the whole world because it actually extends to the whole world." Boersma, *Violence, Hospitality, and the Cross*, 71.

6. Lightner, *Death Christ Died*, 110. See also Erickson, *Christian Theology*, 852.

truth are Isaiah 53:4-6; John 1:29; 3:16-17; 4:42; 6:51; 12:46-47; 2 Corinthians 5:14-15, 18-21; 1 Timothy 2:4-6, 4:10; Titus 2:11; Hebrews 2:9; 2 Peter 2:1; 1 John 2:2; and 4:14. We will exegete and explain what these passages teach concerning the extent of the atonement in four sections: Isaiah 53:4-6, the Johannine literature, the Pauline literature, and the General Epistles. Following this biblical defense of Christ's payment for all sin we will explain why a complete and unlimited payment for sin does not entail universalism. Throughout the chapter we will also take special care to respond to the arguments of particular redemption against an unlimited scope in the atonement.

ISAIAH 53:4-6

Isaiah 52:13-53:12[7] is the fourth "Servant Song" in the book of Isaiah (following Isa 42:1-9; 49:1-13; and 50:4-11), and one of the most well known passages of Scripture that describes the substitutionary death of Jesus Christ, the Servant, in the place of sinners.[8] Isaiah 53 explains how Israel can be reconciled to God despite their sin; God will satisfy his justice through the vicarious suffering and death of the Servant for the sins of the people. As John Oswalt states, "This poem expresses the means of salvation that is anticipated in Isaiah 49-52 and in which the people are invited to participate in chs. 54-55."[9] The passage is divided into fives stanzas: 52:13-15; 53:1-3, 4-6, 7-9, and 10-12, and each stanza expresses a different facet of the Servant's person and work.[10] The third stanza is the one that speaks to the extent of the atonement, as it describes whose sins God put upon the Servant.

Isaiah 53:4-6 states, "Surely our griefs He Himself bore, And our sorrows He carried; Yet we ourselves esteemed Him stricken, Smitten of God, and afflicted. But He was pierced through for our transgressions, He was crushed for our iniquities; The chastening for our well-being *fell* upon Him, And by His scourging we are healed. All of us like sheep have gone astray, Each of us has turned to his own way; But the LORD has caused the iniquity

---

7. This passage will be referred to as "Isaiah 53" throughout the book.

8. For a defense of the view that the servant in this passage is Jesus Christ, see Chisholm, Jr., "Christological Fulfillment," 387-404.

9. Oswalt, *The Book of Isaiah: Chapters 40-66*, 385.

10. "In 52:13-15, he is exalted but shocking; in 53:1-3, he is rejected and despised; in 53:4-6, he suffers for sinners ('us'); in 53:7-9, his ministry is unrecognized; and in 53:10-12, he is the sacrificial victor. In this regard, we see the destiny of servanthood, the results of servanthood, the burden of servanthood, the outcome of servanthood, and the goal of servanthood." Oswalt, "Isaiah 52:13-53:12," 90.

of us all To fall on Him." The Servant here suffers, not for his own sins, but for the sins of others. He bears the griefs, sorrows, transgressions, and iniquities of others, and through that suffering others can be healed from their sin, highlighting the substitutionary nature of the Servant's work.[11] The question that arises in this passage concerning the extent of the atonement is who these "others" are. Does this passage affirm that the Servant atones for the sins of only his elect people, thereby leading to particular redemption, or does he atone for the sins of all people, leading to an unlimited atonement?

In order to answer this question we need to understand whom the first person plural pronouns are referring to throughout this passage. There are three possible referents: the nations of 52:13–15, the nation of Israel through the voice of Isaiah, or the collective voice of the prophets.[12] The third possibility does not fit into the context of 53:3–6 and can be rejected, but the other two options are both possible. The first option, however, seems to require an understanding of the Servant as the nation of Israel instead of Christ, and therefore can also be rejected. The second referent seems most likely for three reasons. First, the normal referent for "we" throughout the book (e.g., 16:6; 24:16; 42:24; 64:5–6) is the nation of Israel.[13] Second, there is nothing in the context that shows the passage moving from recording the reactions of the nations in 52:13–15 to recording what they say in 53:1–9.[14] Third, the New Testament seems to support this interpretation with how John 12:38 and Romans 10:16 quote Isaiah 53:1. In this chapter Isaiah describes what the Servant does on the behalf of and in the place of the nation of Israel.

This understanding seems to support an unlimited extent of the Servant's sacrifice. If the servant bore the sins of the entire nation of Israel, he bore the sins of both the elect remnant and those who rejected God. Those who hold to particular redemption are forced to understand Isaiah as only speaking of the elect remnant in 53:4–6.[15] This understanding of the text not only contradicts the referent of the first person plural pronouns, but it also seems to contradict the use of the word "all" in 53:6. In this verse, Isaiah states that all have gone astray, that all have sinned. He then states that God laid the iniquity of all upon the servant. The "all" who have sinned is equated with the "all" whose sins God laid upon the servant. As Millard

---

11. Jeffery, Ovey, and Sach, *Pierced for Our Transgressions*, 54.
12. Oswalt, *The Book of Isaiah: Chapters 40–66*, 381.
13. Delitzsch, *Biblical Commentary on the Prophecies of Isaiah*, 2:310–11.
14. Oswalt, *The Book of Isaiah: Chapters 40–66*, 381.
15. E.g., Wells, *A Price for a People*, 73–75.

Erickson states, "This passage is especially powerful from a logical standpoint. It is clear that the extent of sin is universal; it is specified that *every one* of us has sinned. It should also be noticed that the extent of what will be laid on the suffering servant exactly parallels the extent of sin. It is difficult to read this passage and not conclude that just as everyone sins, everyone is also atoned for."[16] The members of the elect remnant are certainly not the only people who have sinned against the Lord.

In using the word "all" Isaiah also moves from just referring to the nation of Israel to referring to the entire human race. That the "all" in 53:6 is universal, and that the passage is referring to the sins of humanity instead of just the sins of Israel, is made clear from the broader context of the passage. Isaiah speaks of the servant's mission as being a light to the nations (Isa 42:6; 49:6) and as establishing the rule of God among the nations (Isa 42:1, 4), indicating that the Servant's ministry is not only for Israel, but for all people.[17] The outcome of the Servant's sacrifice also involves people from all nations, as the Servant will "justify the many" and "bear their iniquities" (Isa 53:11). The "many" referred to in this verse includes the nations mentioned in Isaiah 52:13–15.[18] Jesus' statement that he came to give his life as a ransom for many (Matt 20:28; Mark 10:45) alludes to this verse and indicates that Jesus thought of himself as the Suffering Servant who gave his life for all peoples.[19] Christ is the Servant who dies for Israel's sins, but he also dies for the sins of the Gentiles in order to bring together both Gentiles and Jews into the church, the people of God (Eph 2:11–22). Christ's death on the cross as the Suffering Servant also inaugurated the New Covenant (Luke 22:20), which, while clearly for Israel (Jer 31:31–34), is potentially for all people (Heb 8–10), and which replaced the old covenant that was only for

---

16. Erickson, *Christian Theology*, 847.
17. Oswalt, *The Book of Isaiah: Chapters 40–66*, 384.
18. Gentry, "Atonement," 37.

19. Many advocates of particular redemption appeal to the word "many" in these verses as proof of particular redemption, that Christ only dies for the "many," and not for all. E.g., Nicole, "Definite Atonement," 201; Owen, *The Death of Death*, 45; and Wells, *Price for a People*, 73–75. This interpretation is one possible understanding of Jesus' statement, but if it is correct than it seems to be pitting Isa 53:11 against Isa 53:6. The emphasis within Isaiah 53, moreover, is on Jesus bearing the sins of "all" or the "many," and the use of "many" in 53:11–12 is not meant to be restrictive in any sense. See Oswalt, *The Book of Isaiah: Chapters 40–66*, 403–8. It is likely that the term "many" as used in Matt 20:28 and Mark 10:45 (and Isa 53:11–12) refers to a great host of people that cannot be numbered, and is therefore emphasizing the unlimited extent of Christ's ransom. As D.A. Carson states, "'The many' underlines the immeasurable effects of Jesus' solitary death; the one dies, the many find their lives 'ransomed, healed, restored, forgiven,' a great host no man can number." Carson, *Matthew*, 434.

the nation of Israel. Isaiah 53 proclaims that the elect and the nonelect from all races have their sins paid for by the Servant's substitutionary sacrifice.

THE JOHANNINE LITERATURE

The Gospel of John

A repeated emphasis in John's Gospel is that Jesus' death was for the "world." In John 1:29 John the Baptist, upon seeing Jesus, proclaims that he is the "Lamb of God who takes away the sin of the world!" John 3:16–17 states that God, out of his love for the world, gave his Son so that all who believe in whom would have everlasting life, that the world through him might be saved. The Samaritan villagers at Sychar call Christ the "Savior of the world" in John 4:42. Jesus said that he is the bread from God which "gives life to the world" (John 6:33) and that he gives his flesh "for the life of the world" (John 6:51). In John 12:47 Jesus states that he did not come to judge the world, but to save the world. What these verses teach concerning the extent of the atonement depends on the referent of the term "world" (*kosmos*) in these verses.

Advocates of particular redemption often insist that seemingly universal terms such as "world" must be understood in their contexts and not simply understood as referring to all people.[20] This is certainly true, as the term "world" is flexible, and can be used in a number of different ways. It is necessary for us to understand all of the ways in which John's Gospel uses the term, and then to understand how it uses the term in each of the specific verses referenced above. John, in his Gospel, uses the term *kosmos* in three different ways.[21] First, *kosmos* sometimes refers to the totality of creation, or everything that exists (John 17:5; 21:25). Second, John uses *kosmos* to refer to the world of humanity (John 1:10, 29; 6:33, 51; 12:19; 14:17, 19; 16:20; 17:21). Third, and most often, *kosmos* refers to the world of humanity that is in opposition to God, that is lost and separated from its creator (John 7:7; 8:23; 12:31; 14:22, 27, 30; 15:18–19; 16:8, 11, 33; 17:6, 9, 14). D. A. Carson makes this clear:

> Although some have argued that for John the word *kosmos* ('world') sometimes has positive overtones ('God so loved the world,' 3:16), sometimes neutral overtones (as here [1:9]; cf. also 21:24–25, where the 'world' is simply a big place that can hold a lot of books), and frequently negative overtones ('the world

---

20. E.g., Nicole, "Definite Atonement," 205.
21. Harris III, "An Out-of-this-World Experience," 7–10.

did not recognize him,' 1:10), closer inspection shows that although a handful of passages preserve a neutral emphasis the vast majority are decidedly negative. There are no unambiguously positive occurrences. The 'world,' or frequently 'this world' (e.g., 8:23; 9:39; 11:9; 18:36), is not the universe, but the created order (especially of human beings and human affairs) in rebellion against its Maker (e.g., 1:10; 7:7; 14:17, 22, 27, 30; 15:18–19; 16:8, 20, 33; 17:6, 9, 14). . . . In fact, the 'world' in John's usage comprises no believers at all. Those who come to faith are no longer of this world; they have been chosen out of this world (15:19). If Jesus is the Savior of the world (4:42), that says a great deal about Jesus, but nothing positive about the world.[22]

Nowhere in his Gospel does John use *kosmos* to refer to a limited group of people, such as believers or the elect, or Gentiles as opposed to Jews. In order to be consistent with their view, however, advocates of particular redemption must understand *kosmos* in a limited sense. For example, John Owen argues at length that *kosmos* does not refer to all people in any of the verses quoted above. According to Owen, John 1:29 refers to Christ bearing sin that is common to all. The term "world" in John 3:16 refers only to the elect. In John 4:42 and 6:51 the use of "world" simply means that Christ is the only Savior for sin, and that he is the Savior of all who are saved.[23] Similarly, William Shedd notes that the term "world" sometimes refers to believers (as in John 6:33, 51), it sometimes refers to those who are contrary to the church, and it sometimes refers to nations in distinction from the Jews (as in John 3:16).[24] Louis Berkhof believes "world" denotes the nations as opposed to Israel in John 1:29; 6:33, 51.[25] I. Howard Marshall offers a good response to these interpretations when he states, "It is not possible to limit 'world' to mean 'all without distinction but not all without exception'; the plain sense of the sayings is that salvation is available for all and is offered to all and can be received by those who believe."[26]

John's use of *kosmos* means that when Christ's death is spoken of in relation to the "world," it is spoken of in relation to all people or to all lost people who are opposed to God and the ways of God. Either way, John continually speaks of Christ's atoning death as unlimited in extent, and not only for the elect or for believers. John the Baptist's proclamation in John 1:29

22. Carson, *Gospel of John*, 122–23.
23. Owen, *Death of Death*, 209–31.
24. Shedd, *Dogmatic Theology*, 2:479–80.
25. Berkhof, *Systematic Theology*, 395–96.
26. Marshall, "For All," 338.

stresses that Christ's atoning sacrifice as the Lamb of God is for all people. As F. F. Bruce states, "Here the sin which is removed by the Lamb of God is that of 'the world' (*kosmos*); the universal note so struck is heard again in the course of this Gospel (e.g., 3:16 f.; 4:42; 6:51) and in the First Epistle (2:2; 4:14). The reader of the Gospel as a whole finds John's proclamation much less cryptic than its first hearers must have done with no such context to guide them in its meaning. The 'world' embraces all without distinction of race, religion, or culture (cf. John 12:32)."[27] Similarly, the Samaritans' statement in John 4:42 that Christ is the "Savior of the World" emphasizes the universality of his work. Jesus is not the Savior of the Jews alone, but he came to be the Savior of all people, Jews and Gentiles.[28] Jesus' statement in John 6:33, that he is the bread of God who gives life to the world, carries the same meaning; Jesus is not the Savior of Israel alone, but he has come to offer life to all people who are lost.[29] When Jesus says that he gives his flesh for the life of the world in John 6:51, he means that he gives his life (i.e., he dies) so that all people might have life.[30] Jesus again makes salvation available to all people when he states that he did not come to judge the world, but to save the world in John 12:47.[31] John repeatedly emphasizes that Jesus' mission was to give his life as an atoning sacrifice that paid for the sins of all people so that all people might be saved.[32]

John 3:16–17 is particularly clear in relating the death of Jesus to all people. The reason God gave his Son to the world is because he loves the world. The purpose behind God's giving the Son is so that whoever believes

---

27. Bruce, *Gospel of John*, 53. For a defense of this verse as referring to substitutionary atonement, see Morris, *Apostolic Preaching*, 129–43.

28. Koester, "'The Savior of the World,'" 668.

29. Bruce, *Gospel of John*, 152; and Carson, *Gospel of John*, 287.

30. Some commentators see an allusion here to Isa 53, heightening the universality of the sacrifice, as Jesus suffers for the iniquity of all. See Bruce, *Gospel of John*, 158; and Carson, *Gospel of John*, 295. J. Ramsey Michaels, an advocate of particular redemption, states that "this is about as close as the Gospel of John ever comes to universal (as distinct from definite) atonement." Michaels, "Atonement," 108.

31. Köstenberger, *John*, 303.

32. Wayne Grudem, an advocate of particular redemption who recognizes the meaning of *kosmos* in the Johannine literature, understands these verses in John to simply be saying that sinners in general will be saved, and that verses speaking of Christ dying for the world are referring to the free offer of the gospel. Therefore unlimited atonement is not a necessary conclusion from these passages. Grudem, *Systematic Theology*, 598. While Grudem is correct to note that Jesus did die for sinners and to freely offer the gospel, John's language in these verses is in no way restrictive. There is no warrant in these verses for making a distinction between sinners in general and all sinners, other than a preconceived notion of particular redemption. Not only that, but, as we will see in chapter 4, a universal gospel offer demands an unlimited atonement.

in him can have eternal life. By sending the Son into the world, God's saving will is shown to be for the world, or all people "without distinction or exception."[33] This verse so clearly expresses God's love for the world and Jesus' mission as pertaining to the world that many advocates of particular redemption insist that the term 'world' in these verses must refer to the elect only.[34] This understanding of 'world' not only contrasts with John's usage of *kosmos*; it does not make sense within the context of the verses. Robert Lightner highlights this incongruity:

> Let us follow through with the limited view and interpretation of the world 'world' in such a simple and familiar passage as John 3:16. If 'world' means the elect only, then it would follow that he 'of the elect' that believeth may be saved and he 'of the elect' that believeth not is condemned (cf. John 3:18). This absurdity would contradict the most basic point of Calvinism, namely, that God has elected from eternity past certain individuals and they alone will be saved. Whoever heard of elect people being damned, and yet that is precisely what the limited interpretation leads to in John 3:16–18 when the limited concept is followed through.[35]

In John 3:16–17 God declares his love towards sinful humanity, and out of this love he sends his Son to die in the place of sinful humanity so that sinful humanity might be saved and have eternal life. This interpretation is so plain that some contemporary advocates of particular redemption recognize the universal nature of John's "world" language in this passage, even if they refuse to understand the atonement as paying for the sins of all of sinful humanity.[36]

---

33. Bruce, *Gospel of John*, 89.

34. Owen actually paraphrases the verse as follows: "God so loved the elect, that he gave his only-begotten Son, that whosoever believeth in him should not perish." Owen, *Death of Death*, 214. See also Long, *Definite Atonement*, 9–13.

35. Lightner, *Death Christ Died*, 70.

36. Some speak of Christ dying for sinners in general, instead of sinners in particular. John Frame, for example, states, "Since all people who are apart from Christ are cursed for their unbelief and disobedience (John 3:36), *world* includes everybody apart from grace. It is a universal term. . . . My conclusion is that God sent his Son, motivated by his love for the world." Frame, *The Doctrine of God*, 418. John MacArthur is another example: "So the context of John 3:16 requires the verse to speak of God's love to sinful mankind in general." MacArthur, Jr., "The Love of God for Humanity," 13. It is difficult, however, to understand how Christ died for sinners in general if he did not die specifically for all sinners. Robert Letham and R. B. Kuiper understand the term *kosmos* in John 3:16 to be referring only to the evil quality of the world, and therefore as not reflecting on the question of the extent of the atonement. Kuiper, *For Whom Did*

1 John

The meaning of the term 'world' in John's first epistle is no different than it is in John's Gospel. Just as he did in the Fourth Gospel, John states that Christ's atoning sacrifice is for the world. This thought is expressed in two verses: 1 John 2:2 and 4:14. The latter of these verses states, "We have seen and testify that the Father has sent the Son *to be* the Savior of the world." The designation "Savior of the world" is unique to the Johannine literature, occurring only one other time in John 4:42. In that context the phrase emphasizes that Jesus is the Savior of all the people of the world, not just the Jews. The context of the statement in 1 John is different, however, because the question of whether Jesus was the Savior of the Jews only or of all humanity was not a pressing issue for John's readers.[37] John most likely uses this phrase here to emphasize that Jesus has come in the flesh as the atoning sacrifice for all sin, which includes the sin of all people. This emphasis was necessary as a response to heretics who believed that salvation was an intellectual exercise involving deliverance from ignorance instead of sin, and that faith in Jesus' death as an atoning sacrifice was not necessary for salvation.[38] Jesus Christ, as the Savior who has been sent by the Father, is the Savior of the world, including even the heretics to whom John is referring. The term "world" is used here to denote humanity in opposition to God, ascribing the widest possible scope to the saving purposes and activity of God.

First John 2:2, like 1 John 4:14, also ascribes the widest possible scope to Christ's death. It is one of the clearest expressions in all of Scripture that the atonement is not for believers only. First John 2:1–2 states, "My little children, I am writing these things to you so that you may not sin. And if anyone sins, we have an Advocate with the Father, Jesus Christ the righteous; and He Himself is the propitiation for our sins; and not for ours only, but also for *those of* the whole world." One of the reasons John is writing this epistle is so that his readers will not sin. In case they do sin, however, John encourages them with the truth that Jesus Christ the righteous one is their advocate before the Father, interceding on their behalf. His readers can take comfort in the surety of Christ's advocacy because he is the propitiation for their sins.[39] John adds to this encouragement by proclaiming that Christ is

---

Christ Die?, 30; and Letham, *The Work of Christ*, 240–41. John's use of *kosmos*, however, even when it has a negative connotation, refers to people who are evil. The question of whom Christ died for in these verses cannot be avoided.

37. Kruse, *The Letters of John*, 164.
38. Smalley, *1, 2, 3 John*, 253.
39. The translation of the word *hilasmos* in this verse is controversial, with the words "propitiation" and "expiation" both attested as possible meanings. The word

not only the propitiation for their sins, but he is the propitiation for the sins of the whole world.[40] Christ is the propitiation for "our sins" in the same way that he is the propitiation for "the sins of the whole world," as the verb "is" (*estin*) is in the present tense and the indicative mood, and therefore governs both clauses. In stating that the Son has propitiated the sins of the whole world, John emphasizes that Christ's propitiation for sin is not only for believers (or the elect), but also for the sins of all people, elect and non-elect. His use of the adjective *olou*, or "whole," is particularly meaningful, because it rules out the idea that only a portion of the world's sins are in view.[41] Just as he did in 4:14, John stresses that Christ's saving work encompasses the sins of all people so that even the heretics in the community would know that their sins were forgivable on the basis of the atonement.

If the term "world" in 1 John 2:2 refers to unsaved humanity as explained above, then Christ has propitiated the sins of unsaved humanity,

---

"propitiation" depicts God as the object of the atonement and understands his wrath as placated by the atonement. The word "expiation" depicts God as the subject of the atonement, as he is the one who removes the defilement of sin by covering it. C. H. Dodd is the most famous defender of translating *hilasmos* as "expiation." He based this translation primarily on linguistic evidence, arguing that Hellenistic Judaism as depicted in the Septuagint did not regard sacrifices as means of pacifying the Deity, but as means of delivering people from sin. Therefore the New Testament occurrences should be interpreted in the same way. See Dodd, *The Epistle of Paul to the Romans*; idem, "Hilaskesthai," 352–60; and idem, *The Johannine Epistles*. Dodd's conclusions have been challenged, however, most notably by Leon Morris and Roger Nicole. Both demonstrate that the linguistic evidence Dodd produces is not conclusive, and that the Old and New Testaments both refer to propitiation. See Morris, *Apostolic Preaching*, 144–213; and Nicole, "C. H. Dodd and the Doctrine of Propitiation," 117–57. "Propitiation" is to be preferred in 1 John 2:2 for two reasons. First, the notion of propitiation includes expiation, while expiation does not include propitiation. The former is inclusive while the latter is not. See Michaels, "Atonement," 114–16; and Smalley, *1, 2, 3 John*, 38–40. Second, the context of 1 John 2:2 makes God the object of the propitiation, as Jesus Christ is the advocate with the Father. That Jesus is our advocate, interceding for our sins before the Father, implies that the Father is displeased with sin. As I. Howard Marshall states, "There can be no doubt that this [propitiation] is the meaning. In the previous verse the thought was of Jesus acting as our advocate before God; the picture which continues into this verse is of Jesus pleading the cause of guilty sinners before a judge who is being asked to pardon their acknowledged guilt. . . . In order that forgiveness may be granted, there is an action in respect of the sins which has the effect of rendering God favorable to the sinner." Marshall, *The Epistles of John*, 118.

40. "The repeated *peri* ('for') in this final phrase [of 1 John 2:2] makes it clear that the *sins* of the world are the concern of the 'atoning sacrifice' made by Jesus, rather than 'the world' in general." Smalley, *1, 2, 3 John*, 40, emphasis the author's.

41. "The sacrificial offering of Christ is effective not just for the sins of the 'world' (which could refer to a section of it), and still less for 'our' sins (those of John's immediate circle) alone, it embraces the sins of the *whole* world." Ibid., 40, emphasis the author's.

and John without question teaches that the atonement is unlimited. Advocates of particular redemption have made several attempts, however, to explain how the term "world" in this verse does not refer to unsaved humanity, and therefore how John's statement does not contradict particular redemption. One understanding has been to interpret the phrase "the propitiation for our sins" as referring to Jewish believers and the phrase "the sins of the whole world" as referring to Gentile believers; therefore Christ is the propitiation for the elect from all races.[42] This interpretation has fallen out of favor, however, because it misunderstands the context of 1 John.[43] Another possibility is that John was indicating that Christ's sacrifice in not confined to one generation, but is applicable to all generations, although this understanding of the verse does not do justice to the meaning of the term *kosmos*.[44] Some advocates of particular redemption hold that John's statement emphasizes the exclusiveness of Christ's propitiation; there is only one way of salvation in the entire world and that is Christ.[45] This interpretation is correct to note that John is saying all sins can be forgiven on the basis of Christ's sacrifice, but incorrect to limit the verse to just teaching this, because this understanding does not do justice to the intensive "*olou*" (whole) or the meaning of *kosmos*. Others maintain that John is simply stating that Christ is the propitiation who is available to pay for the sins of anyone in the world.[46] Again, this statement is true as far as it goes, but if Christ's propitiation only paid for the sins of the elect, then how is it available to pay for the sins of anyone in the world, unless the term "world" is only referring to the elect? Another possible explanation is that John wanted to emphasize that Christ's atonement was not only for the disciples or those who came under apostolic influence, but was in fact for people from all nations, though this

---

42. Bavinck, *Sin and Salvation*, 465; Letham, *Work of Christ*, 242; Long, *Definite Atonement*, 117–19; Owen, *Death of Death*, 220; and Pink, *The Sovereignty of God*, 258–59.

43. Michaels explains: "But his [Pink's] attempt to show that 1 John is addressed to Jewish Christians is unconvincing. 1 John is written to a Christian community without reference to its ethnic background, whether Jewish or Gentile or both. Its concern, as we have seen, is with the sins of Christian believers after their conversion." Michaels, "Atonement," 116–17.

44. Murray, *Redemption Accomplished and Applied*, 73–74; Nicole, "Definite Atonement," 206; Smeaton, *The Apostle's Doctrine*, 460; and Wells, *Price for a People*, 56–57.

45. Michaels, "Atonement," 117; Murray, *Redemption Accomplished and Applied*, 73; and Nicole, "Definite Atonement," 206. This understanding has the verse saying the same thing as John 14:6 and Acts 4:12.

46. Grudem, *Systematic Theology*, 598–99; Hodge, *Systematic Theology*, 2:558–59; and Letham, *Work of Christ*, 242. The term 'world' here, however, is referring to unbelieving humanity in contrast to believers, or the elect.

again seems to contradict the meanings of *olou* and *kosmos*.⁴⁷ Finally, some state that John is referring to "eschatological universalism," in that Christ will have a saved world to present to the Father when the gospel has subdued it.⁴⁸ While the idea of "eschatological universalism" is biblical (Eph 1:10; Col 1:20), it is simply not present in 1 John 2:2.

It is telling that many advocates of particular redemption offer more than one of these possible explanations when discussing 1 John 2:1–2, as none of these proposals does justice to the meaning of the text.⁴⁹ In these verses John indicates that Jesus' saving work is for all of humanity, just as he does in 1 John 4:14. In particular, 1 John 2:2 states that Christ is the propitiation for the sins of believers and unbelievers. There is no clearer statement in Scripture indicating that Christ died to pay the penalty for the sins of all people. The Son, by his atonement, satisfied the wrath of the Father regarding the sins of the elect and the nonelect. First John, just as the Gospel of John, uses the term *kosmos* in relation to Christ's atoning work in order to indicate that Jesus' saving work is for all people, elect and nonelect alike.

THE PAULINE LITERATURE

2 Corinthians 5:14–15

In the first seven chapters of 2 Corinthians Paul defends the integrity of his gospel ministry. Second Corinthians 5:11–21 is a significant passage in this first part of the letter, as Paul here attempts to persuade the Corinthians that his ministry is a credible apostolic ministry (vv. 11–12). Paul explains in verses 14–15 why he was devoted to serving God and the Corinthians (v.13). Second Corinthians 5:14–15 reads, "For the love of Christ controls us, having concluded this, that one died for all, therefore all died; and He died for all, so that they who live might no longer live for themselves, but for Him who died and rose again on their behalf." The reason that Paul ministered to the Corinthians was because the love of Christ compelled him to do

---

47. Berkhof, *Systematic Theology*, 396; Calvin, *Commentaries on the Catholic Epistles*, 173; Murray, *Redemption Accomplished and Applied*, 73; Nettles, *By His Grace and for His Glory*, 299; and Shedd, *Dogmatic Theology*, 2:480.

48. Warfield, *Selected Shorter Writings*, 1:167–77. See also Kuiper, *For Whom Did Christ Die?*, 35–36.

49. Many advocates of particular redemption offer two or three of the possible interpretations of 1 John 2:2 and do not conclusively state what the passage is saying. E.g., Letham, *Work of Christ*, 242; Long, *Definite Atonement*, 101–19; Murray, *Redemption Accomplished and Applied*, 72–75; Nicole, "Definite Atonement," 206; and Tiessen, *Who Can Be Saved?*, 488.

so. The reason that Paul was convinced of Christ's love was because he died for all. After expressing this conviction Paul then states two consequences of Christ's death for all. First, the consequence of Christ dying for all is that all died; his death involved their death (v. 14).[50] Second, the purpose of Christ's death was so that those who live in him should live for him (v. 15).

The pertinent interpretive question in this passage for the extent of the atonement is how extensive the term "all" (*pantes*) is, as each of the three uses of *pantes* is referring to the same group of people.[51] A related question is who is included in the group "they who live." Are "they who live" the same group as the "all," or is Paul referring to a different group of people here? Advocates of particular redemption understand all four expressions (the three uses of "all" and "they who live") as referring to believers.[52] The "all" that died are those who died to sin when Christ died for them on the cross. The "all" are the same people as "they who live" because Christ's death and resurrection are a unity, and all for whom Christ died are the same people for whom he rose.[53] This understanding is supported by an appeal to Romans 6:4–8, which asserts that those who died with Christ in the likeness of his death are also made to live with him in the likeness of his resurrection.[54]

The other possible meaning for *pantes* is that it refers to all people without exception, or the whole of humankind. The phrase "they who live" may then refer to all people without exception as well, or it may refer to those in Christ. It seems clear that they phrase "they who live" refers to believers. This is so for three reasons: because this is how Paul describes believers elsewhere (Rom 6:4), because this would be an odd way to refer to all human beings, and because if this were true, universalism would result.[55] If "they who live" are believers, however, then it strongly suggests that *pantes* refers to all people without exception, and not to believers. Paul introduces a new category of people with the phrase "they who live," and this category is distinct from the "all." As Murray Harris states, the addition of the expression "they who live" "suggests that a new, distinct category is

---

50. The two deaths clearly took place at the same time. Harris, *Second Epistle to the Corinthians*, 421.

51. Ibid., 420.

52. For example, Bavinck, *Sin and Salvation*, 465; Berkhof, *Systematic Theology*, 396; Kuiper, *For Whom Did Christ Die?*, 29–30; Letham, *Work of Christ*, 241; Murray, *Redemption Accomplished and Applied*, 69–72; Nicole, "Definite Atonement," 205; Owen, *Death of Death*, 238–40; Shedd, *Dogmatic Theology*, 2:480; Tiessen, *Who Can Be Saved?*, 488–89; and Wells, *Price for a People*, 76–82.

53. Letham, *Work of Christ*, 241.

54. Murray, *Redemption Accomplished and Applied*, 71–72.

55. Harris, *Second Epistle to the Corinthians*, 421; and Martin, *2 Corinthians*, 132.

being introduced; while all persons 'died' when Christ died, not all rose to new life when he rose from the dead."[56] If Paul had meant to indicate that "all" and "they who live" were the same group of people, then why did he not simply continue to use the word "all?"

Paul in these verses states that Christ died for all so that all died. This death that all died was not a death to sin or self, as this would indicate that all of humanity is saved. It is also not a potential death, as the language here indicates an actual death. The death that all die in Christ's death is most likely the death that all deserve because of their sin. All have died in the sense that Christ in his death suffered the penalty for all sin, and therefore for all death.[57] Christ also died for all so that those who live (believe in him) should no longer live for themselves, but for him, the one who died and rose on their behalf. These verses therefore affirm Christ's substitutionary death for all people without exception, holding together the universality and the particularity of the cross.[58]

2 Corinthians 5:18–21

Second Corinthians 5:18–21 builds upon and completes the truths expressed in 5:14–15. Second Corinthians 5:16–17 describes two consequences of Christ's death for those who believe (cf. 5:15). First, for believers there is now a completely different way of viewing reality (v. 16). Second, anyone who is in Christ is a new creation, and a part of Christ's new order for the universe (v. 17). All of these benefits of being in Christ are from God (v. 18a), as God is the one "who reconciled us to Himself through Christ and

---

56. Harris, *Second Epistle to the Corinthians*, 421.

57. As R. V. G. Tasker states, "Christ's death was the death of all in the sense that they should have died; the penalty of their sins was borne by him (1 Cor 15:3; 2 Cor 5:20); He died in their place." Tasker, *The Second Epistle to the Corinthians*, 86. See Garland, *2 Corinthians*, 279; and Harris, *Second Epistle to the Corinthians*, 422.

58. Harris elaborates: "While all persons died, in one sense, when the Man who represented them died, not all were raised to new life when he rose. Paul is not suggesting that irrespective of their response and attitude, all people have new life in Christ or experience selfless living. There is universalism in the scope of redemption, since no person is excluded from God's offer of salvation; but there is a particularity in the application of redemption, since not everyone appropriates the benefits afforded by this universally offered salvation." Harris, *Second Epistle to the Corinthians*, 423. This truth accords with Rom 6:4–8, where Paul is speaking of believers who die and rise with Christ because they are united with him through baptism (which is the evidence of faith). Paul does not speak of unbelievers in Rom 6:4–8. Advocates of particular redemption are correct to understand the unity of dying and rising with Christ for believers from Rom 6:4–8, but they are incorrect when they say that Rom 6:4–8 demands that only believers died with Christ in 2 Cor 5:14–15.

gave us the ministry of reconciliation, namely, that God was in Christ reconciling the world to Himself, not counting their trespasses against them, and He has committed to us the word of reconciliation" (2 Cor 5:18b-19). These verses state that God reconciled the world to himself through Christ, and the results of this reconciliation are the forgiveness of sins and the preaching of the cross.[59]

Reconciliation is a distinctly Pauline idea, as he is the only author in the New Testament who uses the word group that relates to reconciliation in a redemptive context (Rom 5:10-11; 11:15; 2 Cor 5:18, 19, 20; Eph 2:16; Col 1:20, 22). Most broadly reconciliation refers to God's work in which, out of his love, he acts to reverse the estrangement brought about by humanity's sin and bring about harmonious relations between himself and his creation. God reconciles through Jesus Christ, on the basis of Christ' s atonement. It is primarily an objective act; it is something that God has done for humanity in the cross of Christ. As George Ladd states, "A close examination of the passages in Romans 5 and 2 Corinthians 5 leads to the inescapable conclusion that reconciliation is not primarily a change in humanity's attitude toward God; it is, like justification, an objective event that is accomplished by God for humanity's salvation. Reconciliation was wrought first by God for human beings, not in human beings."[60] It is also a subjective act, however, because human beings must subjectively experience for themselves the reconciliation that God has wrought in order to have fellowship with him. Ladd also makes this clear when he states, "Until God's offer of objective reconciliation has been received in an attitude of glad surrender, no person is in fact reconciled to God; she or he is still a sinner and in the last day will suffer the full and awful outpouring of the wrath of a holy God. The content of reconciliation, therefore, while first of all the objective act of God, is also the affirmative reaction of people to the proffer of reconciliation."[61] Both the objective and the subjective senses of reconciliation are present in 2 Corinthians 5:18-21.

Second Corinthians 5:18-19 are parallel statements, in that verse 19 repeats and amplifies the thoughts of verse 18.[62] The objective work of reconciliation appears at the beginning of each verse, in that God has reconciled "us" (v. 18) or "the world" (v.19) to himself. The need for a subjective receiving of God's reconciliation is highlighted at the end of each verse, as Paul

---

59. Ibid., 444.
60. Ladd, *A Theology of the New Testament*, 493.
61. Ibid., 496.
62. Barnett, *Second Epistle to the Corinthians*, 305.

speaks of the ministry and the message of reconciliation.[63] This ministry and message of reconciliation is clarified in verse 20, which states "Therefore, we are ambassadors for Christ, as though God were making an appeal through us; we beg you on behalf of Christ, be reconciled to God." In light of God's reconciling act and consequent entrustment of the message of reconciliation to Paul, Paul describes himself (and others who follow after him) as Christ's ambassador. God makes his appeal through his ambassadors, and people need to believe this appeal in order to be reconciled to God; they need to subjectively experience the objective reality of God's reconciliation in order to have a relationship with God.[64] Second Corinthians 5:21 returns to the objective idea of reconciliation and describes how God accomplished reconciliation in Christ. The verse states, "He made Him who knew no sin *to be* sin on our behalf, so that we might become the righteousness of God in Him."

The interpretive issue that impacts the debate over the extent of the atonement is whom the term "world" is referring to in 2 Corinthians 5:19. There are several possible meanings of this term. Some understand it to be referring to all believers, as only believers are actually reconciled and do not have their trespasses counted against them.[65] Similar to this understanding is that Paul, in his use of "world," is enlarging upon the "us" in verse 18, which refers to "Jews," and that "world" refers to Gentile believers.[66] A third possibility is that Paul uses "world" to refer to all of creation (cf. Col 1:20).[67]

---

63. The message and the ministry of reconciliation are the same. As Harris remarks, "The ministry is the proclamation of the message. Whether God is said to 'give the ministry of reconciliation' (v. 18) or 'to entrust the message of reconciliation' (v. 19) to Paul and others, the emphasis is on the privilege and obligation of the task of proclaiming that reconciliation." Harris, *Second Epistle to the Corinthians*, 445.

64. Many commentators understand the appeal in v. 20 as directed toward the Corinthians believers who were antagonistic toward Paul and whom Paul was therefore calling on to turn back to him. This is seen as an immediate application of God's reconciling work. E.g., Barnett, *Second Epistle to the Corinthians*, 310–312; Garland, *2 Corinthians*, 298–300; Martin, *Reconciliation*, 109. It is better, however, to understand this appeal as the summation of the message of Christ's ambassadors. This interpretation construes "reconciliation" in its soteriological sense, which is what Paul is talking about in this passage. It also allows for a broader application of being an ambassador for Christ, whereas the former view restricts being an ambassador to Paul. Paul makes his specific appeal to the Corinthian believers in 6:1, not 5:20. See Harris, *Second Epistle to the Corinthians*, 447–49; and Marshall, "The Meaning of Reconciliation," 123–24.

65. Kuiper, *For Whom Did Christ Die?*, 36; Long, *Definite Atonement*, 121–30; Nicole, "Definite Atonement," 205; Owen, *Death of Death*, 227–28; and Wells, *Price for a People*, 119–20.

66. Berkhof, *Systematic Theology*, 396; Kruse, *Second Epistle of Paul to the Corinthians*, 127; Shedd, *Dogmatic Theology*, 2:480; and Tiessen, *Who Can Be Saved?*, 487.

67. Barnett, *Second Epistle to the Corinthians*, 302; Martin, *2 Corinthians*, 158; and

Jesus Christ's Payment for the Sins of All People in the Atonement

A fourth option understands Paul as referring to all of humanity with the term "world."[68]

The fourth option seems to be the best option for three reasons. First, it harmonizes with the understanding of 2 Corinthians 5:14–15 presented above. Paul has already indicated that Christ died for all humanity, so it would be natural for him to repeat this thought when he discusses reconciliation a few verses later. Second, the first two options above, which understand the term "world" to be referring to believers only, do not fit the context of the passage. Not only has Paul emphasized Christ's death for all, but he emphasizes the objective and subjective sides of reconciliation. Only those "who live" and those who are "in Christ" are subjectively reconciled to God through faith, but all people are objectively reconciled to him. As Marshall makes clear, "'God reconciles the world to himself' thus means: God acts in Christ to overlook the sins of mankind, so that on his side there is no barrier to the restoration of friendly relations. The message of the Christian preacher is a declaration of this fact."[69] The understanding that Paul is referring to Gentiles in distinction to Jews also has no basis in the context, as the word "us" in verse 18 includes the Corinthians, who were not all Jews.[70] Third, Paul is clearly referring to humanity with the pronouns "their" and "them," and with his reference to "transgressions." The movement from the "us" of v. 18 to the "world" of v. 19 "with regard to the objects of reconciliation is not a movement from the anthropological to the cosmological, but from the narrower to the wider anthropological focus."[71] God did not count the transgressions of humanity against them, but instead reconciled them to himself in Christ; making forgiveness available to all people (this is essentially the same thought as 5:21). This language rules out the option of understanding "world" in a cosmological sense. Throughout 2 Corinthians 5:11–21 Paul consistently states that Christ's death, his atoning work of reconciliation, paid the penalty for the sins of all people so that all people might have a relationship with God.

Turner, "Ministry of Reconciliation," 85.

68. Demarest, *Cross and Salvation*, 190; Douty, *Did Christ Die*, 106–10; Garland, *2 Corinthians*, 293–94; Harris, *Second Epistle to the Corinthians*, 443; Lightner, *Death Christ Died*, 65–66; Marshall, "Meaning of Reconciliation," 123; and Walvoord, "Reconciliation," 3–5.

69. Marshall, "Meaning of Reconciliation," 123.

70. Whether one takes the word "us" in v. 18 as referring to believers only or to all of humanity, it includes the Corinthians. The church at Corinth was not made up exclusively of Jews. See Acts 18:1–17.

71. Harris, *Second Epistle to the Corinthians*, 443.

The Pastoral Epistles

There are three statements in the Pastoral Epistles that describe the atonement as being for all people. The first of these is 1 Timothy 2:3–6, which states, "This is good and acceptable in the sight of God our Savior, who desires all men to be saved and to come to the knowledge of the truth. For there is one God, *and* one mediator also between God and men, *the* man Christ Jesus, who gave Himself as a ransom for all, the testimony *given* at the proper time." In 1 Timothy 2:1–8 Paul[72] is encouraging prayer for all people (v. 1), including kings and those in authority (v. 2), because such prayer is good and pleasing to God our Savior (v. 3),[73] who desires all people to be saved (v. 4).[74] The reasons that God desires for all people to be saved are because he is the one and only God, and because Jesus Christ is the one and only Mediator between God and humanity (v. 5). Jesus is the one who was a ransom for all (v. 6), and the one whom Paul was appointed to preach to the Gentiles (v. 7). Therefore Paul desires that all people pray everywhere without wrath or dissension (v. 8).

The primary interpretive issue in this passage that impacts the debate over the extent of the atonement is the meaning of "all" in verses 4 and 6. Advocates of particular redemption argue that "all men" refers to "all sorts of men," or "all kinds of men"; essentially this passage is stating that God's desire and Christ's ransom encompass not only the Jews, but Gentiles as

---

72. We will assume that Paul was the author of the Pastoral Epistles, as they state (1 Tim 1:1; 2 Tim 1:1; Titus 1:1). For a defense of this position, see Earle, *1 Timothy*, 341–43.

73. The phrase "God our Savior" appears 6 times in the Pastoral Epistles (1 Tim 1:1; 2:3; 4:10; Titus 1:3; 2:10; 3:4). In this context the phrase is clearly soteriological, as "God our Savior" desires the salvation of all, and the verses following speak of Christ as the one Mediator and as a ransom for all. See Baugh, "Savior of All People," 338–40; Marshall, "Universal Grace and Atonement," 55; and Mounce, *Pastoral Epistles*, 84–85.

74. In light of the universality of the statement "God desires all men to be saved," some have tried to argue that this verse is not speaking of God's absolute will or purpose. Instead it merely speaks of his wish or his preference. This is based on a supposed difference between the word *thelo* (used here in 1 Tim 2:3), which means "wish" or "desire" and the word *boule*, which means "intend." While it is theologically correct to distinguish between God's "decretive will" and his "permissive will" (see Piper, "Are There Two Wills in God?," 107–31), there is no linguistic argument for weakening God's desire for the salvation of all, as 2 Pet 3:9 states the same thing using the verb *boule*. The two verbs have different nuances, but they are essentially synonymous. God genuinely desires the salvation of all. Owen understood that this was the verb's meaning and therefore argued that "all" could only refer to believers, because he believed that everything God desired would be accomplished. Owen, *Death of Death*, 232–33. See Marshall, "Universal Grace," 55–57; and Mounce, *Pastoral Epistles*, 85–86.

well.[75] On the other hand, advocates of unlimited atonement assert that "all men" means "all people"; God's desire and Christ's ransom are for all people without exception.[76] In defense of the first option, appeal is often made to 1 Timothy 2:1–2, where Paul encourages prayers for all people, and then mentions specifically two groups of people, kings and those in authority. The mention of groups of people in 1 Timothy 2:2 is understood as clarifying what Paul meant by "all men" in 1 Timothy 2:1.[77] First Timothy 2:2 is better understood, however, as a parenthetical reference, instead of explaining what Paul meant in 2:1. The point of the entire passage is that salvation is for all; therefore praying for all is good and pleasing to God.[78]

In addition to the appeal to 1 Timothy 2:1–2, Steven Baugh offers three more arguments in support of the understanding of "all men" as "all kinds of men."[79] First, he asserts that the mention of one God and one Mediator (v. 5) echoes Deuteronomy 6:4, which demonstrates that God's salvation is not only for the Jews but for the Gentiles as well. This statement is certainly true; that there is only one God and one Mediator demonstrates that God desires the salvation of Gentiles as well as Jews, but it also stands in opposition to the synagogue's beliefs that God hates the sinner, that God only wants to save the righteous, and that salvation is only for a select few who have the right knowledge (cf. the statement that God wants all to come to the knowledge of the truth in v. 4). Therefore v. 5 does not support the meaning of "all sorts of people," but rather indicates that God desires the salvation of all people without exception; sinners as well as the righteous and Gentiles as well as Jews.[80] Baugh's second argument is that the phrase "in his own time" emphasizes the eschatological nature of Christ's ransom as reaching out to all peoples, and not all people. While there is an eschatological nuance to this phrase, this is no way demands that God's ransom is only for the

---

75. Baugh, "Savior of All People," 338–40; Bavinck, *Sin and Salvation*, 465; Berkhof, *Systematic Theology*, 396–97; Knight, *The Pastoral Epistles*, 119, 122; Letham, *Work of Christ*, 242–43; Long, *Definite Atonement*, 142; Nettles, *By His Grace*, 299–300; Nicole, "Definite Atonement," 204; Owen, *Death of Death*, 233–36; Tiessen, *Who Can Be Saved?*, 489; and Wells, *Price for a People*, 121–24.

76. Chafer, "For Whom Did Christ Die?," 324; Demarest, *Cross and Salvation*, 190–91; Douty, *Did Christ Die*, 113–15; Earle, *1 Timothy*, 358; Lea and Griffin, Jr., *1, 2 Timothy, Titus*, 89–91; Marshall, "For All," 326–33; Miethe, "The Universal Power of the Atonement," 79–80; Mounce, *Pastoral Epistles*, 84–85, 89–90; Picirilli, *Grace, Faith, Free Will*, 133–37; Sailer, "A Wesleyan View," 192–93; and Towner, *The Letters to Timothy and Titus*, 183–86.

77. Knight, *Pastoral Epistles*, 119.

78. Mounce, *Pastoral Epistles*, 85; and Lea and Griffin, *1, 2 Timothy, Titus*, 88–89.

79. Baugh, "Savior of All People," 339–40.

80. Mounce, *Pastoral Epistles*, 85.

groups of the Jews and Gentiles and not all people. This phrase can be accurately understood in its context just as easily if "all men" means "all people without exception." His third argument is based on Titus 1:1–3, where Paul proclaims that his commission to preach to the Gentiles is confirmation of God's purpose to include Gentiles in salvation through Christ, and this proclamation explains Paul's zeal in defending his apostolic calling in verse 7. Again, Baugh is correct to note this emphasis, but the emphasis can just as easily support an unlimited atonement view of this passage, as Paul's passionate defense of his ministry could be intended to teach the Ephesian church that the gospel is for all people, including the Gentiles.[81]

The second option, that "all men" refers to "all people" and not to "all kinds of people," seems preferable for four reasons. First, as we have seen, it correctly understands 1 Timothy 2:1 as instructing believers to pray for all human beings, and not various classes of human beings. Second, it makes better sense of Paul's argument regarding one God and one Mediator. God is the only God and Christ is the only Mediator, and therefore God is the God of all and Christ is the Mediator for all. These statements are true of all people without exception. As William Mounce states,

> In Paul's day, sectarian Judaism emphasized 'our' in an exclusive sense, and the opponents in the PE were making the same mistake. As a corrective, Paul's usage goes back to the original emphasis of the Shema on 'one' God as opposed to 'many' gods. God is not the God of the opponents alone but is the only God and consequently the God of all. . . . In Rom 3:29–30 Paul argues that because there is only one God, all people will be justified in relation to their faith. Likewise here Paul argues that because there is only one God, all people must be the object of prayer since all can be saved through the one God and the one mediator.[82]

Third, the focus of Paul's reasoning in this passage is that Christ is the ransom *for all*. Most commentators understand verse 6 as referring to the thought of Mark 10:45,[83] which emphasizes the immeasurable greatness of Christ's ransom.[84] The fourth reason, and perhaps the most decisive one,

---

81. Lea and Griffin, *1, 2 Timothy, Titus*, 92–93.

82. Mounce, *Pastoral Epistles*, 87.

83. Kelly, *The Pastoral Epistles*, 63–64; Knight, *Pastoral Epistles*, 121–22; Lea and Griffin, *1, 2 Timothy, Titus*, 91; Marshall, "Universal Grace," 59; Morris, *Apostolic Preaching*, 51–52; and Mounce, *Pastoral Epistles*, 89–90.

84. Explaining the difference between the "many" in Mark 10:45 and the all in 1 Tim 2:6, Marshall states, "It appears to be firmly established that in Hebrew the word for 'many' often has the sense of 'a great many as opposed to a few,' rather than 'only

is that this meaning harmonizes with Paul's statement in 1 Timothy 4:10, which states "For it is for this we labor and strive, because we have fixed our hope on the living God, who is the Savior of all men, especially of believers." This statement is similar to the one in 1 Timothy 2:3-4, and it is extremely difficult to understand "all men" as "all sorts of men" in this verse; it seems clearly to refer to all people without exception. In light of these four reasons, 1 Timothy 2:3-6 states that Christ's atonement is for all people without exception because God desires the salvation of all people without exception.

The controversy concerning 1 Timothy 4:10 is not over the meaning of "all men" but instead concerns the meaning of "Savior." Since this verse unambiguously states that God acts as Savior toward two groups of people, all men (all people) and believers, advocates of particular atonement argue that the term "Savior" in this context is not soteriological.[85] Instead, the term "Savior" is understood in a broad sense as "Preserver," or "Provider."[86] This interpretation understands the verse as talking about God's common grace as opposed to his salvific grace.[87] Paul uses the phrase "Savior of all men" to assert that God is the one who provides for all people because his common grace embraces the whole world.

---

some as opposed to all.' Thus 'all' is the appropriate paraphrase. It is the natural word to use in moving from a crassly literal rendering of the Hebrew to more idiomatic Greek." Marshall, "Universal Grace," 59.

85. There is a way, however, to preserve the soteriological meaning of Savior and to avoid understanding 1 Tim 4:10 as stating that God acts as Savior toward all people. It is possible that the word *malista*, normally translated "especially," should be translated "namely" in 1 Tim 4:10. On this understanding the verse would state that God is the Savior of all people, namely those who believe. See Knight, *Pastoral Epistles*, 203-04; and Skeat, "'Especially the Parchments,'" 174-75. The word *malista* is used 8 times by Paul (Gal 6:10; Phil 4:22; 1 Tim 4:10; 5:8, 17; Titus 1:10; 2 Tim 4:13; and Phlm 16), and in all but 2 Tim 4:13, Titus 1:10, and the verse under discussion it certainly means "especially." *Malista* possibly means "especially" in the latter three cases. It seems that in 1 Tim 4:10 Paul is distinguishing two groups of people, and therefore that the translation "especially" is preferable here. This understanding fits the context, as 1 Tim 4:10 is most likely deliberately echoing the universality of 1 Tim 2:3-6. It also fits Paul's normal usage of the word, as the two other passages that approximate 1 Tim 4:10 in Paul are Gal 6:10 and Phil 4:22, both of which require "especially" as opposed to "namely."

86. Baugh, "Savior of All People," 333-38; Calvin, *Sermons on the Epistles to Timothy and Titus*, 398-99; Grudem, *Systematic Theology*, 599; and Turretin, *Turretin on the Atonement of Christ*, 130.

87. Baugh, "Savior of All People," 333. Both Berkhof and Kuiper, for example, discuss 1 Tim 4:10 in the context of common grace and not in the context of the extent of the atonement. Berkhof, *Systematic Theology*, 434-44; and Kuiper, *For Whom Did Christ Die?*, 81.

Although the ideas of "preserver" and "provider" fit the semantic domain of *soter* ("Savior"),[88] it is doubtful that this is the idea that Paul had in mind when he used this term. The phrase "God our Savior" appears six times in the Pastoral Epistles (1 Tim 1:1; 2:3; 4:10; Titus 1:3; 2:10; 3:4), and in every other place it is used, the meaning is clearly soteriological. Paul also seems to be repeating the same thought he introduced in 1 Timothy 2:3–6: the gospel is for all people without exception.[89] Understanding *soter* as "Savior" also fits the soteriological context of the passage, as Paul speaks of the promise of eternal life that comes from godliness in 4:8. Furthermore, the interpretation of "Preserver" either leads to the idea that God bestows more of his common grace upon believers (which seems to contradict the idea of common grace and verses such as Matthew 5:45) or that the noun *soter* be understood in two different ways in regards to "all men" and "believers." Instead, 1 Timothy 4:10 asserts that the Living God acts as Savior toward all people, but especially toward believers. As this verse echoes 1 Timothy 2:3–6, it almost certainly seems to be saying that God desires the salvation of all people, and he has provided that salvation for all people in the ransom of Christ, but that he acts as Savior toward believers in a much more profound, deeper sense because it is only they who enter a saving relationship with him.[90] First Timothy 4:10, like 1 Timothy 2:3–6, offers strong support for understanding Christ's atonement as being for all people without exception.[91]

The third statement in the Pastoral Epistles that indicates the atonement is for all people is found in Titus 2:11. Titus 2:11 states, "For the grace of God has appeared, bringing salvation to all men."[92] The issue with this verse, like 1 Timothy 2:3–6, is the meaning of "all men." Advocates of partic-

---

88. Baugh, "Savior of All People," 334–38.

89. "The second line of the faithful saying closely parallels Paul's introduction to the second faithful saying (1 Tim 2:3–4) in its description of God as Savior and as making the offer of salvation to all. . . . There is no exclusivism in Paul's gospel, contrary to his opponents' teachings (cf. 1 Tim 2:1–7)." Mounce, *Pastoral Epistles*, 256.

90. Lea and Griffin, *1, 2 Timothy, Titus*, 136

91. Millard Erickson believes this verse to be one of the strongest supports for unlimited atonement. Concerning the teaching of 1 Tim 4:10, he states "Apparently the Savior has done something for all persons, though it is less in degree than what he has done for those who believe." Erickson, *Christian Theology*, 851.

92. There is a translation issue in this verse. The KJV and the NIV both make the adjective "bringing salvation" (*soterios*) modify "the grace of God," which would result in "the grace of God that brings salvation has appeared to all men." This translation is most likely not correct, however, because the adjective is in the predicate position, and therefore it describes the effects of the appearing. This interpretation results in the NASB translation quoted above.

Jesus Christ's Payment for the Sins of All People in the Atonement

ular atonement understand the phrase as meaning "all classes of men," and therefore as only referring to believers.[93] This interpretation of the phrase is based upon the supposition that Paul uses the phrase in the same way in the two passages discussed above, and on the understanding that "all men" is equivalent to "us" in 2:14.[94] If the above interpretations of 1 Timothy 2:3–6 and 4:10 are correct, however, then Paul is most likely using the phrase in the same way to mean "all people." Furthermore, it is difficult to understand why Paul would use the limited interpretation in this verse. The point of 2:11–14 is to give the theological reasons for the ethical instruction to various groups in 2:1–10. Why would Paul first instruct all of the groups in the correct ways of Christian conduct, and then stress that all of the groups were included in God's saving plan, as if there was some sort of confusion over that issue?[95] Instead, the point of the passage is to indicate how Paul's ethical instructions are based upon God's purposes in Christ's saving work, as the "grace of God" that appeared was Jesus Christ in his birth, life, death, and resurrection.[96] This grace has made salvation available to all people (v. 11), and has resulted in the redemption of believers (v. 14). Therefore this passage (just like 1 Tim 4:10) presents both Christ's unlimited payment for sin and his particular intention to save the elect, just as the multi-intentioned view asserts. Titus 2:11, like 1 Timothy 2:3–6 and 4:10, indicates that God has made salvation available to all people through Christ's atoning sacrifice for all people.

THE GENERAL EPISTLES

Hebrews 2:9

Hebrews 2:9 states, "But we do see Him who was made for a little while lower than the angels, *namely*, Jesus, because of the suffering of death crowned with glory and honor, so that by the grace of God He might taste death for everyone." This verse is a significant one in its context, as it sums up 2:1–8 and provides the foundation for 2:10–18. In 2:1–4 the author of Hebrews states that because Christ is superior to the angels (the point of Heb 1:4–14)

---

93. Bavinck, *Sin and Salvation*, 465; Berkhof, *Systematic Theology*, 396; Knight, *Pastoral Epistles*, 319; Nicole, "Definite Atonement," 205; and Tiessen, *Who Can Be Saved?*, 489.

94. Knight, *Pastoral Epistles*, 319.

95. Marshall, "For All," 330.

96. Hiebert, *Titus*, 439; Lea and Griffin, *1, 2 Timothy, Titus*, 310; Knight, *Pastoral Epistles*, 318–19; Marshall, "For All," 330; and Mounce, *Pastoral Epistles*, 422.

we ought to pay attention to Christ's message of salvation. The author than goes on in 2:5–9 to demonstrate that Christ is superior to the angels because he is the one to whom the world is subjected. Psalm 8:4–6 is quoted as proof: humanity was meant to subject the world, and actually has subjected the world (v. 8). Currently, we might not see all things subjected to humanity, but we know that they are and one day will be because Jesus has fulfilled this prophecy.[97] The one who was made a little lower than the angels in his incarnation is now crowned with glory and honor because of his death, and it was in the sufferings of his death that, by the grace of God,[98] Jesus tasted death for everyone. The idea of "tasting" is here used metaphorically as "experiencing," and it is not used to indicate that Jesus' death was quick or short. Jesus' "tasting death" is equivalent to his "suffering death" and refers to his substitutionary atonement.[99] The author then explains in 2:10–18 why the death of Jesus is part of his greatness: it is on the basis of and through Jesus' death that God saves people.

This verse is an important one in the debate over the extent of the atonement because it states that Jesus tasted death for everyone. The question therefore concerns whether "everyone" refers to all people or only to the elect. Those who prefer the latter option come to that conclusion by equating "everyone" with the "many sons brought to glory" (v. 10), "those who are sanctified" (v. 11), those who are the "brethren" of Christ (v. 12), those who are the "children of God" (vv. 13, 14), those who are delivered from the bondage of death (v. 15), and those who are God's people (v. 17).[100] The former interpretation of "everyone" as "all people," is to be preferred, however, for the following reasons. First, Christ's death for everyone in Hebrews 2:9 is not only the explanation for how the elect are saved, it is also the explanation of how all things are subjected to him. Christ is the fulfillment of Psalm 8:4–6, a prophecy given to humanity, because he is united with all people in his incarnation and his death.[101] It is also difficult to understand

---

97. Lane, *Hebrews 1–8*, 48.

98. There is an alternative reading "apart from God" for the phrase "by the grace of God" in some ancient manuscripts. The traditional reading "by the grace of God" seems more likely because it is better attested. For a discussion of the options and evidence, see Ellingworth, *The Epistle to the Hebrews*, 155–57. Whichever reading one takes, however, has no effect on the understanding of this verse for the extent of the atonement.

99. Ellingworth, *Epistle to the Hebrews*, 157; and Johnson, *Hebrews*, 92.

100. Bavinck, *Sin and Salvation*, 465, 489; Berkhof, *Systematic Theology*, 396–97; Calvin, *Hebrews*, 599; Kuiper, *For Whom Did Christ Die?*, 28–29; Lane, *Hebrews 1–8*, 55; Murray, *Redemption Accomplished and Applied*, 61; Nettles, *By His Grace*, 300; Nicole, "Definite Atonement," 205–06; Owen, *Death of Death*, 237–38; Shedd, *Dogmatic Theology*, 2:479; and Wells, *Price for a People*, 93–94.

101. Douty, *Did Christ Die*, 118; Ellingworth, *Epistle to the Hebrews*, 153–57;

how all things can be subjected to Christ if he did not pay for the sins of all people, as we will see when we explore Christ's cosmic triumph over sin in the next chapter. Second, the word used for "everyone" in Hebrews 2:9 (*pantos*) seems to suggest that Christ's death was for each and every human being. The best translation of the word is "every (or each) person," as *pantos* is used in the singular and should be translated as "each" or "every." The context also makes it clear that the word is referring to human beings and not the entire universe, which is semantically possible.[102] Hebrews 2:10–18 certainly speaks of Christ's death saving the elect, but this is another example of the multiple intentions in Christ's atonement, moving from the general to the particular (cf. 2 Cor 5:14–15; 1 Tim 4:10: Titus 2:11–14; 1 John 2:1–2). Hebrews 2:9 indicates that Christ's atonement was for each and every human being, meaning that Christ died to pay the penalty of sin for each and every human being.

2 Peter 2:1

One of the primary reasons that Peter[103] wrote his second letter was to warn the churches about false teachers in their midst. These false teachers are first mentioned in 2 Peter 2:1, which reads, "But false prophets also arose among the people, just as there will also be false teachers among you, who will secretly introduce destructive heresies, even denying the Master who bought them, bringing swift destruction upon themselves." The false teachers are the subject of the entire second chapter of the letter, with 2 Peter 2:1–3 serving as an introduction to their denunciation. The false teachers are similar to the false prophets of the Old Testament (v. 1a), and they stand in sharp contrast to the men who spoke from God as they were moved by the Holy Spirit (2 Pet 1:21). These false teachers were already among the Christian community to whom Peter wrote, and as 2 Peter 2:1 indicates they were secretly introducing destructive heresies, denying the Master who bought them, and bringing swift destruction upon themselves.[104] These actions

---

Johnson, *Hebrews*, 89–93; Lightner, *Death Christ Died*, 71–72; and Morris, *Hebrews*, 25.

102. Johnson, *Hebrews*, 92; and O'Brien, *The Letter to the Hebrews*, 100.

103. We will assume that Simon Peter was the author of 2 Peter, as the letter states (2 Pet 2:1), although there are plausible evangelical explanations as to why this might not be the case. See the discussion in Bauckham, *Jude, 2 Peter*, 158–62; and Davids, *The Letters of Jude and 2 Peter*, 123–30.

104. Peter uses the future tense when speaking of the false teachers, but it is clear from the context (2:13, 15, 17) that the false teachers were present in the community. Schreiner, *Jude, 2 Peter*, 327.

characterize the false teachers and clearly communicate that the false teachers were unbelievers.[105]

Advocates of unlimited atonement consider 2 Peter 2:1 to be one of the strongest statements supporting an unlimited redemption, because the verse seems to be saying that Christ died for those who deny him, and are therefore lost. Therefore Christ's atonement is not only explicitly said to be for who do not believe in him, it is said to be for the worst kind of heretics who deny Christ and his atonement. This understanding of the verse is based upon the phrase "denying the Master who bought them," with "Master" referring to Jesus Christ and "bought" referring to soteriological redemption, but not to actual salvation. This understanding is contested, however, with the two main issues being the meaning of the terms "Master" and "bought."[106]

The word translated "Master" in 2 Peter 2:1 is *despotes*, which is used ten times in the New Testament. In four of these instances the word clearly refers to masters of households or slave owners (1 Tim 6:1, 2; Titus 2:9; 1 Peter 2:18). *Despotes* is clearly used of God the Father three times (Luke 2:29; Acts 2:24; Rev 6:10), with each reference stressing the Father's absolute sovereignty. The word occurs in 2 Timothy 2:21, where it most likely refers to Jesus Christ and stresses his ownership and sovereignty over believers.[107] Most significant for our understanding of 2 Peter 2:1, *despotes* refers to Jesus Christ in Jude 4, which states, "For certain persons have crept in unnoticed, those who were long beforehand marked out for this condemnation, ungodly persons who turn the grace of our God into licentiousness and deny our only Master and Lord, Jesus Christ." Not only does the phrase "our only Master and Lord, Jesus Christ" seem to fit the Granville Sharp rule (meaning that "Master" and "Lord" most likely both refer to Jesus Christ because the words are governed by the same article), but the word *despotes* was used of Jesus in Palestinian circles, and this would have been known by Jude.[108] Second Peter 2:1 parallels Jude 4, which means that the term almost certainly refers to Jesus Christ in 2 Peter 2:1 as well.[109] Furthermore, no matter

---

105. Bauckham, *Jude, 2 Peter*, 240–41; Davids, *Jude and 2 Peter*, 220–21; and Hiebert, "Portrayal of False Teachers," 258–60.

106. Long, *Definite Atonement*, 91–99; and Chang, "Second Peter 2:1," 56–60 both discuss four different interpretations of the phrase "Master who bought them," while Kennard, "Petrine Redemption," 401 lists six different interpretations.

107. Chang, "Second Peter 2:1," 53.

108. Bauckham, *Jude, 2 Peter*, 39–40; Davids, *Jude and 2 Peter*, 45; Kennard, "Petrine Redemption," 403; and Schreiner, *Jude, 2 Peter*, 439–40.

109. Bauckham, *Jude, 2 Peter*, 240; Blum, *2 Peter*, 276; Chang, "Second Peter 2:1," 53–54; Davids, *Jude and 2 Peter*, 221; Hiebert, "Portrayal of False Teachers," 259;

how it is understood, the phrase "bought them" almost certainly refers to a work of Christ rather than a work of the Father.[110]

The exact meaning of "bought them" in this context is also disputed, however. The word translated "bought" is *agorazo*, which when used in a soteriological sense is one of the words used in the New Testament to denote redemption. The word is used six times in regards to people (1 Cor 6:20; 7:23; 2 Pet 2:1; Rev 5:9; 14:3–4), and except for the disputed use in 2 Peter 2:1 it plainly refers to soteriological redemption. The word is also used 24 times in a nonsoteriological sense, however, in reference to commercial purchases.[111] This has led some to argue that the usage in 2 Peter 2:1 is nonsoteriological, and should mean "acquire." Gary Long, for example, offers six reasons why the use of *agorazo* in 2 Pet 2:1 is not soteriological: the word is never used in the Septuagint Old Testament to translate redemption words, the word is never used in a salvation context in the New Testament without the mention of a price, whenever the word is used of people it always refers to believers, the word by itself does not include a payment price and cannot be used soteriologically without the mention of one, *agorazo* is better translated "acquire" or "obtain" when no payment price is stated, and the word is never used in the New Testament in a hypothetical sense.[112] The meaning of this word is almost certainly soteriological, however, for four reasons. First, as noted above, whenever the word refers to people as the object of purchase in the New Testament, it is always used soteriologically, unless 2 Peter 2:1 is the lone exception.[113] Second, the context of the verse is clearly soteriological.[114] Third, *agorazo* is used soteriologically in Revelation

---

Kennard, "Petrine Redemption," 403; Long, *Definite Atonement*, 85; and Schreiner *Jude, 2, Peter*, 329.

110. Schreiner, *Jude, 2, Peter*, 329. See also Davids, *Jude and 2 Peter*, 221; and Kennard, "Petrine Redemption," 403. There are some advocates of particular redemption that understand *despotes* in this verse as referring to God the Father, but this is a minority view. See Owen, *Death of Death*, 251; and Nettles, *By His Grace*, 300–02.

111. Morris, *Apostolic Preaching*, 53–55.

112. Long, *Definite Atonement*, 86–87.

113. Chang, "Second Peter 2:1," 55; and Kennard, "Petrine Redemption," 402.

114. "The context clearly develops soteriological issues. Within this development there is a major emphasis on lifestyle, which is quite appropriate to Petrine redemption. For example, those who have knowledge of Christ are to abundantly appropriate in their lives faith, moral excellence, knowledge, self-control, perseverance, godliness, brotherly kindness and love (2 Pet 1:2–7). This meaningful way of life assures the believer that he shall bear fruit and enter into the eternal kingdom (2 Pet 1:8–11). This meaningful way of life is the reverse of the preredemptive, futile, sinful way of life (1 Pet 1:18; 2 Pet 1:9). So *agorazo* here is best seen as soteriological redemption." Kennard, "Petrine Redemption," 402.

14:3–4, and there is no mention of a price in those verses.[115] Fourth, there is no reason to understand *agorazo* hypothetically; Christ actually did redeem the false teachers, but they are not in Christ through faith (they deny him with their words and their actions) and therefore they do not subjectively experience that redemption. Just as Christ objectively reconciled the world but not all people are subjectively reconciled to him (2 Cor 5:18–21), Christ objectively redeemed the world, though all are not subjectively redeemed by him.[116]

The meanings of "Master" and "bought" in 2 Peter 2:1 lead to the conclusion that Jesus Christ redeemed the false teachers who deny him; which means that in his atonement he paid the price for their sins. Therefore 2 Peter 2:1 states that Christ paid the penalty for the sins of unbelievers. The language and context of 2 Peter 2:1 rule out the interpretations of the verse that understand *despotes* to refer to God the Father, or Christ as "Sovereign Creator," which results when one understands *agorazo* in a non-redemptive sense. They also rule out interpretations that understand the verse to be referring only to physical or temporal deliverance.[117] Neither are the false teachers charitably treated as professing Christians, a view commonly espoused by advocates of particular redemption.[118] The verse is also clearly speaking of those who are unbelievers, which means that the false teachers are not apostate Christians or former Christians who have lost their

---

115. "The lack of a mentioned price is no reason to overthrow this soteriological meaning since half of the NT soteriological meanings of this word omit any mention of a price (2 Pet 2:1; Rev 14:3–4)." Ibid., 402.

116. As Chafer states (though I do not agree with the distinctions he makes between *agorazo* and *exagorazo*), "There is, then a redemption which pays the price, but does not of necessity release the slave, and there is a redemption which is unto abiding freedom." Chafer, "For Whom Did Christ Die?," 313.

117. This view states that Peter refers to the temporary deliverance of the false teachers from the pollutions of the world because of "their knowledge of the Lord" (2 Pet 2:20). See Owen, *Death of Death*, 251–52. Not only does this view misunderstand the meaning of *agorazo*, it also requires that the false teachers be professing believers. There is no support for this view in the text, and as we have seen there is good reason to believe that the false teachers were not professing believers.

118. Berkhof, *Systematic Theology*, 397; Kuiper, *For Whom Did Christ Die?*, 38; McCartney, "Atonement in James, Peter, and Jude," 178–79; Nicole, "Definite Atonement," 204; Schreiner, *Jude, 2, Peter*, 329; Shedd, *Dogmatic Theology*, 2:481; ." Smeaton, *Apostle's Doctrine*, 447; Tiessen, *Who Can Be Saved?*, 490; and Wells, *Price for a People*, 90–93. The problem with this view is that there is no basis for it in the text. As with the temporal deliverance view, the text gives no evidence that these false teachers were treated as believers, and much evidence that they were not. See Blum, *2 Peter*, 276–77; Chang, "Second Peter 2:1," 60; Davids, *Jude and 2 Peter*, 221; and Sailer, "A Wesleyan View," 193.

Jesus Christ's Payment for the Sins of All People in the Atonement

salvation.[119] Peter in this verse speaks of unbelieving false teachers who deny Jesus Christ, their Master and the one they should have trusted in and served because he is the one who redeemed them from their sins through his death on the cross.

A UNIVERSAL PAYMENT FOR SIN DOES NOT RESULT IN UNIVERSALISM

The primary theological argument that advocates of particular redemption advance against Christ's payment for the sins of all people, elect and non-elect, is that this understanding of the extent of the atonement demands universalism. Berkhof is representative when he states, "It should also be noted that the doctrine that Christ died for the purpose of saving all men, logically leads to absolute universalism, that is, to the doctrine that all men are actually saved. It is impossible that they for whom Christ paid the price, whose guilt he removed, should be lost on account of that guilt."[120] This argument is behind much of the particular redemption understanding of the verses we explored above, as alternate interpretations of those verses are deemed necessary to avoid universalism. As Tom Wells states,

> When Christ is said to do these things for "all" or for "the whole world" we must either reduce the redemption words, making them say much less than they say, or reduce the universal terms such as "all" and "the whole world." You can't say, "We won't do either!" unless you are prepared to say that Christ redeemed and reconciled and turned the wrath of God away from all men at the cross. But that is just to say that all men will be saved! As I said before, we would like to believe that, but the Bible will not let us do so.[121]

Advocates of particular redemption support the assertion that a universal payment for sins entails universalism with several arguments. The most common one is that when the Bible speaks of Christ's death, it speaks of it actually accomplishing salvation instead of just making it possible. If Christ actually paid for the sins of all people, if he actually redeemed all people, reconciled all people, and propitiated the wrath of God for all

---

119. Views advanced by Bauckham, *Jude, 2 Peter*, 240; and Kennard, "Petrine Redemption," 403–05.
120. Berkhof, *Systematic Theology*, 395
121. Wells, *Price for a People*, 52.

people, then all people would be saved.[122] Supporters of particular redemption also assert that since God is completely sovereign, and His will can never be thwarted, all people would be saved if Christ died for all people, hence unlimited atonement logically results in universalism.[123] They claim that if Christ paid for all peoples' sins God would be unjust to send anyone to hell, because He would then be making them pay for sins that had already been paid for by Christ.[124] If even the sin of unbelief has been paid for, then God would be unjust to punish sinners for their unbelief.[125] Finally, since Christ died to actually secure salvation for His people (Eph 5:25; Titus 2:14; Heb 2:10), He could not have died for all people because not all people are saved.[126]

Christ's universal payment for sin does not entail universalism, however, for two reasons. First, as the exegesis throughout this chapter has shown, the Bible consistently differentiates between Christ's objective work in the atonement and the subjective application of that work to the believer. Christ's atonement actually accomplished reconciliation, redemption, and propitiation for all people, but all people are not saved because all people do not subjectively appropriate what Christ has done for them. In order to experience the reconciliation and redemption that Christ has accomplished in the atonement, one must be in Christ through faith. As William Shedd states, "Atonement in and by itself, separate from faith, saves no soul. Christ might have died precisely as he did, but if no one believed in him he would have died in vain."[127]

Proponents of particular redemption combine the provision and application of the atonement into the same act, denying the strong distinction between Christ's objective work in the atonement and the subjective application of that work to the believer, and primarily use two arguments in defense of this. The first is that Christ procured the gift of saving faith in the atonement, and therefore only those whom Christ died for can have saving faith.[128] There is no reason, however, why Christ could not have secured the gift of saving faith only for the elect through his death for all, as one of his particular intentions in the atonement. Marshall makes this point: "To say that God provides the means of acceptance, namely faith and the gift of the

---

122. Nicole, "Definite Atonement," 201.
123. Owen, *Death of Death*, 233.
124. Grudem, *Systematic Theology*, 595.
125. Owen, *Death of Death*, 61–62.
126. Berkhof, *Systematic Theology*, 395.
127. Shedd, *Dogmatic Theology*, 2:477.
128. Nicole, "Definite Atonement," 202.

Spirit, does not require that God, having given Christ for the sins of the world, should act to save every individual."[129] The second argument is that Christ only intercedes for the elect, and therefore he died only for the elect because his death and intercession are coextensive.[130] Christ certainly does only intercede unto salvation for the elect (John 17; Rom 8:34; Heb 7:25; 1 John 2:1), but like the rest of the blessings of the atonement, intercession unto salvation is something that is available to all but only effectual for those who are in Christ. Scripture also seems to indicate that Christ does intercede in at least one instance for the nonelect (Luke 23:34), and Paul encourages believers to intercede for them as well (1 Tim 2:1–2; cf. Rom 9:1–5). Furthermore, Christ's role as advocate for the saved involves his pleading against Satan, the Accuser of the brethren (Rev 12:10). This advocacy is possible because Jesus gained victory over Satan at the cross, and Jesus' victory over Satan is only possible because his atonement was the payment for all sin (as we will see in Chapter 4). Christ procuring the gift of faith only for the elect or interceding unto salvation only for the elect does not require that his atoning death be only for the elect; the particular and general intentions of the atonement do not have to be coextensive. Advocates of particular redemption err by collapsing the application and the provision of the atonement into the same act when the Bible separates them. In his atonement Christ provided salvation for more people than he purposed to save.[131]

Supporting this distinction between the objective work of the atonement and the subjective application of it is the necessity of faith on the part of believers for salvation. If those who believe in particular redemption are correct, and the application and provision of the atonement are coextensive because the atonement actually saved the elect, then it seems to follow logically that nothing else is necessary for the elect to be saved. Robert Picirilli puts it this way, "The point is that if propitiation, say, or reconciliation were actually finished on the cross, then all those whose sins were actually propitiated were on the day Christ died removed from the wrath of God and reconciled to Him. Indeed, those elect not yet born would therefore never be under the wrath of God or estranged from Him in their real lifetimes.[132] The Bible makes it clear, however, that faith in Christ is absolutely necessary for salvation, and that without faith in Christ even the elect are subject to God's wrath. In Ephesians 2:1–10, Paul writes about the nature of the salvation

---

129. Marshall, "For All," 341.
130. Letham, *Work of Christ*, 236–37.
131. Demarest, *Cross and Salvation*, 191.
132. Picirilli, *Grace, Faith, Free Will*, 94.

that the Ephesian believers possessed. He begins this section by noting that before their conversion they were dead in sin (Eph 2:1), they were followers of the devil (Eph 2:2), and they used to be children of wrath who deserved nothing but the judgment of God, like all other unbelievers (Eph 2:3). In other words, before they put their faith and trust in Jesus Christ, they were in the same state as the rest of fallen humanity.[133] The question then is: how could Paul write that the Ephesian believers were once children of wrath if their salvation had been actualized in Christ's atonement? How could he write that they had been saved by grace, through faith (Eph 2:8)? How can those who were saved at the cross be described as sinners under the wrath of God who need to put their faith in Him in order to be saved? As Bruce Ware states,

> Is not saving faith required *for the elect to be saved*? If so, how can it be said of the death of Christ *in itself* that by his death *alone* he saved those for whom he died? As long as one believes that all people (including the elect) are born into this world with the sin of Adam so that until anyone savingly believes in Christ he or she remains *unsaved* and under God's wrath, then we cannot speak correctly of Christ's death as actually and certainly *saving* the elect. No, even here, the payment made by his death on behalf of the elect renders their salvation *possible* (and because of their election, a future *certain* reality) while that salvation becomes *actual* only upon their exercising saving faith. If Christ's death, then, is a payment for sin that makes *possible* the salvation of people, which salvation *actually* occurs only when they savingly believe, then there is no problem saying Christ's death paid the penalty of the sin of *all* the people in the whole world, because until any believes, he or she is not saved.[134]

This biblical truth also effectively responds to the particular redemption arguments that God would be unjust to send sinners to hell or punish them for their unbelief if Christ paid for their sins. Without being in Christ by grace through faith all people are culpable for all of their sin (including unbelief) and all people face eternal punishment in hell. Since all people, including the elect, are children of wrath and culpable for their sin before

---

133. "The children of wrath, then, are those who are doomed to God's wrath because through their condition of sinful rebellion, they deserve his righteous judgment. As does Paul in Rom 1:18–3:20, the writer makes this category cover all humanity outside Christ.... What was once true of the readers (vv 1, 2) was also once true of all believers (v. 3a), and what was once true of all believers is also true of the rest of humanity (v. 3b)." Lincoln, *Ephesians*, 98–99.

134. Ware, "Extent of the Atonement," 5, emphasis the author's.

their salvation in Christ, it seems that no person is rescued from hell until he or she is saved, and therefore the "double payment" argument loses its force. If advocates of particular redemption employ this argument, then they need to explain how they escape it in the case of the elect before the elect are actually saved.

The second reason that Christ's payment for the sins of all people does not necessitate universalism is because there are multiple intentions in Christ's atonement. Christ's unlimited atonement does not thwart God's sovereign will because God intended to accomplish both general and particular purposes in the atonement, and this required payment for the sins of all people. As we will see in chapter 4, God does several things for his creation and/or unbelievers through Christ's payment for the sins of all people. As we will see in chapter 5, God also accomplishes the certain salvation of the elect through Christ's payment for the sins of all people. God's particular saving work on the cross does not rule out His general work for the non-elect, and is in fact consistent with it. The multi-intentioned view of the extent of the atonement, which is based upon Christ's payment for the sins of all people, does not result in or in any way demand universalism.

CONCLUSION

Jesus Christ's payment for the sins of all people, elect and nonelect, is a truth affirmed throughout Scripture. Though there are not many passages in the Old Testament that speak of the extent of the atonement, Isaiah 53:6 stands out as one text that affirms Christ's atonement is for the sins of all people. The New Testament, centered as it is upon the good news of Christ's death and its implications for humanity, is much clearer about the extent of the atonement. John's Gospel repeatedly describes the atonement in universal terms, as Jesus came to be the Savior of the world (John 4:42) in order to take away the sins of the world (John 1:29). First John is no less emphatic, as Christ is described as the propitiation for the sins of believers and of unbelievers (1 John 2:1-2). Paul's position on the extent of the atonement is the same as John's; Christ's death was a ransom for all (1 Tim 2:3-6) and resulted in the reconciliation of the world (2 Cor 5:18-21). The author of Hebrews also describes Christ as tasting death for everyone (Heb 2:9). Finally, Peter makes it clear that even unbelieving false teachers owe their allegiance to Christ, because he bought them in his atonement (2 Pet 2:1).

Although the New Testament consistently confirms Christ's payment for the sin of all people, it never teaches universalism. It makes a consistent difference between the objective accomplishment and the subjective application of the atonement. Even the elect do not receive the salvific benefits of the atonement until they subjectively appropriate them by grace through faith. Christ's payment for the sin of all people on the cross did not secure the salvation of all people, but instead only secured the salvation of the elect in accordance with the Father's electing will and the Holy Spirit's effectual saving work. Christ's procurement of salvation for the elect in his atonement was one of the multiple intentions that God had in the atonement. The atonement also had several general purposes, which flow out of Christ's universal payment for sin. Christ's payment for all sin was for specific purposes and accomplished exactly what God intended for it to accomplish, and therefore the universality of the atonement in no way diminishes the value or the power of Christ's atonement as some proponents of particular atonement contend.[135] Christ's payment for all sin is instead at the very heart of the atonement's glory and majesty.

---

135. Bavinck, *Sin and Salvation*, 468–69; Murray, *Redemption Accomplished and Applied*, 63–64; and Nicole, "Definite Atonement," 203.

CHAPTER 4

The General Intentions of the Atonement

INTRODUCTION

THE MULTI-INTENTIONED VIEW HOLDS that God the Father, in sending his Son to die on the cross, had both particular and general purposes for the atonement. The general purposes of God are those purposes that have reference both to the elect and to the nonelect, (and in some cases all of creation), while the particular purposes are those which concern only the elect. In accordance with the Father's will, the Son died to pay for the sins of all people, the elect and the nonelect, in order to accomplish these multiple purposes. Based upon the Son's atoning death on the cross, the Spirit then works to apply the atonement in both particular and general ways. In this chapter we will demonstrate, both exegetically and theologically, what God's general purposes in the atonement are. The general intentions of the atonement were to make the universal gospel call possible, to make common grace (and not only salvific grace) possible, to provide an additional basis of condemnation for those who reject the gospel, to serve as the supreme revelation of God's character, and to make Christ's cosmic triumph over all sin possible. Through this examination we will not only establish the biblical and theological validity of the multi-intentioned view, but we will also demonstrate the necessity of Christ's payment for the sins of the nonelect.

A GENUINE UNIVERSAL GOSPEL CALL

One of the Father's primary intentions in sending the Son to die for the sins of all people was to make it possible for the gospel to be genuinely and rightly offered to all people. Even though not all people will be saved, Christ died to provide the basis by which all people could be saved if they would trust in Christ. The genuineness of the offer for all people to be saved through Christ's atoning work is necessary because God desires that all people know of his saving love towards them in the atonement (John 3:16), and because there is a sense in which he desires for all people to experience the salvation that only the atonement brings (1 Tim 2:4; 2 Pet 3:9). God offers the universal gospel call because he wants all people to hear the good news of the gospel, turn from their sin, and come to him through his Son.[1] As D. A. Carson states, "However much God stands in judgment over the world, he also presents himself as the God who invites and commands all human beings to repent."[2] The universal gospel call genuinely demonstrates God's love toward all of humanity, even if it does not result in salvation for all who hear it.

The Nature of the Universal Gospel Call

The universal gospel call is "the invitation or summons to salvation conveyed through cognitive encounter with the Gospel message," and it includes a presentation of the plan of salvation, an invitation to come to Christ in faith and repentance, and the promise of forgiveness and salvation.[3] The basis of the universal gospel call is the universal invitation to come to God issued in both the Old and the New Testaments. The prophets in the Old Testament continually called both the children of Israel and the nations of the world to come to God. Psalm 22:27 states, "All the ends of the earth will remember and turn to the LORD, and all the families of the nations will worship before You." Isaiah 45:22 is another example, "Turn to Me and be saved, all the ends of the earth; For I am God, and there is no other" (cf. Isa 55:1; 65:2). This verse makes it clear that "If the Lord is the sole God of the

---

1. The universal gospel call is for all people because it is meant to go out to all people, not because every single person will eventually hear it (Matt 28:18–20). See Piper, *Let the Nations Be Glad*, 171–81.
2. Carson, *The Difficult Doctrine of the Love of God*, 17–18.
3. Demarest, *Cross and Salvation*, 218.

whole world and if he is a savior (v. 21), then he must be the savior of the whole world as well."[4]

In the New Testament John the Baptist continued the practice of the Old Testament by calling all people to come to God for salvation (Matt 3:1–12; Mark 1:3–8; Luke 3:2–20; John 1:6–8; 19–34), emphasizing the universality of Jesus' salvific work with statements like "Behold, the Lamb of God who takes away the sin of the world!" (John 1:29). Jesus did the same thing, inviting all people to enter the kingdom of God through repentance and faith (Matt 11:28; 22:1–14; Luke 5:32; 14:16–24; John 7:37–38). He then commanded his disciples to preach his name throughout the ends of the earth in the Great Commission (Matt 28:18–20; Mark 16:15; Luke 24:47; Acts 1:8). Acts records the early Christian evangelists offering the gospel indiscriminately to all people (e.g., Acts 2:38–39; 4:12; 8:22; 17:30). However, this call did not always end with its hearers accepting salvation, but was often resisted and rejected (Luke 13:34; Acts 7:51; 13:46; 17:32), demonstrating that the gospel call goes out to the nonelect just as it does to the elect. As Jesus stated, "For many are called, but few are chosen" (Matt 22:14). That the universal gospel call can be rejected illustrates the difference between this call and the Spirit's particular, effectual calling.[5]

All supporters of unlimited atonement agree that the gospel call is universal, in that it is meant for all people.[6] They typically understand the

---

4. Oswalt, *The Book of Isaiah: Chapters 40–66*, 223.

5. Effectual calling is "the Spirit's call to sinners to hear and to believe the gospel, rendered effectual by his supernatural enlivening work, or as the Spirit's provision of grace resulting in saving faith, rendered irresistible against all blindness, hardness, and unbelief." Ware, "Effectual Calling and Grace," 204. The effectual call is always issued through the proclamation of the gospel (2 Thess 2:14), but it is distinct from the general invitation of the gospel (e.g., Isa 45:22; Matt 11:28), which goes out to all people, because it always results in salvation.

6. There are some advocates of unlimited atonement who believe that one of the implications of an unlimited atonement is that all people have an opportunity to accept or reject God's salvation, whether they have heard the gospel or not. E.g.,, "The gracious love that intends salvation for all of humanity also at the same time confronts every person with a genuine choice regarding the meaning of one's present existence and the nature of the ultimate future." Guy, "The Universality of God's Love," 45. Another way this belief is stated is with the idea that God knows who would accept him if they would have heard the gospel, so those people end up being saved, even though they never actually heard the gospel. As Donald Lake states, "A valid offer of grace has been made to mankind, but its application is limited by God's response rather than God's arbitrary selection. God knows who would, under ideal circumstances, believe the gospel, and on the basis of his foreknowledge, applies that gospel even if the person never hears the gospel during his lifetime." Lake, "He Died for All," 43. The problem with this idea is that Scripture consistently presents the proclamation, hearing, and acceptance of the gospel as absolutely necessary for the Holy Spirit's work of salvation to take place. The

universal gospel call as one of the strongest proofs for the truth of unlimited atonement.[7] Supporters of particular redemption also typically believe in the universal gospel call (with some notable exceptions),[8] although they deny that the universal gospel call necessarily results in an unlimited extent of the atonement. Berkhof is typical when he states, "The universal offer of the gospel does not consist in the declaration that Christ made atonement for every man that hears the gospel, and that God really intends to save each one."[9] As we will demonstrate, however, the Bible makes it clear that Jesus' payment for the sins of all people, elect and nonelect, was necessary for the universal gospel call to be possible. Both the content of the gospel and the motivation for the gospel demand an atonement that was for the sins of all people. The Holy Spirit's work in taking the gospel to all people also suggests a universal payment for sin, as the Spirit's work is closely tied to the Son's. Finally, an offer of salvation to all would seem to imply that provision has been made for the salvation of all, indicating that an atonement for all people is necessary for the universal gospel call to be genuine.

The Content of the Gospel

Paul gives a succinct account of the gospel he preached in 1 Corinthians 15:1–5. These verses state, "Now I make known to you, brethren, the gospel which I preached to you, which also you received, in which also you stand, by which also you are saved, if you hold fast the word which I preached to you, unless you believed in vain. For I delivered to you as of first importance what I also received, that Christ died for our sins according to the

---

Spirit, as the Spirit of the Father (Matt 10:20; Luke 11:13; 1 John 4:2) and the Spirit of the Son (Rom 8:9; Gal 4:6; Phil 1:19; 1 Pet 1:11), only saves people by explicitly applying the atonement of Jesus Christ through the gospel of Jesus Christ. The atonement's payment for all sin did not procure an opportunity for anyone to be saved apart from hearing the gospel, which is part of the reason the gospel needs to be proclaimed to all people. I defend the necessity of the gospel for salvation in further detail in Shultz, Jr., "The Necessity of the Gospel," 73–84.

7. Chafer, "For Whom Did Christ Die?," 315–16; Douty, *Did Christ Die*, 45–49; Lake, "He Died for All," 43–44; Lightner, *Death Christ Died*, 114–18; Marshall, "For All," 345–46; Miethe, "The Universal Power of the Atonement," 83–85; and Picirilli, *Grace, Faith, Free Will*, 115–18.

8. These exceptions include Joseph Hussey (1660–1726), John Gill (1697–1771), John Brine (1703–1765), Klaas Schilder (1890–1765), and Herman Hoeksema (1886–1925). Nicole, "Covenant, Universal Call," 407. However, these are exceptions, and most supporters of particular redemption adamantly uphold the universal gospel call. See Nicole, "Covenant, Universal Call," 410–11; and Packer, *Evangelism and the Sovereignty of God*, 26–27.

9. Berkhof, *Systematic Theology*, 397–98.

Scriptures, and that He was buried, and that He was raised on the third day according to the Scriptures, and that He appeared to Cephas, then to the twelve." This gospel is the message that the Corinthians heard from Paul, received, and believed; and it was through their belief in this message that they were saved (vv. 1–2). At the heart of the gospel is the atoning death of Christ on the cross and his subsequent resurrection, as verses 3–4 state (cf. also 1 Cor 1:18, 21, 23, 14). In order for a person to be saved, he or she must believe that "Christ died for our sins."

The importance of this explanation of the gospel for the extent of the atonement is that the heart of Paul's gospel is the phrase "Christ died for our sins." This phrase indicates that Christ died a substitutionary death for the sins of humanity, the elect and the nonelect, believers and unbelievers. The reason this is so is because it is the gospel message that was preached to unbelievers to lead them to salvation. The Corinthians were not saved at the moment the atonement occurred, but were saved when they believed in the gospel message that "Christ died for our sins" (1 Cor 15:2). Paul, as he preached this message in Corinth, certainly did not preach it only to the elect, but also preached the gospel to those who would reject it and never be saved. This is the way that the early church preached the gospel as well, considering the likelihood that Paul was passing on the message he had already received.[10] If the atonement were limited only to the elect, than how could Paul and the early church preach to a group of unbelievers that "Christ died for our sins"? The word "our" includes both the preacher and those to whom he is preaching. If the atonement was only for the elect, to preach this message to the nonelect would at best be giving them a false hope and at worst would be untrue. The content of the universal gospel call includes the fact that Christ died for all sins, and is therefore based upon an atonement that was for all sins. Part of the gospel message is telling unbelievers that "Jesus died for you."[11]

The Motivation for the Gospel

Paul not only states that the content of the gospel is Christ's payment for the sins of all people, but he also states that Christ's payment for all people is the motivation for preaching the gospel. He makes this clear in 2 Corinthians 5:11–18. In this passage Paul defends his ministry to the Corinthians by explaining his motivation for the ministry. Paul first states that his motivation

---

10. Morris, *The First Epistle of Paul to the Corinthians*, 201.

11. Contra Berkhof, *Systematic Theology*, 397; Nicole, "Covenant, Universal Call," 410; Packer, "Introductory Essay," 16–22; and Waldron, "Biblical Confirmation," 49–50.

for ministry is the fear of the Lord (v. 11), that his reverential awe for God compels him to persuade others of the gospel. A few verses later Paul states that another motivation for his ministry is the love of Christ, which is demonstrated in Christ's death for all people (v. 14).[12] As Paul Barnett explains, "In the second part of the verse Paul explains that he knows of, and is controlled by, 'the love of Christ,' because he became 'convinced' that 'one died for all.' In other words, Paul's sense of ongoing compulsion to evangelize ('controls') arose from his considered judgment ('we are convinced') when he understood that '[Christ had] died for all.'"[13] Paul's motivation for his ministry is Christ's payment for the sins of all people; it is what compels him to serve the Lord.

This motivation becomes even clearer in 2 Corinthians 5:18–20, which states, "Now all *these* things are from God, who reconciled us to Himself through Christ and gave us the ministry of reconciliation, namely, that God was in Christ reconciling the world to Himself, not counting their trespasses against them, and He has committed to us the word of reconciliation. Therefore, we are ambassadors for Christ, as though God were making an appeal through us; we beg you on behalf of Christ, be reconciled to God." This passage highlights the objective and subjective aspects of reconciliation with God.[14] Christians have the ministry of reconciliation and the word of reconciliation (subjective), and this word and ministry is that God was in Christ reconciling the world to himself (objective). God wrought a universal reconciliation, therefore he issues a universal gospel call, and therefore Christians are to be ambassadors for him (2 Cor. 5:20). Not only are the fear of God (2 Cor 5:11) and the love of God (2 Cor 5:14) the motivation for preaching the gospel, the universal reconciliation that Christ accomplished on the cross ought to drive all gospel preaching.[15] Christians ought to take the gospel to all people because Christ died for all people.

---

12. For a defense of understanding "all" in 2 Cor 5:14 as "all people without exception," see our discussion of this passage in chapter 3.

13. Barnett, *Second Epistle to the Corinthians*, 288.

14. For an explanation of the objective and subjective aspects of reconciliation in this passage, and for a defense of the word "world" as referring to "all people without exception," see our discussion of this passage in chapter 3.

15. It is possible that 2 Tim 2:10 could be used to contradict this assertion. This verse states, "For this reason I endure all things for the sake of those who are chosen, so that they also may obtain the salvation which is in Christ Jesus *and* with *it* eternal glory." In this verse Paul states that he endures hardship in his gospel ministry (2 Tim 2:8–9) for the sake of those who are chosen, so that they may obtain salvation. Paul here describes his motive for preaching the gospel as the salvation of the elect. As this motivation only refers to believers, it is particular, as opposed to universal. This motivation need not contradict, however, the motivation of God's love for all people in

The Spirit's Work in the Gospel Call

While the Holy Spirit effectually calls the elect to salvation through the gospel, he also works to call an innumerable amount of people in the universal gospel call. The Holy Spirit works to take the gospel to the world just as he works to take it to believers. Perhaps the most significant passage of Scripture describing the Holy Spirit's work in taking the gospel to all people is John 16:7–11, which states, "But I tell you the truth, it is to your advantage that I go away; for if I do not go away, the Helper will not come to you; but if I go, I will send Him to you. And he, when he comes, will convict the world concerning sin and righteousness and judgment; concerning sin, because they do not believe in me; and concerning righteousness, because I go to the Father and you no longer see me; and concerning judgment, because the ruler of this world has been judged." In this passage, Jesus tells his disciples why it is to their advantage that he go away, because when he goes away he will send the Holy Spirit to them. The Holy Spirit, when he comes, will then convict the world of sin, righteousness, and judgment. These words of encouragement are in light of the disciples' responsibility to testify to the world about Christ, even though the world hated Christ and his followers (John 15:18–16:4). The Holy Spirit would assist their testimony amidst suffering.

Concerning the nature of the universal gospel call, this passage makes two things clear. First, this passage emphasizes that the Spirit convicts the *world* concerning the message of Christ. The word "world" here refers to all unbelievers. This can be seen from the context of the passage (John 15:18–16:6). The world is hostile toward God, opposes the purposes of God, and hates God. Elsewhere Scripture states that these characteristics are true of all unbelievers (Rom 1:18–32; 3:9–20; Eph 2:1–3). It is all unbelievers whom the Holy Spirit works to convict. Concerning this convicting work of the Spirit, Bruce states, "The Spirit bears witness to the world (not least through the witness of Jesus' followers, as was affirmed in John 15:16ff.) that Jesus, rejected, condemned, and put to death by the world, has been vindicated and exalted by God. His rejection, condemnation, and execution expressed in violent clarity the world's refusal to believe in him; that unbelief is now

---

the atonement or the universal reconciliation wrought by the atonement. Paul's gospel ministry can certainly be motivated both by God's general intentions in the atonement, as well as his particular, salvific intentions for the elect. Rather than contradict the findings above, 2 Tim 2:10 complements them, and fits into a multi-intentioned view of the extent of the atonement.

exposed as sin."[16] Jesus in this passage explains the Holy Spirit's role in taking the gospel to unbelievers, or the universal gospel call.

Second, in this passage the Bible explicitly connects the Holy Spirit's work of convicting the world through the gospel to Christ's work on the cross. Jesus went away from his disciples through his death, resurrection, and ascension, and just as he promised in this passage it was only after those experiences that he sent the Spirit (Acts 1:8; 2:1–4, 33). This means that all of the Spirit's work in convicting the world of the gospel is tied to Christ and occurs because of Christ's atonement. As John 16:7–11 explains, the Holy Spirit's work in the world is not only for the elect. Since the Holy Spirit's work of taking the gospel to all unbelievers, elect and nonelect, is based upon Christ's atonement, it seems that Christ's atonement cannot be limited to the elect. As Robert Lightner states, "The Holy Spirit's work could not reach out beyond the elect if the death of Christ did not have this universal scope since the Spirit's ministry was procured in and through the cross. In other words, how could a part of the work of Christ on the cross be universal if the whole of it was not? . . . The problem really centers in the convicting work of the Holy Spirit since this is His principle ministry towards the unsaved. How can the Spirit be said to have a ministry toward the entire world in showing all men their need of Christ if the death of Christ did not reach out to the entire world?"[17] Limiting Christ's atonement to the elect results in separating part of the Spirit's work in the world from the Son's work on the cross.

The Genuineness of the Gospel Call

In light of the command throughout Scripture to preach the gospel to all people, those who hold to particular redemption seem to have a dilemma. Lewis Sperry Chafer articulates, "A very difficult situation arises for the limited redemptionist when he confronts the Great Commission, which enjoins the preaching of the gospel to *every* creature. How, it may be urged, can a universal gospel be preached if there is no universal provision? To say on the one hand that Christ died only for the elect and on the other hand that His death is the ground on which salvation is offered to all men is perilously near contradiction."[18] This contradiction is one that even some advocates of particular redemption recognize. As Thomas Crawford states, "That there is great difficulty in the way of harmonizing the general invitations with the

16. Bruce, *Gospel of John*, 319.
17. Lightner, *Death Christ Died*, 130–31.
18. Chafer, "For Whom Did Christ Die?," 315, emphasis the author's.

Gospel on the one hand with the special reference of the atonement to those who shall eventually be partakers of its benefits on the other hand—it would be altogether fruitless to disguise."[19]

Supporters of particular redemption attempt to resolve this contradiction in one of three ways. First, some hold that particular redemption, far from undermining the universal gospel call, actually supports the sincere offer of the gospel, and that authentic evangelism would be impossible without it.[20] Second, some maintain that the extent of the atonement has nothing to do with evangelism; whether Christ died for all or some does not concern the matter of a universal gospel call.[21] Sinners simply need to be told of what God has done in the atonement, not what he has done specifically for them.[22] Third, some assert that the Bible teaches both particular redemption and a universal gospel call, and although these may seem contradictory, they both need to be held because the Bible clearly teaches both.[23]

Each one of these resolutions has problems, and they are all unnecessary in light of the multi-intentioned view. First of all, the sincere offer of the gospel does not necessitate particular redemption because Christ died both to secure the salvation of His elect (his particular intention) and to pay for the sins of all people (his general intention). Christ procured the offer and provision of salvation for all people on the cross, and he also procured the definite application of salvation for the elect on the cross.[24] God's multiple intentions in the atonement alleviate the concerns of a vacuous gospel offer; there is an objective salvation that Christ accomplished that is certain for the elect and available for all. Second, the extent of the atonement is related to evangelism and does take into consideration the matter of the universal gospel call, as the content of the gospel call makes clear (1 Cor 15:3–5). Third, if one believes that Christ died for all people on the cross, there is no need to believe that the universal gospel call and the particularity of the

---

19. Crawford, *Respecting the Atonement*, 510. R. B. Kuiper, who holds to particular redemption, calls the universal gospel call and particular redemption a "paradox." Kuiper, *For Whom Did Christ Die?*, 86.

20. Nicole, "Covenant, Universal Call," 410; and Murray, *Redemption Accomplished and Applied*, 65.

21. Packer, *Evangelism and the Sovereignty of God*, 68; and Berkhof, *Systematic Theology*, 397–98.

22. Berkhof, *Systematic Theology*, 397; Nicole, "Covenant, Universal Call," 410; and Packer, "Introductory Essay," 16–22.

23. Crawford, *Respecting the Atonement*, 510; Grudem, *Systematic Theology*, 597–603; and Kuiper, *For Whom Did Christ Die?*, 86.

24. We will defend this truth in chapter 5.

atonement are contradictory. Rather, the universality of the gospel call is one of God's general purposes in the atonement.

The crux of the issue is how the gospel can be genuinely offered to the non-elect if God made no payment for their sins. As Lightner states, "If Christ died only for the elect, then why take that message to the non-elect? An even more sobering question would be, 'Why does God invite all men if Christ did not provide for all?' It is *His* invitation which is universal and man merely takes it to men."[25] If Christ did not pay for the sins of the non-elect, then it is impossible to genuinely offer salvation to the non-elect, since there is no salvation available to offer them. In a sense, when offered the gospel, the non-elect would be offered something that was never there for them to receive in the first place. There must be a genuine payment for all people, who can, if they so choose, receive it. The need for a genuine gospel call that offers an available salvation to all people, as well as the content of the gospel, the biblical motivation for sharing the gospel, and the Holy Spirit's work in taking the gospel around the world, demonstrate that the universal gospel call is based upon and presupposes Christ's payment for the sins of all people, elect and nonelect.

AN ADDITIONAL BASIS OF CONDEMNATION

Christ's payment for all sin not only made the universal gospel call possible, but it also provided an additional basis of condemnation for those who explicitly reject his payment for their sins. In addition to demonstrating God's desire for the salvation of all people and his love toward all people, the universal gospel call also results in an additional basis of condemnation for those who hear the genuine offer of the gospel and then reject it. The universal gospel call therefore not only reveals the grace and love of God, but also reveals his justice. Those who reject Christ's atonement for all are judged and condemned already because of their unbelief (John 3:18). This unbelief is not the only reason that people are condemned, as many advocates of unlimited atonement argue,[26] but it results in additional condemnation when

---

25. Lightner, *Death Christ Died*, 114.

26. Many Arminians believe that Christ's atonement redeemed all people from the guilt of Adam's sin and therefore the only reason people go to hell is because they explicitly reject Christ's atonement for them. As Olson states, "People go there [hell] not because their punishment was not suffered by Christ but because they reject the amnesty provided by God through Christ's substitutionary death." Olson, *Arminian Theology*, 65. Moderate Calvinists do not believe that Christ's atonement has redeemed all people from Adam's sin, but many argue that the atonement changed the basis for which people are judged. Walvoord is typical when he states, "A person now proceeds to eternal punishment not

unbelievers stand before the judgment seat of God to answer for all of their deeds (Rev 20:12). Christ paid for all sins on the cross, including unbelief, and therefore people go to hell because they are sinners not in Christ (1 John 5:11–12), as it is in Christ that salvation and every spiritual blessing is found (Eph 1:3).[27] The additional basis of condemnation for those who explicitly reject Christ's atonement is evident from the Holy Spirit's work of convicting unbelievers and Peter's description of the false teachers plaguing the church in 2 Peter 2.

The Holy Spirit's Work of Convicting Unbelievers

In addition to describing the Holy Spirit's role in taking the gospel to the world, John 16:7–11 also tells us that the Holy Spirit actually convicts unbelievers of their sin, righteousness and judgment. Not all of the unbelievers who experience the conviction of the Holy Spirit are elect. Believers are not the only ones convicted of their sin prior to their salvation; unbelievers also experience conviction that does not result in salvation. The word translated "convict" in John 16:8 (*elegko*) is also used in reference to unbelievers in 1 Corinthians 14:24 and Jude 15. First Corinthians 14:24–25 states "But if all prophesy, and an unbeliever or an ungifted man enters, he is convicted by all, he is called to account by all; the secrets of his heart are disclosed; and so he will fall on his face and worship God, declaring that God is certainly among you," explaining that an unbeliever in the midst of the church assembly might be convicted of his own sinfulness and forced to acknowledge God's work in the assembly. Jude 14–15 is even clearer in regard to the conviction of unbelievers, as it speaks of the Lord coming to "convict all the ungodly of all their ungodly deeds which they have done in an ungodly way, and of all the harsh things which ungodly sinners have spoken against Him." The ungodly in this passage are those who are convicted of their own sinfulness but who are not brought to repentance and faith.[28] Conviction of sin, although it is necessary for salvation, is not in itself effectual in bringing people to trust in Christ for salvation.

---

because God has failed to provide, or because the love of God has been ineffective, but rather because he has rejected that which God has provided.... The condemnation of the sinner now is not simply because he is a sinner, but because he has rejected God's provision to care for his sin." Walvoord, "Reconciliation," 11.

27. This negates the argument that with unlimited atonement sinners are condemned only for their unbelief, because Christ has paid for all of their sins. For further discussion see Erickson, *Christian Theology*, 1209; Grudem, *Systematic Theology*, 1142–43; and Moore, "Personal and Cosmic Eschatology," 898.

28. Davids, *Letters of Jude and 2 Peter*, 81.

The Holy Spirit's convicting ministry among the nonelect is explicitly tied to Christ's work in John 16:7–11. The Holy Spirit only convicts people through special revelation, or the gospel. This means that like the universal gospel call, the Holy Spirit's convicting ministry demonstrates God's saving love toward all people. As D.A. Carson states, "This convicting work of the Paraclete is therefore gracious: it is designed to bring men and women of the world to recognize their need, and so turn to Jesus, and thus stop being 'the world.'"[29] The Holy Spirit's convicting ministry also means, however, that those who experience and reject it by refusing the gospel experience additional condemnation and judgment. There are different levels of punishment in hell, and they seemed to be based upon a sinner's knowledge of God's will for him or her, including knowledge of the gospel (Luke 12:47–48; Heb 10:29), as "greater revelations bring greater responsibility."[30] Christ's payment for the sins of all people results in the Holy Spirit's work among both the elect and the nonelect, and this work brings both grace and justice as it is received or rejected.

The Destiny of the False Teachers in 2 Peter 2

Second Peter 2 states that the explicit rejection of the gospel results in further condemnation for unbelievers. Second Peter 2:1 tells us that those who deny their Master who bought them are "bringing swift destruction upon themselves."[31] This phrase "closely relates their crime with their sure doom. 'Bringing,' a present active participle, indicates that their persistent denial of their Master promotes a process which will culminate in their ruin. 'Upon themselves,' underlines that their fate is self-inflicted."[32] The rest of the chapter goes on to describe the sins and judgment of those "false teachers." Second Peter 2:20–21 expresses their end, "For if, after they have escaped the defilements of the world by the knowledge of the Lord and Savior Jesus Christ, they are again entangled in them and are overcome, the last state has become worse for them than the first. For it would be better for them not to have known the way of righteousness, than having known it, to turn away from the holy commandment handed on to them." As Blum states, these verses assert that the false teachers "who have for a time escaped from

---

29. Carson, *Gospel of John*, 537.
30. Moore, "Personal and Cosmic Eschatology," 899.
31. Those who deny their Master are those whom Christ died for, and those that reject him and are therefore condemned. We defend this understanding of 2 Pet 2:1 in chapter 3.
32. Hiebert, "Portrayal of False Teachers," 260.

The General Intentions of the Atonement 101

worldly corruption through knowing Christ and then turn away from the light of the Christian faith are worse off than they were before knowing Christ."[33] These false teachers are unbelievers who once made false professions of faith without ever experiencing regeneration.[34] They are justly condemned all the more because of their knowledge and explicit rejection of the Christian faith, which includes the death of Christ for their sins (2 Pet 2:1).

Just as the people of Isaiah's time and Jesus' time heaped condemnation upon themselves because of their rejection of God's messages (Isa 6:9–10; Matt 13:11–6), so too do the nonelect who reject the gospel message. The reason that this results is because in rejecting the gospel, people are rejecting the atonement of Jesus Christ, which is the provision of salvation that he made for them when He paid for their sins on the cross. Those who purposely reject the preaching of the gospel will be justly held accountable for their actions, and it will result in great condemnation at the judgment. As John Calvin states, "When he first shines with the light of his Word upon the undeserving, he thereby shows a sufficiently clear proof of his free goodness. Here, then, God's boundless goodness is already manifesting itself but not to the salvation of all; for a heavier judgment remains upon the wicked because they reject the testimony of God's love."[35]

THE PROVISION OF COMMON GRACE

Throughout the New Testament God's grace is presented as the basis of his salvific work for the elect (e.g., John 1:16; Acts 11:23; 15:11; 20:24; Rom 3:24; 4:16; 5:15; 1 Cor 15:10; 2 Cor 4:15; Gal 1:15; Eph 2:8–9; 2 Thess 2:16; Titus 2:11; Heb 2:9; 1 Pet 1:13). Scripture also presents God's grace in non-salvific contexts, however, and speaks of God's grace toward unbelievers (e.g., Gen 4:15; Pss 66:5, 7; 104:10–11, 14–15; 145:16–17; Matt 5:43–47; Acts 14:16–17). Experience also demonstrates that God's grace is not restricted to those who are Christians; good things happen to unbelievers, and unbelievers are not as sinful as they could be. These differences in God's grace, as it is displayed salvifically towards the elect and non-salvificially towards the elect and the nonelect, have led theologians to distinguish between God's special (or saving) grace and his common grace.

Special grace begins with the Holy Spirit's effectual calling of a person and results in that person's salvation; therefore only the elect experience

33. Blum, *2 Peter*, 282.
34. Ibid., 282–83; and Schreiner, *Jude, 2 Peter*, 360–65.
35. Calvin, *Institutes of the Christian Religion*, 967.

special grace. They experience special grace through special revelation, or the gospel of Jesus Christ (Acts 14:3; Col 1:5–6), which means that special grace is only possible because of the atonement. Common grace, on the other hand, is grace that is not confined to the elect. While everyone experiences common grace to some degree, God does not necessarily dispense his common grace equally, nor does everyone experience all of the aspects of common grace in the same way. Common grace differs from special grace because it can come through general revelation, it can be successfully resisted, and it does not result in salvation.[36] It is like special grace, however, in that it is a work of the Holy Spirit. As John Walvoord notes, "The entire work of the Holy Spirit on behalf of the unsaved world is sometimes given the terminology common grace."[37] Common grace is also like special grace in that it is based upon and flows out of Christ's atonement.

Many advocates of particular redemption agree that common grace is a result of the atonement, but do not believe that common grace requires an atonement that pays for the sins of the nonelect.[38] They describe common grace as an indirect benefit to the nonelect that comes about because of Christ's particular atonement for the elect. R. B. Kuiper is representative when he states, "The blessings of common grace, although resulting only indirectly from the atonement, were most surely designed by God to result from the atonement. The design of God in the atoning work of Christ pertained primarily and directly to the redemption of the elect, but indirectly and secondarily it also included the blessings of common grace."[39] This explanation, however, does not do justice to the truth that non–salvific grace goes out to the nonelect on the basis of the atonement or to the Holy Spirit's role in common grace, as we have already seen in discussing the universal gospel call. The idea of the universal sufficiency of the atonement in particular redemption does not allow for common grace, because the universal sufficiency is related to the intrinsic merit of Christ's sacrifice and not to his intention to pay for all sin, as we saw in the last chapter.[40] Neither does the idea that common grace is an indirect benefit of an atonement meant only for the elect explain all of the different ways that God displays his common grace. Common grace typically includes three elements: God's giving

---

36. Hodge, *Systematic Theology*, 2:674.
37. Walvoord, *The Holy Spirit*, 107.
38. Bavinck, *Sin and Salvation*, 470; Berkhof, *Systematic Theology*, 398–99; Boettner, *The Reformed Doctrine of Predestination*, 160–61; Kuiper, *For Whom Did Christ Die?*, 81–84; Murray, *Redemption Accomplished and Applied*, 61–62; and Nicole, "Definite Atonement," 199.
39. Kuiper, *For Whom Did Christ Die?*, 83–84.
40. Boersma, *Violence, Hospitality, and the Cross*, 71.

of natural gifts, God's restraining of sin and evil in human affairs, and God's patience in exercising judgment.[41] As we will demonstrate, each of these elements of common grace is only possible because of Christ's payment for all sin on the cross.

God's Giving of Natural Gifts

God is presented in Scripture as the giver of all good gifts (Jas 1:16–17), and he is also the one who "causes his sun to rise on the evil and the good, and sends rain on the righteous and the unrighteous" (Matt 5:45; cf. Acts 14:17). We refer to these gifts of God as natural gifts because they are not salvific in nature. The Old Testament presents God as the one who all people should look to for their provision. "The eyes of all look to you, and you give them their food in due time. You open your hand and satisfy the desire of every living thing." (Ps 145:15–16).[42] God is surely abundant in goodness and truth towards all people (Exod 34:6). In the New Testament Jesus is the light that enlightens every person (John 1:9). This statement likely means that Christ allows enlightenment and understanding to come to all people; all people are able to know true things about God and the universe.[43] God gives natural gifts to people that are manifest in the physical world and in human society. These gifts include the amazing feats of intellect, strength, and beauty that human beings are able to accomplish. He does all of this on the basis of the atonement.

That God bestows his good gifts indiscriminately upon humanity because of Christ's atonement is evident because of why and how God bestows common grace. All of the grace that God bestows upon humanity is undeserved because all people have sinned against God and deserve nothing but his righteous judgment (Isa 64:6; Rom 3:9–20; Rom 6:23; Eph 2:1–3). The reason that God forestalls his judgment is because his wrath against humanity has been satisfied in the atonement. As Augustus Strong states, "If

---

41. Mouw, *He Shines in All That's Fair*, 9.

42. Common grace is just as evident in the Old Testament as it is in the New Testament. It is still only possible, however, on the basis of the atonement. Just as salvation (special grace) in the Old Testament is bestowed by God in anticipation of the cross, so is common grace.

43. Commenting on John 1:9, Leon Morris states, "There is a general illumination of the whole race, and it is the common teaching of the New Testament writers that God has revealed something of himself to all people (Rom 1:20), sufficient at least for them to be blameworthy when they take the wrong way instead of the right way. John attributes this general illumination to the activity of the Word." Morris, *The Gospel According to John*, 84.

it be asked in what sense Christ is the Savior of all men, we reply: that the atonement of Christ secures for all men a delay in the execution of the sentence against sin, and a space for repentance, together with a continuance of the common blessings of life which have been forfeited by transgression."[44] Therefore every blessing that a person receives, including life and all of the gifts that come with the sustaining and enrichment of life, is due first and foremost to God's grace displayed in the atonement. If the atonement were only for the elect, this could have resulted in a delay of God's judgment to allow for the saving of the elect, but it would not account for the ways in which God has continued to bless the nonelect with his natural gifts throughout history.

God's Restraining of Sin and Evil

God not only shows his love and kindness towards all people with his gifts; God also shows love and kindness towards all by restraining sin and evil in their lives. He did this for Cain (Gen 4:15), the people at the Tower of Babel (Gen 11:1–9), and King Abimelech (Gen 20:6). He does this in the life of unbelievers before he gives them over to their sinful lusts for continually rejecting him (Rom 1:24, 26, 28). He does this through the influence of the church in the world, which is to be continually fighting the forces of hell (Matt 16:18) as it stands up for the truth (1 Tim 3:15). He does this through institutions such as human government, which is "a minister of God to you for good" (Rom 13:4; see also Gen 9:6; Rom 13:1–3; 1 Pet 2:13–14). Also, almost all people, including the non-elect, show kindness to others to one degree or another, and there have been very few, if any, people who have been as evil as they possibly could be.

All of this restraining of sin is due to the influence of the Holy Spirit, who during this present age restrains lawlessness (2 Thess 2:7).[45] As Charles Hodge states,

> To the general influence of the Spirit (or to common grace), we owe—(1) All the decorum, order, refinement, and virtue existing among men. Mere fear of future punishment, the natural sense of right, and the restraints of human laws, would prove feeble barriers to evil, were it not for the repressing power of the

---

44. Strong, *Systematic Theology*, 772.

45. There are a number of competing interpretations of this verse centering on the identification of "the one who restrains." For a defense of the interpretation that this is the Holy Spirit, see Thomas, *1 & 2 Thessalonians*, 324–35; and Walvoord, *Holy Spirit*, 114–16.

Spirit, which, like the pressure of the atmosphere, is universal and powerful, though unfelt. (2) To the same divine agent is due specially that general fear of God, and that religious feeling which prevails among men, and which secures for the rites and services of religion in all its forms, the decorous or more serious attention which they receive.[46]

It is because this restraining of sin and evil is a work of the Holy Spirit that it results from the atonement, as all that the Holy Spirit does to restrain sin and pour grace upon the world flows from the Son's atoning death. In the same way that God's natural gifts for the nonelect are a result of the atonement that includes the nonelect, the Holy Spirit's restraining work among the nonelect is only possible because of the atonement for the nonelect.

God's Patience in Judgment

God is also gracious toward all people in that he does not instantly judge their sin. God did not instantly damn the human race when Adam and Eve fell into sin, but instead postponed his judgment on the basis of Christ's atonement. As Robert Duncan Culver remarks concerning Christ's atonement, "This 'reconciliation,' in part, affects God's treatment of the sons of Adam from Eden onward. If God had 'imputed' (KJV) 'their trespasses against them' fully the full execution of death would have put an end to the human race. Now, since Calvary, it is clear why. The reconciliation in promise only (Gen 3:15, the *protoevangelion*) became fulfillment at Calvary."[47] Romans 3:23-25 makes this clear when it states, "For all have sinned and fall short of the glory of God, being justified as a gift by His grace through the redemption which is in Christ Jesus; whom God displayed publicly as a propitiation in His blood through faith. *This was* to demonstrate His righteousness, because in the forbearance of God He passed over the sins previously committed." These verses explain that all people have sinned against God (v. 23) and can only be justified on the basis of Christ's redemption and propitiation, or the atonement, through faith (v. 24-25a). Christ's atonement, and the justification of sinners on the basis of it, demonstrates God's justice in showing patience toward sinners (v. 25b). It is because of the atonement that God can justly forbear from punishing sin for as long as he desires, because sin has been punished in Christ. Therefore all people are allowed to live this life, even though they are sinners who deserve nothing but damnation, because of Christ's atonement.

46. Hodge, *Systematic Theology*, 2:671.
47. Culver, *Systematic Theology*, 585. See also Strong, *Systematic Theology*, 772.

One of the primary reasons that God is kind, forbearing, and patient in judgment is so that people might repent and enter into a relationship with him (Rom 2:4). Second Peter 3:9 declares that "The Lord is not slow about His promise, as some count slowness, but is patient toward you, not wishing for any to perish but for all to come to repentance" (cf. 2 Pet 3:15). God lovingly delays his judgment because there are people still yet to be saved. John Frame states, "Now we learn that God's decision to wait [in judgment] is not arbitrary, nor is it mainly in the interest of creating a more interesting story. Rather, it is a function of God's love and grace.... So his decree to lengthen the temporal sequence genuinely reflects his knowledge of, and love for, those he intends to create."[48] God's patience in judgment is bound up with his desire that all people be saved and that all people hear about his salvation in the universal gospel call. Therefore it is one of the aspects of grace and love that God demonstrates toward the nonelect in the atonement.

All people, elect and nonelect, are able to enjoy the blessings and benefits of this life and have an opportunity to repent of their sins and experience the blessings of salvation because God's delays his judgment upon sin. He did this in the time of the Old Testament, overlooking human ignorance before the coming of Jesus Christ (Acts 17:30), and he does it in the present time as well. This patience of God in judgment demonstrates his goodness, mercy, justice, glory, love, and grace (Ps 145:9; Ezek 33:11; Rom 2:5; Eph 1:4–6). It also demonstrates that God has intentions in the atonement for all people, and therefore that the atonement paid for the sins of all people. God's patience in judgment, which is only possible because of the cross, allows for all people to experience and receive God's good gifts of common grace.

THE SUPREME REVELATION OF GOD'S CHARACTER

God not only intended to provide salvation and grace for all and to secure salvation for the elect in the atonement, but he also intended for the atonement to be the supreme revelation of his character. John's Gospel describes the atonement as the glorification of Jesus Christ, and teaches that Christ's glorification in the atonement glorifies the Father as well (John 12:20–28; 13:30–32; 17:1). The reason that Christ's atonement for sin on the cross is at the same time the glorification of God is because the atonement most fully demonstrates all of God's moral attributes, such as goodness, love, grace, holiness, and justice (or righteousness), which can all be categorized

---

48. Frame, *Doctrine of God*, 432.

as aspects of God's love or God's justice.[49] The atonement demonstrates the wisdom and power of God (Rom 11:33-36; 1 Cor 1:17-2:5), and it does so because the atonement perfectly demonstrates God's love and God's justice at the same time. God's love and justice are seen in the multiple intentions of the atonement, such as the universal gospel call, common grace, the reconciliation of all things, and the salvation of the elect, which demonstrates why Christ's payment for the sin of all people was necessary in order to display God's love and justice fully before his creation.

The Love of God

Scripture emphasizes that the supreme expression of God's love toward people is the atonement. First John 4:9-10 states, "By this the love of God was manifested in us, that God has sent His only begotten Son into the world so that we might live through Him. In this is love, not that we loved God, but that He loved us and sent His Son to be the propitiation for our sins." The way that God, who is himself love (1 John 4:8), reveals his love towards humanity is through sending his Son to be the propitiation for the sins of the world (cf. John 3:16; 1 John 2:2). After explaining this, John then uses God's love in the atonement as the basis of his ethical exhortations to his readers; since God loved us in this way, we ought to love one another (1 John 4:11-5:3; cf. 3:16). John explains that it is only through God's gift of his Son on the cross that the world is able to know what true love is.

Paul expresses the same idea about God's love in the atonement as John. Romans 5:8 states, "But God demonstrates His own love toward us, in that while we were yet sinners, Christ died for us." This verse expresses three truths about God's love.[50] First, it was Jesus Christ, God's Son (cf. Rom 5:10), whom God the Father gave to bear the sins of sinners. One of the wonders of the cross is that the Triune God himself gave himself in the atonement, which is the supreme example of love. Second, God's love manifests itself in Christ's death. It was not merely the incarnation or Jesus' teaching that supremely demonstrated God's love for humanity, but the death of Jesus on the cross. Third, God's love is for sinners. As John Stott states, "But God in giving his Son gave himself to die for his enemies. He gave everything for those who deserved nothing from him."[51] The highest demonstration of God's love is Christ's atoning death for sinners because in it God completely gives of himself for the benefit of others. As J.I. Packer states, "It is a matter

---

49. Bavinck, *God and Creation*, 191-228.
50. Stott, *Cross of Christ*, 209-11.
51. Ibid., 210.

of undisputed history that God is love (*agape*) came new to the world with Christianity, and it should be a matter of undisputed theology that what this means is only known through the atonement."[52]

That the atonement is the supreme expression of God's love seems to suggest that the atonement is for all people, because God's love is for all people (as we have seen when discussing the universal gospel call). The Bible speaks of love in different ways, however, indicating that God displays his love toward different people in different ways through the atonement. D. A. Carson distinguishes five different ways that the Bible speaks of God's love: God's inter-trinitarian love (the love of the Father for the Son and vice-versa), God's providential love for everything he has made, God's salvific love for the fallen world, God's particular love for his elect, and God's relational love that is in some way conditioned upon obedience.[53] Neither particular redemption nor unlimited atonement is able to adequately account for the full biblical nature of God's love. Unlimited atonement rightly stresses the universal love of God, but does so to the detriment of God's particular love, for how can there be particular love in an act that is exactly the same for everyone?[54] Conversely, particular redemption rightly stresses the saving nature of God's love, but does so to the detriment of God's universal love, for how can there be universal love in an act that is only for a certain number of people?[55]

The multi-intentioned view of the extent of the atonement overcomes this dilemma, for it recognizes both the particular and the universal love of God in the atonement by asserting that God accomplished multiple purposes on the cross. Jesus Christ died for all people, but he died for some people with different intentions. This corresponds with how the Scriptures describe God's diverse and varied love. Though stopping short of a multi-intentioned view, D. A. Carson argues along these lines based on God's love,

---

52. Packer, "The Atonement in the Life of a Christian," 424.

53. Carson, *Difficult Doctrine of the Love of God*, 16–21.

54. Almost all proponents of unlimited atonement make the universal nature of God's love one of the central arguments for their view. For example, see Bloesch, *Jesus Christ*, 167–70; Demarest, *Cross and Salvation*, 189–93; Hunt, *What Love is This?*, 293–96; 515–17; Guy, "The Universality of God's Love," 31–49; Lightner, *Death Christ Died*, 111–14; Marshall, "Universal Grace," 51; Olson, *Arminian Theology*, 221–25; and Strong, *Systematic Theology*, 716–17.

55. Almost all proponents of particular redemption appeal to the particular, special love that God has for the elect as one of the central arguments for their view. For example, see Berkhof, *Systematic Theology*, 392–99; Hill, "Atonement in the Apocalypse of John," 191–94; Letham, *The Work of Christ*, 234–36; Long, *Definite Atonement*, 9–13; Nicole, "Particular Redemption," 178; Owen, *Death of Death*, 115–20; and Packer, "Introductory Essay," 12–16.

"Both Arminians and Calvinists should rightly affirm that Christ died for all, in the sense that Christ's death was sufficient for all and that Scripture portrays God as inviting, commanding, and desiring the salvation of all, *out of love* (in the third sense developed in the first chapter). Further, all Christians ought to confess that, in a slightly different sense, Christ Jesus, in the intent of God, died effectively for the elect alone, *in line with the way the Bible speaks of God's special selecting love for the elect* (in the fourth sense developed in the first chapter)".[56] God loves all people in some ways, but he loves some people (the elect) in all ways, and this is "the clear witness of the entire Bible."[57] The supreme revelation of God's love, therefore, can only be made in an atonement that is for both the elect and the nonelect. God's manifestation of his love is a general intention in the atonement because God wants all people, elect and nonelect, to know of his love toward them.

The Justice of God

The atonement not only reveals God's love for the world, but it also supremely manifests God's holy justice toward all people. The Bible often points towards the judgment of God in the eschaton as the vindication of his justice, especially in light of the injustices of this life (e.g., Ps 73; Acts 17:30–31; Rom 2:4; 2 Pet 3:3–9). The Bible also states, however, that God's justice has already been demonstrated in the atonement, where the decisive judgment against sin took place. Paul brings forth this truth in Romans 3:23–26. The atonement, in which Jesus Christ suffered the punishment due to humanity for their sin, vindicated God's justice in light of his delay in judging sin (v. 25). God's justice is also demonstrated in the atonement, however, because he is "the justifier of the one who has faith in Jesus" (v. 26b). Not only is God seen to be just in delaying his punishment for sin (so that people might repent, 2 Pet 3:9), he is seen to be just in saving those who put their faith in Jesus Christ.

The reason that God demonstrates his justice in the salvation of sinners who put their faith in Jesus Christ is the same reason he demonstrates his justice despite his delay of punishing sin; it is because of Christ's redemption and propitiation for sin in the atonement (Rom 3:24–25a). All who hear the gospel have the opportunity to be justified freely through God's grace in Jesus Chris because of his sacrifice on the cross (Rom 3:24), even though all people have sinned and fallen short of God's glory (Rom 3:23). Because of the atonement, all people, the elect and the nonelect, can

---

56. Carson, *Difficult Doctrine of the Love of God*, 77, emphasis the author's.
57. Packer, "The Love of God," 283–84.

potentially see God's righteous justice. God justifies all people who repent of their sin and trust in the truth of the gospel, and this act of salvation demonstrates God's justice because Christ has paid for their sin through his atonement.[58] As John Frame states, "The perfect sacrifice of Jesus is the basis of our righteousness, and when God clears our guilt for Jesus' sake, he is acting justly. Through Christ, God is able both to justify the ungodly (us) and to defend himself against any charge of injustice." God is just to forgive anyone because Christ has earned his or her forgiveness.

This demonstration of God's justice depends upon the fact that Christ's atonement was for all sin, the sin of the elect and the nonelect. The righteousness of the gospel is available to all who believe (Rom 3:22), even though all people are sinners. In order for the gospel to be genuinely offered to all sinners, the atonement must have paid for all sin. As we saw earlier concerning the universal gospel call, if Christ did not pay for the sins of the non-elect, then it is impossible to genuinely offer salvation to the non-elect, since there is no salvation available to offer them. In a sense, when offered the gospel, the non-elect would be offered something that was never there for them to receive in the first place. There must be a genuine payment for all people, who can, if they so choose, receive it. God is just to render it possible for the gospel to be legitimately offered to all people and to save all who accept the truth of the gospel because of Christ's payment for all sin. It is in paying for all sin in the atonement, and not for the sin of the elect only, that God can completely demonstrate his righteousness and justice before the entire creation. Jesus Christ came to reveal God to the world (John 1:14, 18), and his atonement on the cross is the supreme manifestation of God's justice and his love because it is an atonement that has paid for all sin.

THE COSMIC TRIUMPH OVER ALL SIN

The final general intention that God had in the atonement was Christ's cosmic triumph over all sin, or the reconciliation of all things in Jesus Christ. When sin entered the world, it not only marred the relationship between God and humanity, but it disturbed the relationship of all of creation with God, as the creation itself looks forward to its freedom from sin's bondage (Rom 8:19–23). Sin negatively affected everything in God's created universe, necessitating the reconciliation of all things in creation. In order to accomplish this restoration of all creation, God reconciled all things to himself through the atonement of Jesus Christ. Colossians 1:19–20 teaches us this: "For it was the *Father's* good pleasure for all the fullness to dwell

---

58. Frame, *Doctrine of God*, 457.

in Him, and through Him to reconcile all things to Himself, having made peace through the blood of His cross; through Him, *I say*, whether things on earth or things in heaven." The reconciliation of "all things" by the blood of Christ in this passage is coextensive with the creation of "all things" by Christ mentioned earlier in Colossians 1:15–16.[59] The phrase "all things" is also as broad as it possibly can be, as it is described as "things on earth or things in heaven." This means that the work of reconciliation is as broad as it can be, it is on the widest possible scale; all things everywhere are reconciled to God by the atonement.[60]

The reconciliation of all things to God through Christ's atonement is only possible if Christ's atonement was for all sin, and not just for the sin of the elect. Proponents of particular redemption contest this truth. Although they usually agree that Christ's atonement accomplished God's cosmic triumph over sin, they do not believe that this triumph required a universal payment for sin. They advance two typical arguments that attempt to hold together a universal reconciliation and an atonement that is only for the elect. The first is that the "world" at the end of time will consist only of the elect, so that when all things are reconciled, it means that only the elect are reconciled.[61] While it is certainly true that the elect are reconciled, it is difficult to understand the basis for the reconciliation of creation in this argument. This argument also cannot explain what it means to say that the nonelect are reconciled, as Col 1:20 does. The second argument is that Christ's reconciliation of all things is a result of the infinite worth and sufficiency of the atonement.[62] The notion of the sufficiency of the atonement, however, either means that Christ's atonement is sufficient for all people because he paid for the sins of all people (which contradicts particular redemption), or that it is sufficient for all people if God had actually wanted it to be for all people, because Christ's sacrifice considered in and of itself is intrinsically of infinite worth. This second notion of sufficiency (which is what advocates of particular redemption believe) cannot ground Christ's reconciliation of all things, however, because it results in an atonement that still only paid for the sins of the elect. As I. Howard Marshall states, "But to say that the atonement is sufficient for all people but has not been made for

---

59. Bruce, *Colossians, Philemon, and Ephesians*, 74.

60. For an explanation of what universal reconciliation accomplishes, see Shultz, Jr., "The Reconciliation of All Things in Christ," 442–59.

61. Bavinck, *Sin and Salvation*, 474–75; Kuiper, *For Whom Did Christ Die?*, 95–100; and Warfield, *Plan of Salvation*, 100–106.

62. Letham, *Work of Christ*, 246; and Tiessen, *Who Can Be Saved?*, 100.

all is meaningless. How can the atonement be sufficient for people for who it has not been made? This is sheer unconvincing casuistry."[63]

How could Christ reconcile all things to himself and triumph over all sin if he did not pay for all sin on the cross? If Christ only paid for the sins of the elect in the atonement, then it would seem that there would be sin that would be outside of his atoning work, and thus there would be sin outside of His cosmic triumph. That Christ's cosmic triumph over sin is only made possible by his payment for all sin is seen in four ways. First, we can see it in the nature of Christ's victory on the cross over all sin, or in what is often called the *Christus Victor* aspect of the atonement. Second, it is evident in the nature of the reconciliation wrought by the cross, as the elect, the non-elect, and the creation are all reconciled to God, albeit in different ways. Third, the resurrection of all people, the elect and the nonelect, supports this truth. Finally, we see it in Christ's role as King, which is based upon his priestly work in the atonement as a sacrifice for all sin.

Christ's Victory over All Sin in the Atonement

Christ's atonement not only made salvation possible for all people; it also conquered the powers of evil, sin, and death by defeating Satan and the powers of darkness. We refer to this aspect of the atonement as *Christus Victor*, in that Christ through the cross gained victory over Satan and his demons. Scripture predicted Christ's defeat of Satan from its very beginning (Gen 3:15), Jesus looked forward to this victory in his earthly ministry (John 12:31; 14:30; 16:11), and he decisively achieved it at the cross. As Jesus' reconciliation includes the complete victory over all of his enemies, Satan's defeat at the cross was necessary for the reconciliation of all things to take place. Jesus' victory is cosmic in scope, and though it is grounded in the atonement it will ultimately take place at the end of time, when Christ delivers up His kingdom to his Father (1 Cor 15:24–28; Eph 1:9–10).[64] Christ achieved his cosmic victory over all sin and evil and reconciled all things

---

63. Marshall, "For All," 345.

64. While Christ defeated Satan at the cross, Satan is still at work today. This is part of the already/not yet aspect of eschatology. As Clinton Arnold states, "The evil principalities and powers, together with their leader Satan, face a definite point in history when their tyranny will be brought to an end. They now function like vicious dogs on a long leash. When Christ returns, he will tighten the leash to such an extent that they will not be able to cause any harm or instill any fear whatsoever. They will be completely pacified. Paul saw the consummation of history in Christ's act of handing over his kingdom to the Father." Arnold, *Powers of Darkness*, 163.

The General Intentions of the Atonement   113

to himself by paying for all sin in his penal substitutionary atonement.[65] Each Scripture that highlights the *Christus Victor* aspect of the atonement indicates that Christ's payment for sin is the foundation of his victory over Satan.

Colossians 2:13-15 is perhaps the clearest passage in this regard: "When you were dead in your transgressions and the uncircumcision of your flesh, He made you alive together with Him, having forgiven us all our transgressions, having canceled out the certificate of debt consisting of decrees against us, which was hostile to us; and He has taken it out of the way, having nailed it to the cross. When He had disarmed the rulers and authorities, He made a public display of them, having triumphed over them through Him." This passage establishes Christ's payment for sin before it describes his victory over Satan. The Colossian believers, despite their sin natures that leave them spiritually dead, can experience forgiveness and eternal life with Christ because Christ has cancelled the "certificate of debt" that stood against humanity, or paid for the sins of humanity.[66] Christ disarmed the demonic rulers and authorities, publicly shaming and triumphing over them, by canceling out humanity's sins. Satan and the demonic powers can no longer hold people in bondage, because people can now experience forgiveness of their sins through the atoning work of the cross. As Arnold states, "By offering his life and spilling his blood, Christ could extend forgiveness of sin to his people. The powers thus lost their chief mechanism for holding people in bondage."[67]

Several other Scriptures reiterate this truth. First John 3:4-10 states that Jesus' mission was to destroy the devil's work (v. 8). He did this by taking away sins (v. 5). Destroying the devil's work means eradicating sin and lawlessness and freeing people to live righteously through salvation.[68] Jesus defeats the devil because he takes away sin by paying its penalty in his substitutionary atonement. Similarly, the "brothers" of Revelation 12 are able to overcome Satan's accusations against them by the blood of the Lamb (v. 11). Satan no longer has any power to accuse believers of their sin because their sin has been paid for and their guilt has been taken away by the atonement.

---

65. Some theologians believe that the *Christus Victor* aspect of the atonement is the primary aspect of the atonement, and do not believe that it is grounded in penal substitution. E.g, Aulén, *Christus Victor*; and Boyd, "Christus Victor View," 23-49. As we will demonstrate in the next few pages, however, the *Christus Victor* aspect of the atonement is a result of Christ's payment for all sin in his penal substitutionary atonement. Satan is defeated because Christ has paid for all sin.

66. Stott, *Cross of Christ*, 229.

67. Arnold, *Powers of Darkness*, 104-105.

68. Jeffery, Ovey, and Sach, *Pierced for Our Transgressions*, 141.

Hebrews 2:14 also states that Christ, through his death, rendered Satan powerless, so that people might be freed from the fear of death (v. 15). In order to render Satan powerless, however, Christ had to become incarnate so that he could be a faithful and merciful high priest before God, and he was a faithful high priest by making propitiation for the sins of the people (v. 17).

Scripture repeatedly states that Christ's atonement not only paid for sin, but defeated sin in the person of the devil. Christ's payment for sin, his penal substitutionary atonement, is inseparably related to his victory over all of the powers of sin. This relationship strongly suggests that the atonement was for the sin of all people, elect and nonelect. The entire human race fell into sin due to Satan's temptation (Rom 5:12). The sin of the entire human race holds the creation in bondage (Rom 8:19–23) and has marred all relationships between God and every aspect of his creation. The sin of humanity needs to be overcome in order for the devil and his demons to be defeated. If Christ only pays for the sin of the elect, then how does he gain victory over all sin? How is Christ's victory over Satan and the demonic powers in the atonement through canceling out sins (Col 2:13–15) and taking away sins (1 John 3:4–10) possible if only a portion of sins were cancelled out and taken away? Since Christ's payment for sin is the foundation of his victory over all sin, it seems his payment had to be for all sin in order for his victory over Satan to be complete and his reconciliation to be total.

The Nature of the Reconciliation of All Things

It is not only the *Christus Victor* aspect of Christ's cosmic triumph over sin that points toward an unlimited extent of the atonement. The nature of Christ's eschatological reconciliation is also based upon his complete payment for and victory over sin, because this reconciliation encompasses all things (Eph 1:10; Col 1:20). Not only does Colossians 1:20 teach the reconciliation of all things in Christ, but Ephesians 1:10 does as well. Commenting on this verse, Andrew Lincoln states, "Christ is the one in whom God chooses to sum up the universe, in whom he restores the harmony of the cosmos. Earlier, 'in Christ' has functioned to indicate Christ's being the elect representative in whom believers are included, but now it can be seen that God's comprehensive purpose goes beyond simply humanity to embrace the whole created order. This part of the *berakah* helps believers to recognize that to be incorporated into God's gracious decision about Christ is also to be caught up in God's gracious purpose for a universe centered and reunited in Christ."⁶⁹ Christ's payment for the sins of all people was necessary for his cosmic triumph over sin because it allowed for the elect, the nonelect, and the creation to be reconciled to God. That the elect are not the only ones reconciled through Christ's atonement means that the atonement was not only for the elect. God intended, in a non-salvific way, to reconcile the nonelect and the creation in the atonement just as he intended to reconcile the elect salvifically. Reconciliation cannot be the same for the elect and the nonelect because, as we saw in chapter 3, the Bible clearly rules out universal salvation.

God salvifically reconciles the elect to himself when they accept his objective reconciliation through faith, resulting in salvation. Romans 5:10 expresses this truth: "For if while we were enemies we were reconciled to God through the death of His Son, much more, having been reconciled, we shall be saved by His life." This verse mentions both aspects of reconciliation, objective and subjective. First, human beings as sinners, the enemies of God, were reconciled through Christ's death. Second, those who have been reconciled, those justified by faith (Rom 5:1) will be saved by his life.⁷⁰ As George Ladd states, "Until God's offer of objective reconciliation has been received in an attitude of glad surrender, no person is in fact reconciled to God; she or he is still a sinner and in the last day will suffer the full and awful outpouring of the wrath of a holy God. The content of reconciliation, therefore, while first of all the objective act of God, is also the affirmative reaction of people to the proffer of reconciliation. Only then does reconciliation become effective for the sinner; only then is he or she reconciled to God."⁷¹

Colossians 1:21–23 also highlights the difference between salvific reconciliation and cosmic reconciliation: "And although you were formerly alienated and hostile in mind, *engaged* in evil deeds, yet He has now reconciled you in His fleshly body through death, in order to present you before Him holy and blameless and beyond reproach-- if indeed you continue in the faith firmly established and steadfast, and not moved away from the hope of the gospel that you have heard, which was proclaimed in all creation under heaven, and of which I, Paul, was made a minister." Paul

---

69. Lincoln, *Ephesians*, 34.

70. "It would seem that the verb [reconcile] is again used in two senses, first in verse 10a of God reconciling men to himself (passive, of men), and second in verse 10b of men who have actually entered into the state of reconciliation. The contrast is the same as that between 'Christ died for us' and 'being now justified.' No doubt the slight shift in meaning is awkward, but it is by no means intolerable. It is supported by the use of 'we have received the reconciliation' in verse 11, which suggests an existing gift to be received by us." Marshall, "The Meaning of Reconciliation," 125.

71. Ladd, *A Theology of the New Testament*, 496.

has just proclaimed that Christ reconciled all things through his cross, and he now explains how the Colossians themselves were reconciled as believers. Though the Colossians were sinners apart from God (v. 21), they were reconciled through Christ's atonement so that they could be presented holy before God (v. 22), and this reconciliation took place because of the Colossians' faith in the gospel that Paul preached (v. 23). There is clearly a difference between the reconciliation accomplished by Christ in Colossians 1:20 and the reconciliation of the Colossians in 1:21–23. For the elect, the reconciliation that comes through faith in the gospel results in peace with God (Rom 5:1) and peace with one another in the church as all barriers to fellowship are broken down in Christ (Eph 2:14–16).

The reconciliation of the nonelect is vastly different from the reconciliation of the elect. While the elect are subjectively reconciled to God during this life at the moment of their salvation, the nonelect never experience this aspect of reconciliation. They are objectively reconciled in the present only in the sense that God has postponed the full display of His judgment toward them (just as He has done for believers as well) so that they might be saved (Rom 3:25; 2 Pet 3:9). Those who never experience a saving relationship with God, however, will still have a future experience of reconciliation with him. They will participate in an eschatological reconciliation.

At the eschaton the nonelect will be reconciled as God restores cosmic peace to his creation. While the peace wrought by the atonement is freely accepted by the elect and results in eternal life with God, God imposes this peace upon the nonelect. For this reason, F. F. Bruce calls this aspect of reconciliation "pacification."[72] There is no glad surrender of the nonelect, who are suffering in hell as the just punishment for their sin, to the will of God, even though they now realize that they ought to worship God and were wrong to sin against him. Instead, God's reconciliation of the nonelect means that they have been decisively subdued to the will of God and can do nothing but serve his purposes. As Philippians 2:9–11 teaches, all things in heaven and earth and below the earth will bow before Jesus Christ and acknowledge him as Lord. The nonelect in hell will be reconciled in that they are no longer able to rebel against God and because they will acknowledge Jesus for who He is. Henri Blocher clarifies this truth:

> The theory of sin forever flourishing ignores the message of Christ's perfect victory over sin and evil. *Every* knee shall bow and *every* tongue confess. . . (Phil 2:10ff.), those of the lost included. It cannot mean outward, hypocritical, and forced agreement; what sense could there be in any outward show in the light

---

72. Bruce, "Christ Hymn," 109.

of that Day, when all secrets shall be exposed (Rom 2:16), before the God who is Spirit? Sinners are forced, then, to confess the truth, but they are forced by truth itself, but its overwhelming evidence and spiritual authority; they can no longer refuse to see, they cannot *think* otherwise. Through Christ, it has pleased God to reconcile, *apokatallaxai*, the whole universe, including all rebellious spirits (Col 1:20).[73]

After their judgment God will consign the nonelect to the lake of fire with Satan, where for all eternity they will never be able to rebel against God (Rev 20:11–15).[74] There will be peace even between God and the nonelect as a result of the atonement.

The creation also experiences reconciliation with God. The evil personal elements of creation, Satan and his demons, are reconciled in much the same way as the nonelect are. They too will bow down before Jesus and confess his Lordship to the glory of God the Father (Phil 2:9-11). As Homer Kent notes, "This universal acknowledgement will include angels and departed saints in heaven, people still living on earth, and the satanic hosts and lost humanity in hell."[75] At the end of the Millennium, after Satan has attempted one final rebellion against God (Rev 20:7-9), he will be thrown into the lake of fire along with the eternally lost (Rev 20:10), where he will no longer be a threat to God's harmony and peace in creation. Angels will also experience reconciliation with God, although Scripture nowhere hints at what this aspect of reconciliation might entail. They do not need reconciliation to God as human beings do, but as members of the creation estranged from God because of humanity's sin, they too will participate in the reconciliation of all things (Rom 8:19-23). The entire creation will be renewed and cleansed from sin. The elect will dwell in a new heavens and new earth (Rev 21-22) as Christ fulfills the cultural mandate and hands over his

---

73. Blocher, "Everlasting Punishment," 303. This is not a "fourth position" concerning the relationship between hell and salvation (in addition to the traditional view, annihilationism, and universalism), as Stephen Williams posits in "The Question of Hell," 163–83. It is instead a modification of the traditional view, as punishment in hell is eternal, but it is imposed upon those who are eternally remorseful and ashamed, not those who eternally rebel against God. See Blocher, "Everlasting Punishment," 304–12.

74. The reconciliation of all things does not entail annihilationism. The biblical evidence is clear that hell is eternal. See Fudge and Peterson, *Two Views of Hell*, 117–81. While the nonelect are no longer able to thwart God's purposes or rebel against him in hell, neither will they ever long for a relationship with him or repent from their sins. See Moore, "Personal and Cosmic Eschatology," 900–901.

75. Kent, Jr., *Philippians*, 125.

kingdom to God the Father (1 Cor 15:24–28).[76] All of this will take place because Christ's atonement has paid for, conquered, and vanquished all sin.

The Resurrection of the Elect and the Nonelect

Christ's reconciliation of all things to the Father through the atonement also includes the future resurrection of all people, the elect and the nonelect. John 5:26–28 states, "For just as the Father has life in Himself, even so He gave to the Son also to have life in Himself; and He gave Him authority to execute judgment, because He is *the* Son of Man. Do not marvel at this; for an hour is coming, in which all who are in the tombs will hear His voice, and will come forth; those who did the good *deeds* to a resurrection of life, those who committed the evil *deeds* to a resurrection of judgment." Christ stated that all people would experience the resurrection; those who had done good things (as a result of their saving faith) would experience the resurrection of life and those that had done evil things (as a result of their unredeemed sin nature) would experience the resurrection of judgment, or damnation (cf. Rev 20:5–7). Christ possesses power over the resurrection and authority to judge people because the Father has given Him those things. Not only does Christ have power over the resurrection of the elect, but he also has power over the resurrection of the nonelect. As Gerald Borchert states, "A major role of the Son in the eschatology of humanity is his issuance of this decisive call (*phone*), which summons the dead from the tombs (5:28) to one of two destinies."[77] All people will only experience the resurrection because of Christ.

Christ's power over the resurrection is a result of his own resurrection (1 Cor 15:13), which is a result of his atonement.[78] People only experience the resurrection because Christ paid for sin in his atoning work on the cross and therefore gained authority over death. First Corinthians 15:21–22 describes how Christ reversed the order of death that Adam instituted after he sinned: "For since by a man *came* death, by a man also *came* the resurrection of the dead. For as in Adam all die, so also in Christ all will be made alive." Although the context of these verses is concerned with the resurrection of believers, the same way that Christ procured the power over the resurrection of the elect to life (dying on the cross as a payment for sin and being raised from the dead) is the same way He did so for the resurrection of

---

76. Moore, "Personal and Cosmic Eschatology," 912–16.

77. Borchert, *John 1–11*, 241.

78. Christ's death and resurrection are always inseparable from one another. See Gaffin, Jr., *Resurrection and Redemption*.

the nonelect to judgment. Furthermore, if Christ has the power over the resurrection of judgment just as he has power over the resurrection of life, and if he only has this power as the last Adam who defeated death through his payment for all sin, then it seems that not only the elect but also the nonelect are raised from the dead on the basis of Christ's work on the cross. As Robert Lightner states, "As the last Adam (1 Cor 15:45), Christ defeated the power of death incurred by the first Adam; and since the penalty of death extended to all men, Christ's victory over death, proved by his own resurrection, must also be the basis for the future resurrection of all men."[79] Because the nonelect will be raised from the dead by the power of Christ's resurrection just as the elect will, it seems that they must have been included in Christ's atonement just as the elect were.

Jesus Christ as King

The final way Christ's cosmic triumph over all sin results from his atonement for all sin is seen in Christ's work and role as king. Jesus is king because of his atonement and resurrection. He spoke of his crucifixion as something that he had to go through in order to receive his kingdom (Matt 3:11–12; Mark 10:35–40; Luke 12:49–50). The "Lamb who was slain" is the one who is worthy to receive power and glory on the throne (Rev 5:11–14). Christ presently sits at the right hand of the Father (Acts 2:33) and is the "ruler of the kings of the earth" (Rev 1:5) and "head over all things to the church" (Eph 1:22). As Christ sits at the Father's right hand, however, he awaits the time when he will return and consummate his kingdom (Matt 25:31–46). At Christ's return his kingdom will be visibly established over the entire earth (Rev 19:11–20:6), and sin and Satan will be conquered once and for all (1 Cor 15:24–28; Rev 20:7–15). Christ's atonement is inseparable from his rule and reign as king.

The inseparable relationship between Christ's atonement and his rule is also seen in how all things are reconciled to him. Jesus Christ reconciles all things because of his priestly work in the atonement (Col 1:20), but all things are reconciled to Christ as he rules over them. Philippians 2:8–11 states that it is because of Christ's death on the cross (v. 8) that God has highly exalted Jesus (v. 9). On the basis of Christ's humiliation, which climaxed in his atonement, God gave him the name of "Lord." This name means that Christ is now the sovereign ruler over the entire universe.[80] Christ's future exaltation consists of all creatures bowing before Jesus (v.

---

79. Lightner, *Death Christ Died*, 144.
80. Hawthorne, *Philippians*, 123–26.

10) and confessing his Lordship and sovereign rule to the glory of God the Father (v. 11). We also see truth in the basis of Christ's authority to judge the nonelect. As we have established, Christ raises the nonelect for judgment because of his atonement. He is worthy to open the book with the seven seals (a work of judgment) because of his atoning work (Rev 5:9).[81] This judgment is a part of his kingly activity as he works to bring peace to the creation, and it is inseparable from his atonement.

As king, Christ not only saves and rules over his elect, but he will one day visibly rule over all creation, first in the millennial kingdom (Rev 20:1–10), and then in eternity (Rev 21–22). As king, Christ has the right to raise the elect and the nonelect from the dead and to judge them. As king, Christ triumphs over and defeats Satan, sin, and death. All of this kingly work is universal; Christ is the ruler of all creation, and one day all of creation will recognize this truth. This kingly work is also based upon the atonement, which defeated Satan, conquered death, and reconciled all things. Christ's victory is only possible because Christ paid for all sin, which means that Christ's rule and reign over all things is only possible because he paid for all sin. Christ's cosmic triumph over all sin and consequent rule as king depends upon his payment for all sin in the atonement.

CONCLUSION

God had several intentions in the atonement that go beyond the elect. In order to accomplish these intentions, he sent his Son to the cross not only to die for the sins of the elect, but also to die for the sins of all people. God intended for Jesus' general payment for all sin to accomplish five things. First, Jesus' death made the universal gospel call possible. We see this in the way the Bible describes the universal gospel call's basis, content and motivation, in the Holy Spirit's role in the universal gospel call, and in what is necessary for a genuine universal gospel call. Second, Christ's atonement procured an additional basis of condemnation for those who explicitly reject the gospel. The nonelect are so culpable for rejecting the death of Christ for their sins precisely because Christ died for them. Third, Christ's atonement made it possible for God to show common grace toward the nonelect. God graciously bestows his good gifts upon the nonelect, restrains sin and evil in their lives, and exercises patience in judging them because of Christ's atonement for all sin. Fourth, the atonement is the supreme example of God's character, his love and his justice, because it is an atonement that is for all sin. Finally, Christ's general atonement accomplished God's cosmic triumph

---

81. Osborne, *Revelation*, 249.

over all sin. We see this in the basis for Christ's victory over Satan, the nature of the reconciliation of all things, the resurrection of the nonelect, and Christ's rule as King.

These five general intentions, based upon Christ's general payment for all sin, make up the general intentions of the multi-intentioned view of the extent of the atonement. Christ's general payment for sin was for specific purposes; it was not merely to make salvation available to all people. Particular redemption is unable to adequately account for these general intentions because it denies that Christ paid for all sin. The atonement was not only a general payment for sin, however. As we will demonstrate in the next chapter, the Bible also teaches that God intended for the atonement to specially benefit the elect, namely by securing their salvation.

CHAPTER 5

The Particular Intentions of the Atonement

INTRODUCTION

JESUS CHRIST'S ATONEMENT NOT only accomplished God's general intentions for his creation, including the elect and the nonelect, but it also accomplished God's intentions for the elect alone. This is why the atonement has multiple intentions, because God intends for it to affect the elect and the nonelect in different ways. Some of the intentions of the atonement are for all people, such as the universal gospel call, common grace, the reconciliation of all to God, and the resurrection of the elect and the nonelect. Other intentions of the atonement are only for the nonelect, such as the additional basis of condemnation for those who reject the gospel and the pacification of the nonelect in Christ's eschatological triumph over all sin. And yet other intentions of the atonement are only for the elect. Specifically, the atonement secured the sure and certain salvation of the elect alone, those who are saved by faith through the gospel of Jesus Christ.

Our purpose in this chapter is to establish, exegetically and theologically, God's particular intention in the atonement: the securing of the salvation of the elect. We purposely use the word "securing" here, as it preserves the difference between the accomplishment of salvation at the cross and the application of salvation by the Holy Spirit, or the objective and subjective aspects of the atonement. The atonement secured and made certain the salvation of the elect, but it did not technically "save" the elect because no one is saved until he or she puts his or her faith in the gospel of Jesus Christ, an action wrought by the Holy Spirit. In order to establish God's particular intention in the atonement it will first be necessary to demonstrate that God the Father intended for God the Son to secure the salvation of the elect in the atonement. We will do this by examining God's sovereignty throughout salvation (particularly in his unconditional election of the elect), God's special love for the elect, and the Father and the Son's unity in salvation. We will then biblically and theologically establish how Christ secured the salvation of the elect. Christ secured the salvation of the elect in the atonement by dying for their sin in order to send the Holy Spirit to apply salvation to them. On the basis of the atonement, the Spirit applies salvation to the elect through effectual calling, regeneration, conversion, justification, indwelling, Holy Spirit baptism, sanctification, preservation and perseverance, and glorification. Throughout this chapter we will take special care to respond to the arguments of unlimited atonement against particularity in the atonement and to explain how the particular aspects of the atonement do not contradict the universal aspects. This chapter, together with the two previous chapters, establishes the biblical and theological validity of the multi-intentioned view of the extent of the atonement.

SECURING THE SALVATION OF THE ELECT

The doctrine of election concerns God's plan to save sinners,[1] and it refers to his unconditional choice before creation of which people, among all those he has created, will be saved through the atonement of Jesus Christ. When the Bible speaks of salvation as based upon God's purpose and plan (e.g., Rom 8:28–29; 9:11; Eph 1:11; 2 Tim 1:9), it is usually referring to his work of election, or the "divine initiative in human salvation."[2] The Bible does refer to election in contexts that are not salvific, as when it speaks of God's election to service in a corporate sense of the nation of Israel (Deut 7:6–8; 1 Kgs 3:8; Ps 132:13) and also of the church (1 Pet 2:9). The Bible also speaks of God's electing certain individuals for service, such as Abraham (Gen 12:1–3), Moses (Num 16:5–7), and Jeremiah (Jer 1:5). Jesus Christ is sometimes described as God's "elect one" (Isa 42:1). The primary emphasis of election in the Bible, however, particularly in the New Testament, is on sinners' individual election to salvation, as 2 Thessalonians 2:13 illustrates, "But we should always give thanks to God for you, brethren beloved by

---

1. God's salvation plan is for fallen sinners, which means that election is infralapsarian, or after the fall, as opposed to supralapsarian, or before the fall. For a defense of this notion, see Ware, "Divine Election," 47–58.
2. Yarbrough, "Divine Election," 47.

the Lord, because God has chosen you from the beginning for salvation through sanctification by the Spirit and faith in the truth."

There are two primary views of individual election.[3] The first is unconditional election, which can be defined as "that eternal act of God, by which in his sovereign pleasure, and on account of no foreseen merit in them, he chooses certain out of the number of sinful men to be the recipients of the special grace of his Spirit, and so to be made voluntary partakers of Christ's salvation."[4] The second is conditional election, which can be defined as "the view that before the world ever existed God conditionally predestined some specific individuals to eternal life and the rest to eternal condemnation, based on his foreknowledge of their freewill responses to his law and to his grace."[5] The main difference between the two views is God's basis for election. Those who hold to unconditional election believe that the basis for election is God's sovereign will, while those who hold to conditional election believe that the basis is the human response to God's salvation in Christ.

The doctrine of election is closely related to the doctrine of the extent of the atonement, as the former refers to God's plan to save sinners and the latter refers to the enactment of God's plan to save sinners through Jesus Christ. This has led many theologians to assume that one's doctrine of election largely determines the extent of the atonement, and vice versa. A common argument for particular redemption is that it is only consistent with unconditional election,[6] while a common argument for unlimited atonement (from an Arminian perspective) is that it is only consistent with conditional election.[7] There is some truth in this way of thinking, as an atonement that is only particular entails unconditional election, and an atonement that is only universal entails conditional election. It isn't necessary for one's doctrine of election to determine one's doctrine of the extent of the atonement, however. Millard Erickson, for example, appeals to sublapsarianism, the

---

3. There are some who deny any idea of individual election in Scripture, and see election as entirely corporate, but this is a minority view within evangelicalism. See Klein, *The New Chosen People*; and Pinnock, "Divine Election," 276–314.

4. Strong, *Systematic Theology*, 779.

5. Cottrell, "The Classical Arminian View," 72.

6. Boettner, *The Reformed Doctrine of Predestination*, 151, 157–60; Hodge, *Systematic Theology*, 2:547–49; Kuiper, *For Whom Did Christ Die?*, 67–68; Letham, *The Work of Christ*, 234–35; Long, *Definite Atonement*, 21–24; Nicole, "Particular Redemption," 172; Owen, *Death of Death*, 45–62; Packer, "Introductory Essay," 4–8; Tiessen, *Who Can Be Saved?*, 98–99; and Warfield, *The Plan of Salvation*, 96–97.

7. Hunt, *What Love is This?*, 298–300; Lake, "He Died for All," 41–45; Marshall, "Universal Grace," 64–69; Olson, *Arminian Theology*, 63–67; Picirilli, *Grace, Faith, Free Will*, 90, 105–06; and Wiley, *Christian Theology*, 2:295–97.

view that God first chose to send Christ to provide salvation for all and then chose to only save some on the basis of that atonement, and states that one cannot deduce particular redemption from unconditional election because it cannot be proven that the decision to elect only some is prior to the decision to send Christ. Sublapsarianism makes a combination of unlimited atonement and particular redemption logically possible.[8]

Erickson's view of sublapsarianism is correct, and it is certainly possible. By itself, however, this argument does not solve the problem of holding together unlimited atonement and unconditional election. If the Son provided salvation for all, but the Father only intended to save some, then this introduces disjunction into the Godhead, as this implies that the Father and Son have different salvific goals. Most Moderate Calvinists, who hold together unconditional election and unlimited atonement, are open to this charge, and it is one that advocates of particular redemption commonly make.[9] The multi-intentioned view avoids this charge and holds consistently to both unconditional election and an atonement that paid for the sins of all people by asserting that God the Father had multiple intentions for the atonement, and sent God the Son to accomplish these multiple purposes. The atonement not only accomplishes the Father's elective purposes, but his purposes for the creation and the nonelect as well. The Holy Spirit then works among the nonelect and the elect on the basis of the atonement, fulfilling the Father and the Son's intentions. Each person of the Trinity has general and particular intentions for creation, which means the unity of the Trinity is upheld by the multi-intentioned view.

Unconditional election has to do with God's particular purposes, which are accomplished in the atonement, but these particular purposes do not rule out his general purposes, which are also accomplished in the atonement. That God only intends to save some sinners does not mean that he has no purposes for the nonelect, and it does not require that the atonement only be for the elect if the Bible teaches otherwise, as we discovered in chapters 3 and 4. God had general purposes in the atonement that go beyond the elect, which necessitated Christ's general payment for all sin. God also has particular, salvific purposes in the atonement that are only for the elect, and these purposes are consistent with the truth of unconditional election. That God intended for the atonement to secure the salvation of the elect alone differentiates the multi-intentioned view from traditional

---

8. Erickson, *Christian Theology*, 852.

9. Boettner, *Reformed Doctrine of Predestination*, 159–60; Grudem, *Systematic Theology*, 595; Kuiper, *For Whom Did Christ Die?*, 64–70; Nicole, "Particular Redemption," 172; Owen, *Death of Death*, 51; Packer, "Introductory Essay," 4–6; Tiessen, *Who Can Be Saved?*, 98–99; and Warfield, *Plan of Salvation*, 96–97.

unlimited atonement, which is unable to account for any particularity in the atonement because it understands the atonement to be a general payment for all sin that only provides salvation for all, and asserts that the particular, saving acts of God are then found in the Father's election and the Spirit's saving work, but not the atonement. We see the truth of God's securing the salvation of the elect in the atonement in what the Bible teaches about God's sovereignty in salvation, God's special love for the elect, and the unity of the Father and the Son in salvation.

God's Sovereignty in Salvation

The Bible consistently presents God as completely sovereign over all things, including salvation. Perhaps the most straightforward verse in Scripture affirming this truth is Ephesians 1:11, which states, "also we have obtained an inheritance, having been predestined according to His purpose who works all things after the counsel of His will." This verse speaks of the believer's inheritance in Christ (Eph 1:10); an inheritance that believers only have because God has predestined them to have it, according to his purpose. God's "purpose" here is his ultimate plan and design for all things.[10] Predestination to salvation is based upon God's purpose and design; it is not based upon foreseen decisions of faith. As Feinberg states, "'Purpose' (*prothesin*) refers to the goal God intends to accomplish; it is his ultimate design. Paul says that our predestination to salvation was done according to that design or aim. This means that our election wasn't based on what God foresaw about how we would respond when told the gospel. If Paul had meant that, he could have easily said that. Saying that we were predestined according to God's purpose suggests that his decision was based solely on his desires, i.e., it was unconditional."[11] Furthermore, the one who "predestined according to his purpose" is also the one who "works all things after the counsel of his will," which means that God's election is part of God's sovereign plan for all things in his creation.[12] This phrase echoes Ephesians 1:5, which states that "He predestined us to adoption as sons through Jesus Christ to Himself, according to the kind intention of His will."[13] The Bible makes it clear that the basis of salvation is God's sovereign will and pleasure and not any human decision, and that therefore election is unconditional.

---

10. Bruce, *Epistles*, 263–64; and Lincoln, *Ephesians*, 36.
11. Feinberg, *No One Like Him*, 680.
12. Ware, "Divine Election," 23.
13. Lincoln, *Ephesians*, 36.

God's sovereign decision to elect unconditionally some to salvation is absolutely necessary if any are to be saved. All people, as a result of the fall, are dead in their sins (Eph 2:1), blinded by Satan (2 Cor 4:4), and unable to do anything pleasing to God. Apart from a work of God in their lives, people are incapable of doing anything to restore their relationship with God (Rom 3:9–20). This includes putting their faith in the gospel.[14] People must be regenerated, or born again, in order to believe the gospel.[15] This means that it is impossible for election to be based upon a person's future decision to believe in the gospel. Without God's sovereign work of grace in salvation, beginning with election, no one would ever make the decision to believe in the gospel. As Ware states, "It simply cannot be the case that God looks ahead in time and sees those who will believe in Christ and so elects them based on his advanced knowledge of their faith. For apart from regeneration, God would see only unbelief as he looked down the corridors of history."[16] Those who are "appointed to eternal life" are the ones who believe, and not vice versa (Acts 13:48).[17]

God's sovereignty in salvation is also seen in his decision to elect believers "before the foundation of the world" (Eph 1:4; cf. 2 Thess 2:13; 2 Tim 1:9; Titus 1:2). God's decision to choose some people to be saved is made before people are even born, indicating that election is unconditional. This is the point of Romans 9:10–16. In Romans 9 Paul is concerned with why there were so many Jews who were not saved (vv. 1–5). He writes that

---

14. Arminians agree that apart from a work of God it is impossible for anyone to put their faith in the gospel. They believe, however, that this work of God is done for everyone, and is found in prevenient grace. Prevenient grace is grace that enables all human beings to respond freely to the gospel message, and it includes calling, convicting, illuminating, and enabling. See Olson, *Arminian Theology*, 158–61. Prevenient grace is understood as flowing from Christ's unlimited atonement, and Scriptural support for the doctrine is given from John 1:9; 12:32; and Titus 2:11. See Dunning, *Grace, Faith, and Holiness*, 338–39; Grounds, "God's Universal Salvific Grace," 21–30; Wiley, *Christian Theology*, 2:353; and Wood, "The Contribution of John Wesley," 215–20. While there is grounding in the atonement for common grace, there is no biblical warrant for prevenient grace flowing from the atonement. None of the texts used by Arminians in this regard support the doctrine. For a refutation of prevenient grace, see Combs, "Does the Bible Teach Prevenient Grace?" 3–17; and Schreiner, "Does Scripture Teach Prevenient Grace," 229–46.

15. The traditional Calvinist position has been that regeneration precedes faith, although some moderate Calvinists believe that faith does precede regeneration. They still believe that God's special grace is necessary to accept the gospel call; however, they believe this is the work of the effectual call. Either way Calvinists believe that a sovereign work of God upon a person is necessary for that person to put his or her faith in the gospel. Demarest, *Cross and Salvation*, 285–91.

16. Ware, "Divine Election," 21.

17. Bruce, *Acts of the Apostles*, 315.

despite the current situation, God's promise to the Jews had not failed because God continued to save those who were the "children of promise" (vv. 6–9). Paul then uses the illustration of Jacob and Esau to describe God's saving purposes (vv. 10–13). Just as God chose Jacob to be the inheritor of the promise over Esau before the two of them were born, solely on the basis of his sovereign will, so also does he have mercy on (saves) those upon whom he wills to have mercy.[18] God's prerogative as God is to save whomever he wishes to save, depending only upon his own purposes and desires. This truth can also be seen in the fact that God foreknows, or foreordains, who will believe (Rom 8:29; 1 Pet 1:1–2).[19]

The fact that God has unconditionally elected before the foundation of the world those who will be saved requires particularity in the atonement. Christ's atonement must have done something for the elect that it did not do for the nonelect if anyone is to be saved. If God had only general intentions in the atonement, then the atonement provides an objective salvation for all, but it does not enable people to subjectively experience salvation. Arminians put forth the doctrine of prevenient grace in order to solve this problem, but the Arminian view of prevenient grace challenges God's sovereignty in salvation and lacks Scriptural warrant. Furthermore, the Bible asserts that election is "in Christ" (Eph 1:3–5). This means that God the Father, when he elected believers, did so by purposing to save them through the person and work of his Son, Jesus Christ.[20] Christ's atonement is what

---

18. Arminians typically deny that Rom 9 concerns salvation, let alone unconditional election to salvation. They instead interpret Rom 9 as teaching election to service. E.g., Cottrell, "Classic Arminian View of Election," 122–33; MacDonald, "The Biblical Doctrine of Election," 217; and Strauss, "God's Promise," 190–208. This understanding, however, contradicts the language and context of the text. See Schreiner, "Does Romans 9 Teach," 89–106; and Ware, "Divine Election," 9–12.

19. Rom 8:29 and 1 Pet 1:1–2 both assert that God's election is based upon his foreknowledge. Arminians understand these verses to teach that election is based upon God's knowledge of how each person will respond to the gospel. Therefore election is conditioned upon one's faith in the gospel, and is not unconditional. E.g., Cottrell, "Classic Arminian View of Election," 84–93. There are several problems, however, with this understanding of foreknowledge and election. First, it is not found in these verses, but must be read into them. Second, this view contradicts several other passages of Scripture that base God's election upon his own sovereign will, and not the choices of human beings. Finally, this view misunderstands the meaning of foreknowledge, which normally refers to God's personal decision to relate with someone, and is better translated as "foreordain." See Baugh, "The Meaning of Foreknowledge," 183–200; Jewett, *Election and Predestination*, 70–73; and Ware, "Divine Election," 26–29. Therefore, God's foreknowledge in election reiterates his sovereign grace and reinforces the truth that election is completely unconditional.

20. Demarest, *Cross and Salvation*, 133; Hoekema, *Saved by Grace* (Grand Rapids: Eerdmans, 1989), 56–57; Jewett, *Election and Predestination*, 73; and Ware, "Divine

accomplishes the salvation of the elect, and it does so because it secured the salvation of the elect according to the Father's sovereign will.

God's Special Love for the Elect

Not only does God's sovereignty in salvation indicate that Christ's atonement had special reference to the elect, but God's special love for the elect indicates this as well. God does love all people (John 3:16), but he loves his elect in a special way that is different from the way he loves the nonelect. This can be seen in the Old Testament, which consistently speaks of God's particular love for his chosen people, Israel (Deut 4:37; 7:7-8; 10:14-15; 33:3; Hos 11:1-4; Mal 1:2-3). As D. A. Carson states, "God's love is directed toward Israel in these passages in a way in which it is not directed toward other nations."[21] God's particular love is especially demonstrated in his redemption of Israel (Deut 4:37-38; 7:7-9; Ps 89:1-4; Isa 43:3-4). This theme is continued in the New Testament, where God's love is especially directed towards his chosen people who make up the church, the elect in Christ. The "beloved by God" are those whom the Father has chosen for salvation by the Spirit unto the glory of Jesus Christ (1 Thess 1:4; 2 Thess 2:13-14), and it is "in love" that he predestines the elect for salvation through Jesus Christ (Eph 1:4-5). The basis for election is not only God's sovereignty, but also his love.[22] The New Testament also emphasizes that God's particular love is especially demonstrated in the redemption of the elect secured by Christ's atonement (Eph 5:25-27).

Christ's atonement not only demonstrates God's love for the world of humanity (John 3:16; Rom 5:8; 1 John 4:9-10), but it also demonstrates his particular, saving love for the elect, because Christ died to secure the salvation of the elect alone. The very name "Jesus" reflects the truth that the Son of God came to this earth to save "his people from their sins" (Matt 1:21). Jesus is the Greek form of "Joshua," which means "Yahweh saves," and Jesus' people include all Jews and Gentiles who put their faith in him and therefore receive salvation from their sins.[23] Jesus is the "Good Shepherd" who lays down his life for his "sheep" (John 10:11, 14-15). The relationship between

---

Election," 52-54. Arminians understand election "in Christ" as corporate, in that Christ elected the church, but not individuals in the church; as God's goal for all people; or as the quality of believers when they put their faith in Christ. See Cottrell, "Classic Arminian View of Election," 81-83; and MacDonald, "Biblical Doctrine of Election," 219-26.

21. Carson, *The Difficult Doctrine of the Love of God*, 18.
22. Frame, *The Doctrine of God*, 423; and Peterson, *Election and Free Will*, 104-5.
23. Carson, *Matthew*, 76.

Jesus and his sheep in this passage is analogous to the relationship between the Father and the Son, indicating an intimate knowledge and love between Jesus and his sheep. As D. A. Carson states, "However clearly this Gospel portrays Jesus as the Savior of the world (4:42), the Lamb of God who takes away the sins of the world (1:29, 36), it insists no less emphatically that Jesus has a peculiar relationship with those the Father has given him (John 6:37ff.), with those he has chosen out of the world (15:16, 19). So here: Jesus' death is peculiarly for his sheep, just as we elsewhere read that 'Christ loved the church and gave himself up for her' (Eph 5:25)."[24] John 15:12–14 makes the same emphasis when it states, "This is My commandment, that you love one another, just as I have loved you. Greater love has no one than this, that one lay down his life for his friends. You are My friends if you do what I command you." In these verses, Jesus exhorts his disciples to love one another (v. 12), and explains what the standard of love is: to lay down one's life for his friends. Implicitly this verse points toward Jesus' atoning death, and this death was for Jesus' friends, who are his followers (v. 14).[25] Jesus shows no greater love than dying for his friends, his elect followers.

Paul expounds on Jesus' special love for the elect in two passages of Scripture. The first of these is Romans 8:31–39. After explaining how God works all things out for the good of those who love him because all whom God has predestined will be glorified (Rom 8:28–30), Paul bursts into praise for God's redeeming love. This passage only has reference to believers, as it speaks of the impossibility of anyone bringing a charge against God's elect (31–34) or anything separating the elect from the love of Christ (35–39). God is the one who gave his own Son for the elect, and therefore he will give the elect all the blessings that come with salvation. As Romans 8:32 states, "He who did not spare His own Son, but delivered Him over for us all, how will He not also with Him freely give us all things?" The "all" in this verse refers to all of God's believers, the elect, as its context demands.[26] God so loves the elect through Jesus Christ that absolutely nothing can ever separate the believer from God (Rom 8:35, 38–39), including everything in the

---

24. Carson, *Gospel of John*, 387.

25. Bruce, *Gospel of John*, 311; Carson, *Gospel of John*, 522–23; Morris, *Gospel According to John*, 599; and Tenney, *John*, 153.

26. Schreiner, *Romans*, 458. Rom 8:32 does not require particular redemption, however, as some claim. See Berkhof, *Systematic Theology*, 395; Grudem, *Systematic Theology*, 595; Kuiper, *For Whom Did Christ Die?*, 68–69; and Murray, *Redemption Accomplished and Applied*, 66–67. Paul is only referring to believers in this passage, and he has no reason to mention the atonement's intentions for unbelievers. As Norman F. Douty states, "To read him [Paul] as meaning that God delivered Christ for all of us who believe *and for none else*, is injecting into the words what is not there." Douty, *Did Christ Die*, 92, emphasis the author's.

created order and even believers themselves.[27] God's love through Christ enables believers to overcome any adversity that might threaten their salvation. The love presented in this passage comes to believers through Christ's atonement, and it is not shown toward those who do not believe.

The second passage in which Paul speaks of Christ's particular love for the elect is Ephesians 5:22-33. In this passage Paul explains how the Holy Spirit's work of leading believers to "be subject to one another in the fear of Chris" (Eph 5:21) works itself out in marriage. He uses the analogy of the relationship between Christ and the church to show husbands and wives how to relate to one another. Wives are to submit to their husbands just as they submit to Christ, for just as Christ is the head of the church and the church is subject to Christ, the husband is the head of the wife (vv. 22-24).[28] Husbands, on the other hand, are to love their wives in the same way that Christ loved the church (v. 25). Christ loved the church by giving himself up for her on the cross (v. 25). The phrase "gave himself for her" refers to Christ's sacrificial atonement, as is clear from Ephesians 5:2, which states "and walk in love, just as Christ also loved you and gave Himself up for us, an offering and a sacrifice to God as a fragrant aroma."[29] Acts 20:28 also supports this understanding; in this passage Paul tells the Ephesian elders that God purchased the church with his own blood, referring to Jesus Christ's sacrificial atonement for the church.[30] Christ sacrificed himself for the church so that he might sanctify her with his Word (v. 26). The purpose of this sanctification was so that Christ could one day present the entire church to himself at the eschaton as completely holy and blameless (v. 27). Husbands therefore should love their wives in the same way that they love their own bodies (v. 28), because this is the same way that Christ loves his church (vv. 29-30).

What is significant regarding Christ's love in this passage is that Christ's sacrificial love for the church in the atonement is compared to a husband's love for his wife. This indicates that Christ's love in redeeming his church through his atonement is a particular love. Just as husbands are to love their wives above all other women, Christ loves his church, his elect people, above all others.[31] Christ's particular love results in his securing the sanctification (v. 26) and the glorification (v. 27) of his church, and these are things that

27. Morris, *Romans*, 338-42; and Schreiner, *Romans*, 464-67.

28. For a defense of the meaning of "head" as authority and the need for wives to submit to their husbands in the same way that the church submits to Christ, see Grudem, "The Meaning of *Kephalē*," 425-68.

29. Lincoln, *Ephesians*, 312.

30. Bock, *Acts*, 630-31; and Bruce, *Acts of the Apostles*, 434.

31. Ware, "Divine Election," 30-31.

only the elect experience. As Bruce Ware states concerning Christ's love for the church,

> This love, by definition and necessity, then, is a love for his own bride that is different in kind and content from the general love God (or Christ) has for the world. This love, as we see from verses 26–27, leads Christ to save and purify the church. This love impels Christ to make the church 'holy and blameless,' fulfilling what the Father had in election chosen for the church to become in his Son (note: Eph 1:4 and 5:27 use the same phrase, 'holy and blameless'). In short, this richest of all the demonstrations of God's love among human beings is, by necessity, a selective, particular, and discriminate love for just some.[32]

The Bible repeatedly indicates that God shows his saving love toward the elect by securing their salvation through the atonement, as Christ died to save his people, his sheep, his friends, and his church. Paul even specifically states that Christ loved him and gave himself up for him, describing his own personal appropriation of Christ's atonement (Gal 2:20). Paul could so confidently and personally affirm Christ's love and atonement for himself because he was saved by that atonement, indicating that he has Christ's particular, saving love in view in this verse.[33] Advocates of unlimited atonement are correct when they state that these kinds of passages do not demand particular redemption, because verses that limit the extent of the atonement to a particular group can easily be reconciled with verses that speak of Christ's atonement for all people.[34] These passages do demand some kind of special reference to the elect, however, because they indicate that Christ's love resulted in the salvation of the elect. As Roger Nicole states, "The Scripture emphasizes the definite relation of the mission of Christ, and specifically of His death to those whom He actually redeems. . . . These expressions need not be construed as exclusive of others not mentioned—(this is quite manifest in the case of Gal 2:20)—but the specific reference in all these passages certainly indicates that the relationship of the work of Christ to those who are saved is different from that which it bears to those who are lost."[35] The multi-intentioned view is able to account for all of the different ways that the Bible describes God's love, both toward the elect and toward

---

32. Ibid., 31.

33. Bruce, *The Epistle to the Galatians*, 145–46; and Longenecker, *Galatians*, 94.

34. E.g., Douty, *Did Christ Die* 132–35; Erickson, *Christian Theology*, 851; Lightner, *Death Christ Died*, 95–96; Marshall, "For All," 333–36; Picirilli, *Grace, Faith, Free Will*, 90–92; and Sailer, "A Wesleyan View," 190–91.

35. Nicole, "Definite Atonement," 201.

all of humanity (as we saw in chapters 3 and 4), because it recognizes both general and particular intentions in the atonement.

The Unity of the Father and the Son in Salvation

In addition to God's sovereignty in salvation and God's special love for the elect, the unity of the Father and the Son in salvation indicates that the atonement secured the salvation of the elect. In Matthew 11:25–27 (cf. Luke 10:21–22), Jesus praises the Father because he has hidden "these things" from the wise and the intelligent and revealed them to infants; this was the Father's good pleasure. Jesus then goes on to say that all things have been handed over to him by the Father, that no one knows the Son except the Father, and that no one knows the Father except the Son and anyone to whom the Son wills to reveal the Father. These verses state that the Father, the Sovereign Lord of Heaven and Earth (v. 25), both reveals and conceals the good news of the kingdom ("these things") to people as he wills. Jesus delights in the Father's revealing and concealing (v. 26), because, as D. A. Carson states, "Whatever pleases the Father pleases him."[36] Furthermore, Jesus only reveals the knowledge of the Father as the Father wills, according to the Father's authorization (v. 27). Jesus not only praises the Father's sovereign grace in salvation, but he participates in it. The Father and the Son are of one mind in revealing the truth of the gospel to the elect and concealing it from the nonelect. We must realize that this truth in no way rules out the universal invitation to receive Christ in the gospel call. In the very next passage, Matthew 11:28–30, Jesus issues a universal invitation to come to him. At the very least, the Bible considers these two truths to be non–contradictory. As Demarest states concerning Matthew 11:25–27, "Although Matt 11:28–30 likely was spoken at another time in Jesus' ministry, a universal invitation to receive Jesus (v. 28) is not inconsistent with God's purpose to reveal himself to some. This is so because (1) Christ' provision on the cross was universal. And (2) all who respond positively to the invitation will be saved (John 11:26; Acts 10:43; Rom 10:11, 13); but tragically for themselves, depraved sinners are unresponsive to spiritual impulses—hence the need for a supernatural initiative."[37]

The unity of the Father and the Son in salvation is particularly seen in the Gospel of John. In John 5:19–21 Jesus states that he can do nothing of himself, unless it something that he sees the Father doing; because the Son does what the Father does (v. 19). For the Father loves the Son and shows

36. Carson, *Matthew*, 275.
37. Demarest, *Cross and Salvation*, 125.

him all the things that he does (v. 20), and just as the Father gives life to the dead, so does the Son give life to whomever he wishes (v. 21). The analogy in verse 21 is that just as corpses depend upon God's voice to resurrect them, so too do people depend upon the Son's good pleasure to receive salvation.[38] Since the Son only does what the Father does, and since he has received his power from the Father (cf. 5:22, 26, 30), it is clear that Jesus only saves those whom the Father desires for him to save, the elect. As Carson states, "Although the Son 'can do nothing of himself' (v. 19), his will, his pleasure, his choices are so completely at one with the Father that it is no less true to say that the crucial decisions are his. Unlike Elijah, Jesus is no mere instrument of divine power. . . . Just as he chose one man out of the crowd of ill people by Bethesda (v. 6), so he chooses those to whom he gives life."[39]

John 6:37–40 also emphasizes this truth. It states: "All that the Father gives Me will come to Me, and the one who comes to Me I will certainly not cast out. For I have come down from heaven, not to do My own will, but the will of Him who sent Me. This is the will of Him who sent Me, that of all that He has given Me I lose nothing, but raise it up on the last day. For this is the will of My Father, that everyone who beholds the Son and believes in Him will have eternal life, and I Myself will raise him up on the last day." All who come to Jesus and believe in him will receive salvation (John 6:35), but the Galileans Jesus was speaking to did not believe in Jesus (John 6:36), despite his miracles (John 6:26–27). This does not mean, however, that Jesus' mission was frustrated or that it failed. This is because "all" whom the Father had given him would come to him, and Jesus would receive everyone who comes to him from the Father (v. 37). The "all" at the beginning of v. 37 refers to all believers, while the second part of the verse affirms that Jesus will receive each individual believer who comes to him. The verse proclaims both that the whole of the elect (all believers) and all individual believers as being elect (the one who comes to me) will be saved.[40] John 6:37 explains why some people did not believe in Jesus; they did not believe because the Father is completely sovereign over salvation, and he did not give them to him.[41] Jesus goes on to affirm his complete submission to the Father's sav-

---

38. Yarbrough, "Divine Election," 50.

39. Carson, *Gospel of John*, 253.

40. Bruce, *Gospel of John*, 154; and Ware, "Divine Election," 42–43.

41. Grant R. Osborne points out that the Galileans are responsible for their unbelief, because they refuse to believe in Jesus (6:36), and that God's sovereignty in salvation must not be allowed to trump man's responsibility. Osborne, "Soteriology," 248. It is certainly true that all unbelievers are responsible for their unbelief, but this does not undermine God's sovereignty in salvation. Everyone whom the Father desires to come to the Son will come to him, as verse 37 asserts. As Morris states, "The words [of v. 37]

ing will (v. 38). He then explains that the Father's saving will was that Jesus would not lose any of the ones that the Father gives him, but raise them up at the last day (v. 39). Finally, Jesus reaffirms his complete submission to the Father's will as he just explained it in verse 38. Again, the Father's will is that all who believe in Jesus have eternal life, and Jesus in turn will raise them up at the last day, ensuring that they do receive eternal life (v. 40). These verses stress the Father's sovereignty in salvation (unconditional election), and the Son's obedience to this sovereignty by ensuring that the Father's sovereign salvific will is fulfilled. The Father and the Son are of one mind and will when it comes to the salvation of the elect, with the Father choosing some for salvation and the Son accomplishing the salvation of the ones the Father has chosen.[42]

The unity of the Father and the Son in the salvation of the elect is also evident in John 10:26–30. Just as in John 6:37–40, Jesus explains to the Jews he was speaking with why they do not believe in him (John 10:24–25). They do not believe in him because they are not his sheep (v. 26; cf. John 10:11–18).[43] Jesus' sheep hear his voice and follow him, indicating that they are believers (v. 27). Jesus knows his sheep and gives them eternal life; they will never perish because no one will ever snatch them out of his hand (v. 28). Furthermore, no one will ever snatch them out of the Father's hand, and the Father is the one who has given the sheep to Jesus (v. 29). Jesus ends his explanation by reinforcing his unassailable unity with the Father

---

stress the sovereignty of God. People do not come to Christ because it seems a good idea to them. It never does seem a good idea to sinful people. Apart from a divine work in their souls (cf. 16:8), people remain more or less contentedly in their sins. Before they can come to Christ it is necessary that the Father give them to him. This is the explanation of the disconcerting fact that those who followed Jesus to hear him, and who at the beginning wanted to make him a king, were nevertheless not his followers in the true sense. They did not belong to the people of God. They were not among those whom God gave him." Morris, *Gospel According to John*, 325.

42. Bruce, *Gospel of John*, 153–54; and Carson, *Gospel of John*, 290–91.

43. Osborne maintains that the Jews were not Jesus' sheep because they did not believe in him, which seems to reverse the thought of this verse. He bases his interpretation on the larger context of the book and on the succeeding dialogue in 10:31–39, where Jesus invites the Jews to believe. Osborne, "Soteriology," 250–52. Osborne is correct to note that John 10:31–39 is a valid offer of faith, but this does not invalidate God's sovereignty in salvation. All people have the responsibility to accept Christ through faith (the universal gospel call), but all people can only come to Christ in faith if they have been elected to do so. Both of these truths are biblical and Scripture consistently presents them as compatible. As Carson states, "Neither Jesus nor John means to reduce the moral responsibility of the opponents in the slightest. That they are not Jesus' sheep does not excuse them; it indicts them. But the predestinarian note ensures that even their massive unbelief is not surprising: it is to be expected, and falls under the umbrella of God's sovereignty." Carson, *Gospel of John*, 393.

in saving the sheep: "I and the Father are one" (v. 30). This oneness of the Father and the Son refers to their unity in action, will, mind, and purpose, and presupposes their oneness of nature, but does not obliterate the differences between their persons (cf. John 1:1).[44] Once again Jesus asserts that the elect, his sheep, are given to him by the Father, and neither Jesus nor the Father will ever let the sheep go, because Jesus and the Father are one in saving the sheep.

Jesus also expresses the unity of his salvific will with the Father's in his high priestly prayer of John 17. At the beginning of this prayer Jesus states, "Father, the hour has come; glorify Your Son, that the Son may glorify You, even as You gave Him authority over all flesh, that to all whom You have given Him, He may give eternal life" (John 17:1-2). As Jesus prays for his glorification he states that the Father has given him authority over all people so that he may give eternal life to those whom the Father has given him. The Father has given Jesus authority over all people so that he might give eternal life to some, and those people are the ones that the Father has unconditionally elected.[45] The Son glorifies the Father by giving eternal life to those whom the Father has elected, demonstrating the perfect unity of the Father and the Son in salvation. As Jesus continues to pray, he notes that he has manifested the Father's name to those whom the Father has given him out of the world, his disciples, (John 17:6), and he prays specifically for them that the Father would preserve them in their salvation (John 17:9-12).[46] He later states, however, that he also prays this prayer for all future believers (John 17:20), who again are the ones the Father has given him (John 17:24). As Ware states concerning the salvation of these future believers: "Just as the disciples become the disciples because the Father gives these ones to Jesus, so also all future believers come to believe in Christ through the message of the disciples because God has given these to his Son. Belief is necessary, to

---

44. Beasley-Murray, *John*, 174; Bruce, *Gospel of John*, 232–33; Carson, *Gospel of John*, 394–95; and Morris, *Gospel According to John*, 464–65.

45. Bruce, *Gospel of John*, 328–29; Carson, *Gospel of John*, 554–55; Morris, *Gospel According to John*, 335–37; Peterson, *Election and Free Will*, 64; and Ware, "Divine Election," 6.

46. Osborne asserts that apostasy is a valid possibility for believers because Judas, as one of the disciples, was lost (John 17:12). Therefore human action determines salvation just as much as God's sovereignty. Osborne, "Soteriology," 254. This assertion misses the point, however, that Jesus' high priestly prayer for the disciples does not include Judas. As Carson states, "It [v. 12] establishes that Jesus has been utterly faithful to the task assigned him, *viz.* to keep and protect those that the Father has given him (cf. notes on 6:37–38). Jesus' prayer for his disciples, in this context, therefore *excludes* Judas Iscariot, for otherwise one would have to conclude that Jesus failed in the responsibility that had been assigned him." Carson, *Gospel of John*, 563, emphasis the author's.

be sure, but those who believe are those given to Christ by the Father. The unconditional election of the Father, then, accounts for the subsequent faith and salvation of those to whom the Son grants eternal life."[47] Throughout this prayer Jesus consistently ties his redemptive work with the Father's redemptive will. Jesus only secures the salvation of those whom the Father has elected for salvation.

Paul emphasizes the unity of the Father and the Son in salvation just as strongly as John does, most clearly in Ephesians 1:3–14. God the Father is the source of all spiritual blessings in Christ (v. 3). The Father chose believers in Christ (v. 4), and he predestined believers to adoption through Jesus Christ (v. 5). It is in Christ that believers "have redemption through his blood, the forgiveness of our trespasses" (v. 7). It is in Christ that all things are summed up, "things in heaven and earth" (v. 10). Believers have obtained their inheritance in Christ, according to the Father's predestinating purpose (v. 11). These verses demonstrate that all the Father does to save his people he does through Christ, and all that Christ does to save his people he does according to the will of the Father. When it comes to the Father's plan of salvation, Jesus Christ is the "foundation, origin, and executor: all that is involved in election and its fruits depends on him."[48]

God's sovereignty in election, his special love for the elect, and the unity of the Father and the Son in salvation all indicate that Jesus Christ died on the cross to secure the salvation of the elect. Just as Christ died on the cross to accomplish the Father's general intentions in the atonement, so he died on the cross to accomplish the Father's particular, saving purposes in the atonement. We must not only understand why Jesus died on the cross to secure to secure the salvation of the elect, however, but also how he secured this salvation through his atoning work. In accomplishing the Father's particular intention, Christ sent forth the Holy Spirit to apply salvation to the elect. The Holy Spirit only applies the salvation that Christ accomplished through the atonement to the elect, and he does this only according to the will of the Father and the Son. As we will see in the following section, Christ's particular intention for the elect in the atonement is not only confirmed by his fulfillment of the Father's electing will, but also by the Holy Spirit's saving work of bringing people to Christ.

---

47. Ware, "Divine Election," 7.
48. Bruce, *Epistles to the Colossians*, 254–55.

SENDING THE HOLY SPIRIT TO SAVE THE ELECT

Jesus Christ, in fulfilling the Father's intentions for his atonement, accomplished several objective realities that only the elect subjectively experience. As the substitute for sinners (Isa 53:4–6; Col 2:14–15), he was a perfect sacrifice for sin (Eph 5:2; Heb 7:26–27; 9:11–15).[49] In this sacrifice Christ redeemed sinners to God, paying the full price for sin (Acts 20:28; Gal 3:13; Titus 2:14; 2 Pet 2:1; Rev 5:9), and achieved reconciliation between sinners and God, making peace where there once was enmity (Rom 5:10; 2 Cor 5:18–21; 1 Pet 3:18). He was the propitiation for sin (Rom 3:25; Heb 2:17; 1 John 2:2; 4:10), satisfying the just and holy wrath of God against the sin of humanity by being made sin himself so that sinners could be made righteous (2 Cor 5:21). While God intended for these objective realities to accomplish his general purposes in the atonement, he also intended for them to be subjectively applied to the elect, and only to the elect, in order to accomplish his particular purpose in the atonement. In working to fulfill this purpose, Jesus, on the basis of his atonement, sent the Holy Spirit to apply salvation to the elect.

Just as the Holy Spirit's work in the universal gospel call and common grace is evidence of God's general intentions in the atonement, so is his work in applying salvation only to the elect evidence of God's particular intention in the atonement.[50] This is because all that the Holy Spirit does in salvation he does according to the Father's will and on the basis of Christ's atonement.[51] Ephesians 1:3–14 not only describes the unity of the Father and the Son in salvation, but it also describes the Holy Spirit's saving work in unity with the Father and the Son. The Holy Spirit is the one who determines the character of the blessings that the Father bestows through Christ (v. 3).[52] He seals those whom the Father has chosen and the Son has redeemed (v. 13).

---

49. For a detailed explanation of Christ's sacrificial work on the cross, see Letham, *The Work of Christ*, 132–39; Schreiner, "Penal Substitution View," 82–93; and Stott, *Cross of Christ*, 133–62.

50. The Holy Spirit will be referred to using masculine pronouns, as the church has traditionally done. For a defense of the Spirit's masculinity, see Bloesch, *The Holy Spirit*, 60–62.

51. This assertion is contrary to the work of many contemporary theologians who attempt to separate the Spirit's mission from that of Christ's in order to argue for a more inclusive salvation, or a salvation wrought by the Spirit without the gospel of Christ. E.g., Pinnock, *The Flame of Love*; idem, *A Wideness in God's Mercy*; Kärkkäinen, *Pneumatology*; Mangum, "Is There a Reformed Way," 125–34; Sanders, *No Other Name*; and Tiessen, *Who Can Be Saved?*. As the remainder of this chapter will demonstrate, the Spirit's saving work is inseparable from Christ's atonement and the good news of this atonement in the gospel.

52. O'Brien, *Letter to the Ephesians*, 95.

In sealing believers the Holy Spirit serves as a "pledge of our inheritance" (v. 14), guaranteeing Christians' eternal life in Christ. These verses present the Holy Spirit as the one who applies the salvation that the Father planned and the Son accomplished.

The rest of the New Testament also clearly presents the unity of the Spirit with the Father and the Son's saving work. The Holy Spirit's mission, as the Father (John 14:26) and the Son (John 15:26) both send him forth, is to work out salvation in light of the Father's intentions and the Son's accomplishments.[53] The Holy Spirit freely submits himself to carry out the will of the Father and the will of the Son, which are identical (John 6:38). As John Walvoord states, "As the Son is always obedient to the Father, so the Spirit is always obedient to the Father and the Son. This must not be taken to imply any inferiority of the Holy Spirit as to His person, but rather a willing subordination in keeping with His person and the unity of purpose of the Godhead. This subordination of the Holy Spirit is essential to all His ministry and characterizes all that is revealed."[54] The New Testament repeatedly describes the Spirit as the Spirit of the Father (Matt 10:20; Luke 11:13; 1 John 4:2) and the Spirit of the Son (Gal 4:6), or the Spirit of Christ (Rom 8:9; Phil 1:19; 1 Pet 1:11). As the Spirit of Christ, the Spirit's saving work is to unite the believer with Christ and everything that Christ secured for the believer in the atonement. Just as the Father's plan of salvation culminates in Christ and is accomplished through Christ, so the Holy Spirit's application of salvation is inseparably tied to the work and mission of Christ.[55]

Further strengthening the close connection between Christ's atonement and the Spirit's application of the atonement to the elect is that the Spirit now works in the world the way that he does only after and because of Christ's death and resurrection (John 7:39; 16:7; Acts 2:33). Acts 2:33

---

53. At the very least, John 14:26 and 15:26 indicate that the Father and the Son sent forth the Holy Spirit economically, which likely means that the Spirit proceeds from both the Father and the Son eternally as well. This is an affirmation of the *Filioque*. As Sinclair Ferguson states, "The double procession doctrine appears to provide a twofold theological advantage. It underlines the principle that God is in his very being what he reveals himself to be, so that the economic Trinity is a true, however accommodated, reflection of the ontological Trinity. It also indicates a relationship between the Son and the Spirit which is more than economical." Ferguson, *The Holy Spirit*, 75–76. We should note, however, that one's opinion on the *Filioque* does not necessarily determine the relationship between the Son and the Spirit. Rejecting the *Filioque* does not entail the separation of the Son and the Spirit's saving work. There are other biblical and theological reasons grounds for the Son and the Spirit's unity. See Cole, *He Who Gives Life*, 199–202.

54. Walvoord, *The Holy Spirit*, 31.

55. Bloesch, *The Holy Spirit*, 285; and Wellum, "An Evaluation of the Son–Spirit Relation," 17.

states, "Therefore having been exalted to the right hand of God, and having received from the Father the promise of the Holy Spirit, He has poured forth this which you both see and hear." In this verse Peter refers to Pentecost, and Jesus' role in sending forth the Spirit. Bruce Ware makes this clear, "Peter could simply have said that the Father poured forth the Spirit as he had long ago promised, and this would have been accurate. But he states with greater precision and nuance just how Jesus also figures into the sending of the Spirit. The Spirit comes as the Father sends him, to be sure. But the Spirit comes as the Father *first* gives the Spirit to the Son, and *then* as the Son 'has poured out this [i.e., the Spirit] that you yourselves are seeing and hearing.'"[56] Jesus, because he died for the sins of humanity on the cross and rose from the dead, now sits at the right hand of the Father, and therefore he pours forth the Holy Spirit not only to take the gospel message and common grace to the world, but so that the Spirit can do his saving work.

All that Christ accomplished in the atonement for the elect the Spirit now works to apply. As Bruce Demarest states, the Holy Spirit "applies, makes effective, and preserves the redemption Christ bought to those who believe."[57] That Christ's particular intention in the atonement was to secure and make certain the salvation of the elect is seen through every aspect of the Holy Spirit's saving work, what the Bible teaches us about the subjective application of the cross. On the basis of the atonement, the Spirit applies salvation to the elect through effectual calling, regeneration, conversion, justification, indwelling the believer, baptism in the Spirit, sanctification, preservation and perseverance, and glorification. These actions are all part of the Holy Spirit's particular application of the Son's atonement, which is ultimately all that is involved in soteriology. All believers, God's elect, are saved by the work of the Holy Spirit, through the work of Christ, and on account of the Father's initiative.

Effectual Calling

The Holy Spirit begins to apply Christ's atonement to the elect by effectually calling them to believe in the gospel. Effectual calling is the Spirit's work that causes an unbeliever who is dead in his sin (1 Cor 2:14; Eph 2:1) to understand the true meaning of the gospel of Jesus Christ. This call can be defined as "the Spirit's call to sinners to hear and to believe the gospel, rendered effectual by his supernatural enlivening work, or as the Spirit's provision of grace resulting in saving faith, rendered irresistible against all blindness,

---

56. Ware, *Father, Son, and Holy Spirit*, 97, emphasis the author's.
57. Demarest, *Cross and Salvation*, 44.

hardness, and unbelief."[58] It is always issued through the proclamation of the gospel (2 Thess 2:14), but it is distinct from the general invitation of the gospel (e.g., Isa 45:22; Matt 11:28), which goes out to all people, because it always results in salvation.[59] Effectual calling is therefore a work of the Holy Spirit that is specifically for the elect.[60]

This call is articulated perhaps most clearly in Romans 8:28–30, although it is present in a myriad of Scriptures (Luke 14:23; John 6:44; Rom 1:7; 11:29; 1 Cor 1:9, 22–24; Eph 1:18; Phil 3:14; 1 Thess 2:12; 2 Thess 2:14; 2 Tim 1:9; Heb 3:1; 2 Pet 1:10). Romans 8:28 states, "And we know that God causes all things to work together for good to those who love God, to those who are called according to His purpose." Romans 8:30 expounds upon the idea of calling in this verse by clarifying that the called are the same ones who are predestined, justified, and glorified. Thomas Schreiner comments on the meaning of "calling" in this passage:

> "Calling" (*kletos*), must be understood as effectual. It is not merely an invitation that human beings can reject, but it is a summons that overcomes human resistance and effectually persuades them to say yes to God. This definition of "calling" is evident from Rom. 8:30, for there Paul says that "those whom he called (*ekalesen*) he also justified." That text does not say that "some" of those called were justified. It fuses the called and justified together so that those who have experienced calling have also inevitably received the blessing of justification. Now if all those who are called are also justified, then calling must be effectual and must create faith, for "all" those who are called are justified and justification cannot occur without faith (3:21–22, 28; 5:1).[61]

The inseparable relationship between effectual calling, predestination, justification, and the atonement is strengthened when one realizes that the Holy Spirit only effectually calls those whom the Father has given to the Son (John 6:37, 39; 17:2, 6, 9, 12, 24), and that these alone are the ones who

---

58. Ware, "Effectual Calling and Grace," 204.

59. Ibid., 210–11.

60. Cole helpfully points out that there is little exegetical evidence for the Spirit's role in effectual calling. There is a strong theological argument to be made, however, that the work of effectual calling is appropriately attributed to the Spirit as he is the one who works through all stages of salvation to apply that salvation. Cole, *He Who Gives Life*, 215. There is good reason, therefore, to begin the description of the Holy Spirit's application of Christ atonement in salvation with the work of effectual calling.

61. Schreiner, *Romans*, 450–51.

believe and receive eternal life (John 6:40). Only these called ones will be with Jesus forever in glory (John 17:24).

Effectual calling is only possible because Christ, in securing the salvation of the elect in the atonement, sent the Holy Spirit to apply salvation only to those whom the Father had given him. The moral influence theory of the atonement helps us ground the Spirit's drawing of the elect in the atonement itself by emphasizing the subjective impact of the cross.[62] While the moral influence theory is often used to deny an objective accomplishment in the atonement, when seen in light of penal substitution it does highlight an important biblical truth.[63] God does demonstrate his love for humanity in the atonement and expects people to be moved by it and subsequently live by his example (Eph 5:1–2; Phil 2:3–8; 1 Pet 2:21; Heb 12:2). We saw in Chapter 3 that God intends for all people to see the depths and heights of his love in the atonement, but God also effectually intends to move the elect to accept his love and believe in the gospel. John Hammett explains, "Not all respond to the cross in the same way. While it could be argued that the variety of responses is due to human choice, it can also be maintained that the subjective moral influence of the cross is directed by God toward a particular group. By God's intention, the cross does compel a responsive love in them toward the God that first loved them. It is effectual in drawing forth a response of faith and repentance."[64] This clarifies why some see the cross as foolishness and some see it as the power and wisdom of God (1 Cor 1:22–24). Those who respond to the message of the gospel with faith and repentance through the work of the Holy Spirit demonstrate that they are the elect of God (1 Thess 1:4–5). As Hammett states, "Such a response is not universal, but particular."[65]

---

62. The moral influence theory of the atonement is most commonly seen as originating with Peter Abelard in the twelfth century, and more recent proponents include Friedrich Schleiermacher, Horace Bushnell, Hastings Rashdall, and Albrecht Ritschl. This view of the atonement is completely subjective. The atonement saves people by moving them to love others in the same way that Christ loved humanity on the cross. God then saves people because they repent and believe in him as they are moved by Christ's sacrifice. The theory falters, however, in not taking sin seriously and therefore in denying the objective penal substitutionary atonement of Christ. Christ's atonement is only a revelation of God's love (and justice) because it objectively deals with sin, and because it makes salvation available to sinners who do not deserve it. See Eddy and Beilby, "The Atonement," 19–20; and McDonald, *The Atonement*, 174–80.

63. John Stott is an example of someone who recognizes the truth of the moral influence theory when grounded in an objective penal substitutionary atonement. Stott, *Cross of Christ*, 212–19.

64. Hammett, "Multiple Intentions," forthcoming.

65. Ibid.

In fulfilling the directive from the Father and the accomplishment of the Son, the Holy Spirit awakens a person's faith so that she can be united with Christ and experience the full scope and breadth of salvation. Apart from the Spirit's work of effectual calling sinners would be unable to put their faith and trust in the gospel and the Son's accomplishment of salvation in the atonement would never come to fruition in the lives of believers. Bruce makes this clear, "None can come to Christ in faith but those who are persuaded and enabled to do so by the Spirit; but all these will come, drawn by the irresistible grace of heavenly love, and none who comes is rejected."[66]

Regeneration, Conversion, and Justification

While there are some theologians who understand effectual calling and regeneration as synonymous, they can logically, if not chronologically, be considered as two aspects of the Holy Spirit's saving work.[67] Regeneration is "that work of the Spirit at conversion that renews the heart and life (the inner self), thus restoring the person's intellectual, volitional, moral, emotional, and relational capacities to know, love, and serve God."[68] Regeneration is transformational (2 Cor 5:17), it is solely a work of God (Titus 3:5), and it takes place in a person's union with Christ. In the seminal passage in Scripture on regeneration Jesus tells Nicodemus that he must be born of the Spirit in order to see the Kingdom of God (John 3:3–8).[69] Titus 3:5 also makes it clear that God regenerates believers through the Holy Spirit. It states, "He saved us, not on the basis of deeds which we have done in righteousness, but according to His mercy, by the washing of regeneration and renewing by the Holy Spirit." As D. Edmond Hiebert remarks concerning this verse, "This process of renewal in the believer is the work of the Holy Spirit. He alone can produce a new nature that finds active expression in an entirely new manner of life."[70] Furthermore, Titus 3:6 states, "whom He poured out upon us richly through Jesus Christ our Savior," describing the Holy Spirit. The basis of the Holy Spirit's regenerating work is Jesus Christ's work as Savior, or the atonement. The Holy Spirit only regenerates believers because Christ has secured their salvation through his death on the cross.

66. Bruce, *Gospel of John*, 164.

67. For examples of theologians who see regeneration and effectual calling as synonymous, see Hoekema, *Saved by Grace*, 106; and Strong, *Systematic Theology*, 793.

68. Demarest, *Cross and Salvation*, 293.

69. For a defense of the view that Jesus is referring to regeneration in John 3:3–8, see Carson, *Gospel of John*, 187–98.

70. Hiebert, *Titus*, 446.

Regeneration always takes place simultaneously with conversion, which is "the human being's response to God's offer of salvation and approach to the human."[71] Conversion is made up of repentance and faith, or turning away from sin and turning toward God. Although conversion is a conscientious human decision in response to the gospel, it too is presented in Scripture as a work of the Holy Spirit. This is because conversion first cannot take place without effectual calling, and second because it always takes place with regeneration. It is only God who can open blind eyes and awaken dead hearts to repent of sin and put faith in the gospel of Christ (2 Cor 4:4–6). As Bruce Ware states, "Our regeneration and conversion, moving us to repent of sin and trust in Christ, is the work of the Spirit. The Spirit must awaken our hearts to see the beauty of Christ, fall before him, and put our hope and trust in him. God gets all the glory in our conversion. And how is Jesus glorified in this? The Spirit awakens our dead hearts and opens our blind eyes to see Jesus!"[72]

Reinforcing the close connection between regeneration, conversion, and the atonement is the truth that saving faith is a gift from God to the believer, enabling him to believe in Christ, which Christ in his atonement procured only for the elect. Several verses in Scripture point in this direction. First John 5:1a states, "Whoever believes that Jesus is the Christ is born of God." The verb translated "is born of God" (*gegennetai*) is a perfect passive indicative, denoting a past action that continues into the present. This indicates that the one who has been regenerated believes, or that faith is a result of regeneration (cf. John 1:12–13, which teaches the same truth). Acts 13:48 bases faith upon election, while John 6:65 states that people can only come to God as the Father enables them. Philippians 1:29 states that it is has been given to believers to believe on Christ, indicating that believing in Christ is a gracious gift from God.[73] Ephesians 2:8 states that the entire act of salvation, including faith, is the gift of God.[74] Because the Holy Spirit only bestows faith upon the elect, faith must have been secured for the believer by the atonement just as all the other saving works of the Holy Spirit were secured by the atonement.[75]

---

71. Erickson, *Christian Theology*, 955.
72. Ware, *Father, Son, and Holy Spirit*, 121–22.
73. Hansen, *The Letter to the Philippians*, 102.
74. O'Brien, *The Letter to the Ephesians*, 174–76.
75. See Berkhof, *Systematic Theology*, 395; Demarest, *Cross and Salvation*, 262–63; Hoekema, *Saved by Grace*, 143–46; and Ware, "Divine Election," 19–22. It should be noted, however, that the reality of faith as a gift of God procured in the atonement does not demand particular redemption, as many advocates of particular redemption assert (see Chapter 3). Many evangelicals deny that faith is a gift of God for the elect, and insist

In addition to conversion, justification is also a result of the faith that the Holy Spirit gives the believer (Rom 3:26, 28; 5:1; Gal 2:16). It occurs in conjunction with regeneration and conversion in that, having received new life, the believer is now declared righteous in God's sight, his sin being forgiven.[76] Justification is also intimately related to effectual calling, as Romans 8:30 makes clear. While Scripture repeatedly stresses that justification is something that Christ accomplished and that we are only justified on the basis of Christ's atonement (Rom 3:21–30), the Holy Spirit is the one who energizes the faith by which Christians are justified. First Corinthians 6:11 explains this: "Such were some of you; but you were washed, but you were sanctified, but you were justified in the name of the Lord Jesus Christ and in the Spirit of our God."[77] The Spirit's work in justification is to give believers their justifying faith in the Lord Jesus Christ, and the Spirit does this because Christ secured their salvation in his atonement.

Indwelling and Filling

As the Holy Spirit regenerates, converts, and justifies a person, he also indwells him. Although the Holy Spirit's indwelling actually takes place at the same time as his other saving work, it is a distinct ministry of the Holy Spirit to the believer (Rom 8:9, 11; 1 Cor 6:19–20; 2 Cor 5:5; Gal 4:6; 1 John 4:13). The purpose of the Spirit's indwelling is to denote the Holy Spirit's abiding presence with the believer. The Spirit's indwelling is not necessarily experiential, but is meant to result in the filling of the Holy Spirit, and therefore in sanctification.[78] The indwelling of the Spirit in this present age is a result of Christ's atonement. John 7:39 makes this plain when it states, "But this He spoke of the Spirit, whom those who believed in Him were to receive; for the Spirit was not yet *given*, because Jesus was not yet glorified" (cf. John 14:17;

---

that all people are capable of believing the gospel, otherwise the universal gospel call is misleading. They argue that if faith is a gift, then people cannot be held responsible for believing or not believing the gospel. E.g., Geisler, *Chosen But Free*, 188–99; López, "Is Faith a Gift," 259–76; and Miethe, "The Universal Power of the Atonement," 76–77. These arguments fail to understand the seriousness of sin, a person's responsibility for their own sin, God's sovereignty in salvation, and the biblical evidence for faith as a gift.

76. Grudem, *Systematic Theology*, 722.

77. While the NASB here has "in the Spirit of our God," it is possible that the preposition "in" (*en*) could be better translated as "by." This would indicate that the Spirit is also the agent of justification, and would create an even stronger relationship between the work of the Holy Spirit and justification. Thiselton, *The First Epistle to the Corinthians*, 455.

78. Walvoord, *The Holy Spirit*, 155–56.

16:7).[79] It is only as a result of Christ's glorification in the atonement and the resurrection that the Holy Spirit now indwells believers. The Spirit's indwelling, just like effectual calling, regeneration, conversion, and justification, is based upon Christ's particular intention in the atonement for the elect.

The Holy Spirit's filling the believer is a result of his indwelling the believer.[80] Being filled with the Spirit does not take place once and for all, but is something that can and should be repeated, which distinguishes the filling of the Spirit from indwelling and baptism in the Spirit, because those are one-time events. There are several references to believers being filled with the Spirit throughout the book of Acts (Acts 2:4; 4:8; 6:3; 7:55; 11:24; 13:9, 52). Paul also commands believers to be filled with the Spirit in Ephesians 5:18, at least implying that some believers are not filled with the Holy Spirit at points in their lives.[81] The Holy Spirit's filling is "the source of all vital experience in the life of the Christian," and is therefore essential for the believer's sanctification and his empowerment for witness and service.[82] Being filled with the Spirit presupposes knowledge of Christ and his work, as evidence of this filling is seen within the church in "making melody to the Lord," "giving thanks for all things in the name of the Lord Jesus Christ," and being subject to one another "in the fear of Christ" (Eph 5:18–21). The Holy Spirit's filling for empowerment also requires knowledge of the gospel, as it often results in the preaching of the gospel (Acts 2:4; 4:31; 13:9–10).[83] As a result of the Spirit's indwelling and as a part of the Spirit's work of

---

79. Old Testament saints were not indwelt by the Spirit, because the Spirit does this work only in the New Testament age. James Hamilton summarizes the teaching of John 7:37–39 concerning the Spirit's indwelling. "First, the Old Testament promises that in the last days a Spirit-anointed Messiah will come, and also that in the last days the people of God will receive the Spirit. Second, John argues that Jesus is the Spirit-anointed Messiah who ushers in the last days. Third, John adds to the Old Testament expectation of the reception of the Spirit that Jesus must be glorified before believers receive the Spirit. Therefore, believers who lived prior to the glorification of Jesus were not indwelt by the Spirit." Hamilton, Jr., *God's Indwelling Presence*, 120.

80. Certain Old Testament saints were periodically filled by the Holy Spirit for specific purposes (Gen 41:38; Exod 28:3; 31:3; 35:30–35; Num 11:17, 25; 27:18; Judg 3:10; 6:34; 1 Sam 10:9–10; 16:13; Dan 4:8; 5:11–14; 6:3), but all New Testament believers are permanently indwelt by the Holy Spirit and then continually filled by the Holy Spirit on the basis of that indwelling. See Walvoord, *The Holy Spirit*, 155–56.

81. Some understand the command in Eph 5:18 to be filled with the Spirit as referring to the congregation and not to the individual. Therefore this passage is not about sanctification or empowerment, but rather about ecclesiology. See Cole, *He Who Gives Life*, 243–44; and Köstenberger, "What Does It Mean," 233–34.

82. Walvoord, *The Holy Spirit*, 189.

83. Cole, *He Who Gives Life*, 218.

sanctification, being filled with the Spirit is also a result of Christ's particular intentions in the atonement.

Baptism into the Body of Christ

Baptism in the Holy Spirit is concurrent with all of the other activities of the Spirit at the moment of salvation. This assertion is disputed within evangelicalism, though, due to the different ways that people interpret their experience in light of biblical concepts.[84] When Holy Spirit baptism is seen in light of New Testament teaching, however, it seems to be limited to one particular experience, which every believer experiences at the moment of his or her salvation. There are seven verses in the New Testament that mention Spirit baptism. Five of these verses (Matt 3:11; Mark 1:8; Luke 3:16; John 1:33; Acts 1:5) refer to a time in the future when Jesus is going to baptize with the Holy Spirit, with Acts 1:5 indicating a time only a few days away. In Acts 11:16, Peter uses the phrase "baptized with the Holy Spirit" to explain Cornelius' conversion, referring to something that had already taken place.[85] The one event that fits the reference of all these verses is clearly Pentecost, where the Holy Spirit was poured out upon the disciples (Acts 2:4).[86] Acts 2:33 indicates that Jesus received the promise of the Holy Spirit from the Father as a result of his exaltation, and therefore he "poured out" the Holy Spirit upon the church at Pentecost. The seventh reference is 1 Corinthians 12:13, where Paul refers to a past event that all of his readers, who were believers, had experienced.[87] Paul is referring to the baptism of the Holy Spirit that marks every believer's entry into the body of Christ. At the time of their conversion, believers subjectively experience what objectively took place once and for all at Pentecost due to the atonement and resurrection of Jesus Christ: the baptism of the Holy Spirit.[88]

Jesus Christ baptizes believers in the Holy Spirit in order to bring them into his body, and the Holy Spirit, as he is poured out on believers, brings believers into Christ's body by uniting them with Christ.[89] Union with

---

84. E.g., see the five different perspectives on Spirit baptism in Brand, *Perspectives on Spirit Baptism* or Macchia, *Baptized in the Spirit*.

85. Kaiser, Jr., "A Reformed Perspective," 20.

86. Ibid., 20–21; and Stott, *Baptism and Fullness*, 19–31, 38.

87. Ibid., 39.

88. Cole, *He Who Gives Life*, 214; and Stott, *Baptism and Fullness*, 43.

89. This understanding implies a consistent rendering of the preposition *en* in the seven previously noted verses as "in" or "with," not "by." See Kaiser, Jr., "A Reformed Perspective," 21; and Stott, *Baptism and Fullness*, 38–43.

Christ is an over-arching soteriological concept. It is the concept under which John Calvin discusses the whole of his soteriology, and he describes it as the work of the Holy Spirit based upon what Christ has accomplished on the cross.[90] Union with Christ denotes the truth that all believers are in Christ (John 15:4; 1 Cor 15:22; 2 Cor 5:17; 12:2; Gal 3:28; Eph 1:4; Phil 3:9; 1 Thess 4:16; 1 John 4:13) and that Christ is in all believers (Rom 8:10; 2 Cor 13:5; Eph 3:17; Gal 2:20; Col 1:27). As John Murray remarks, "We need to appreciate far more than we have been wont to the close interdependence of Christ and the Holy Spirit in the operations of saving grace. The Holy Spirit is the Spirit of Christ; the Spirit is the Spirit of the Lord and Christ is the Lord of the Spirit (cf. Rom 8:9; 2 Cor 3:18; 1 Pet 1:11). Christ dwells in us if his Spirit dwells in us, and he dwells in us by the Spirit."[91] It is only through being united with Christ by the Holy Spirit that believers can then experience regeneration, justification, sanctification, preservation, and glorification. As with all of these other saving works, baptism in the Holy Spirit and one's subsequent union with Christ are only possible because of Christ's work in securing the salvation of the elect in his atonement.

Sanctification, Preservation, and Perseverance

Sanctification only takes place as the Holy Spirit unites believers with Christ. It is "that gracious operation of the Holy Spirit, involving our reasonable participation, by which he delivers us from the pollution of sin, renews our entire nature according to the image of God, and enables us to live lives that are pleasing to him."[92] There are two aspects to sanctification, definite (or positional) and progressive. Definite sanctification takes place at the moment of a believer's salvation (simultaneously with regeneration, justification, etc.), and is the believer's "being set aside for God's possession and declared holy by faith in Christ's justifying work."[93] We see definite sanctification in 1 Corinthians 1:2, where Paul addresses believers in Corinth as those who were already sanctified in Christ Jesus, and in 1 Corinthians 6:11, where Paul describes sanctification as a completed act akin to justification, done in the name of the Lord Jesus Christ by the Holy Spirit.

It is in progressive sanctification that the Holy Spirit makes the redemption that Christ secured on the cross for the elect effective in their lives. He does this by conforming believers to the image of Christ (Rom

---

90. Calvin, *Institutes of the Christian Religion*, 3.1.1.
91. Murray, *Redemption Accomplished and Applied*, 166.
92. Hoekema, *Saved by Grace*, 192.
93. Demarest, *Cross and Salvation*, 407.

The Particular Intentions of the Atonement   149

8:29). Although progressive sanctification is in Christ, it is a work that Scripture repeatedly attributes to the Holy Spirit. God chose believers for salvation "through the sanctification of the Spirit" (2 Thess 2:13). Believers only become acceptable to God through the sanctification of the Spirit (Rom 15:16). In order to be holy, believers are commanded to walk in the Spirit (Gal 5:16, 25). The Spirit continually works to produce his fruit, the characteristics of Christ, in those whom he indwells and who walk in him (Gal 5:22–23). The Holy Spirit continually fills believers in order that they might be equipped for service (Eph 5:18), giving them spiritual gifts to accomplish the tasks involved with ministering to others (1 Cor 12–14). The Spirit is the one who leads believers to live for God and to grow in righteousness (Phil 2:12–13). Most often, the Spirit sanctifies believers through Scripture, as he inspired the Scriptures for the salvation and edification of believers (2 Tim 3:16–17), and he presently illuminates Scripture to believers so that they can understand and apply them to their contemporary situation (1 Cor 2:10–16). The Holy Spirit's work of inspiring and illuminating Scripture is also inseparably related to the person and work of Jesus Christ, for Jesus Christ is the Word (John 1:1) whose person and work is the central message of Scripture.[94] As an outgrowth of redemption and regeneration, the Holy Spirit's sanctifying work is only possible because Christ secured the salvation of the elect in the atonement.

As the Holy Spirit sanctifies believers, leading them to grow in righteousness, he also preserves them in faith, causing them to persevere and endure in Christ until the end of their lives. The Spirit does this in a number of ways. First, the Holy Spirit seals all believers unto the day of redemption, guaranteeing their inheritance with Christ (Eph 1:13; 4:30). The Holy Spirit is also the believer's *arrabon* (pledge) of future blessing with God (2 Cor 1:22; 5:5; Eph 1:14). As Wayne Grudem states, "When God gave us the Holy Spirit within, he committed himself to give all the future blessing of eternal life and a great reward in heaven with him. . . . All who have the Holy Spirit within them, all who are truly born again, have God's unchanging promise and guarantee that the inheritance of eternal life in heaven will certainly be theirs."[95]

Besides sealing believers, the Holy Spirit also causes believers to persevere by having them consciously reflect on Christ's atoning work on the cross. The Bible uses the sacrificial atonement of Christ as an example to the believer of how she ought to live the Christian life. In Ephesians 5:2 Paul instructs believers to walk in love just as Christ loved them, and the way that

---

94. Cole, *He Who Gives Life*, 259–77.
95. Grudem, *Systematic Theology*, 791.

Christ loved them was by giving himself up to God on the cross. Hebrews 12:1–3 encourages believers to persevere, to "run the race," by setting their eyes upon Jesus. What is pointed out about Jesus in these verses, however, is the way in which he endured the cross and the hostility of sinners against him. First Peter 2:21–25 is another passage where the Bible instructs believers to endure in their walk with God by contemplating the way in which Christ suffered his atoning death. Christ's atonement not only secured the salvation of the elect, but it serves as a concrete example of how believers should love and obey God.

A final way the Holy Spirit causes believers to persevere is by assuring them of their right standing before God in Christ. The Holy Spirit does this as believers live in him, resisting the flesh, obeying God, and advancing in righteousness (Rom 8:5–11).[96] He also does this by bearing witness with believers that they are the children of God. Romans 8:16 states that "The Spirit Himself testifies with our spirit that we are children of God." This is a subjective and internal witness of the Spirit whereby he convinces believers of their right standing before God, that God is their Father.[97] The Holy Spirit continually works to make certain that all whom Christ secured salvation for on the cross are never lost, and that they are brought to glorification (cf. Rom 8:28–30).

Glorification

The present life of the Christian in salvation is but a foretaste of the glory to come. Those who are called, regenerated, converted, justified, indwelt, filled, baptized in the Spirit, united to Christ, sanctified, adopted, and preserved through perseverance will one day be glorified, as the unbreakable chain of Romans 8:28–30 indicates. This is the hope of all Christians (Rom 5:2; 2 Thess 2:14; 1 Pet 5:4). The Holy Spirit guarantees the future glorification of all believers. He ensures that Jesus will never lose any of the ones whom the Father has given to him (John 6:37–40; 10:28–29). As Bruce Demarest states, "Our pilgrimage will issue in a marvelous consummation in which the vestiges of the old self are eradicated and the new self is perfectly realized. Glorification is the bringing to a triumphant conclusion our redemption in Christ. It is the final realization of our unfolding salvation in Christ (Rom 13:11: 1 Pet 1:5)."[98]

---

96. Carson, "Reflections on Assurance," 258–59.
97. Ramm, *The Witness of the Spirit*, 49–57.
98. Demarest, *Cross and Salvation*, 468.

One of the primary aspects of believers' glorification is their resurrection. Believers only experience the resurrection because of what Christ did on the cross. First Corinthians 15:21–22 describes how Christ reversed the order of death that Adam instituted after he sinned. The resurrection and transformation of believers' bodies is a consequence of Christ's exaltation (1 Cor 15:35–50). First Corinthians 15:51 explains that all who are in Christ will be changed, meaning that they will receive a new body. All who receive a new body in Christ, however, do so in the power of the Holy Spirit. Believers will be raised by the Spirit (Rom 8:11) and will receive a Spiritual body (1 Cor 15:44), after the likeness of Jesus Christ (1 John 3:2).[99] Even now, the Holy Spirit causes believers to long for their resurrection bodies (Rom 8:23).

Glorification is the realization of all of the blessings of salvation that were accomplished once and for all in the atonement. All who have the Spirit and who are therefore in Christ can look forward to the redemption of their bodies (Rom 8:23), and to their inheritance that will never fade away or perish (1 Pet 1:3–5). The glorification of the believer includes her ultimate vindication before God at the last judgment, the future manifestation of an already accomplished justification (Rom 5:9–10). It includes a fullness of knowledge that comes with seeing Christ face to face (1 Cor 13:12; 1 John 3:2). Glorified believers will reign with Christ in his eternal kingdom (1 Cor 6:2; Rev 22:3). They will eternally worship God the Father and the Lamb of God (Rev 21:22; 22:3). In glorification the believer is spiritually and morally perfected; freed from sin, both in experience and in nature (Col 1:11; 1 Thess 3:13; Jude 24). Ultimately, all believers will be fully conformed to the image of their Savior, Jesus Christ (Rom 8:29).[100] Being glorified, all believers will dwell together with God in the new heavens and new earth forever (John 14:2–3; Rev 3:12). Glorification is the culmination of the Father's particular, salvific intentions for the elect, in which the Spirit saves all whom the Son sent him to save on the basis of his atonement.

CONCLUSION

The particular intention of the atonement is to secure the salvation of the elect. We discern this particular intention from what the Bible teaches us about God's sovereignty throughout salvation, God's special love for the

---

99. A spiritual body is one that is "consistent with the character and activity of the Holy Spirit . . . completely subject to the will of the Holy Spirit and responsive to the Holy Spirit's guidance." Grudem, *Systematic Theology*, 832.

100. Demarest, *Cross and Salvation*, 473–74; and Erickson, *Christian Theology*, 1010–11.

elect, and the unity of the Father and the Son in purposing to save the elect. The Bible clearly presents both the Father's love and the Son's love toward the elect as unique and particular, resulting in their salvation. Out of this particular love the Father unconditionally elects certain people to be saved before the foundation of the world, based only on his sovereign pleasure. The Father's act of unconditional election is absolutely necessary if anyone is to be saved, because all people are unable to do anything to save themselves. The Father sent the Son to accomplish salvation through his atonement for the sins of the world. In doing so, the Father intended for the Son to not only accomplish salvation by paying for all sin, but to secure the salvation of the elect. The Son did this in his atonement because his saving will is completely in line with the Father's saving will.

The Son secured the salvation of the elect by sending forth the Holy Spirit to apply the salvific benefits of the atonement only to the elect. The Holy Spirit, as the Spirit of Christ, only saves those whom Christ intends for him to save, and those are the same people whom the Father elected. The Holy Spirit applies Christ's atonement through effectual calling, regeneration, conversion, justification, indwelling the believer, baptism in the Spirit, sanctification, preservation and perseverance, and glorification. These benefits of the atonement were intended only for the elect, and the elect are the only ones who experience them. Everything related to salvation has been planned by the Father, accomplished by the Son, and applied (or will be applied) by the Spirit.

This particular intention of the atonement makes up the particular aspect of the multi-intentioned view of the extent of the atonement. Christ's payment for sin did not only accomplish God's general intentions in the atonement, but it also accomplished God's particular intentions. The Holy Spirit not only goes forth to accomplish God's general intentions in the atonement, but he also goes forth to save the elect. The atonement was not exclusively general or exclusively particular; it was both general and particular. God's plan, as the overarching biblical narrative describes, not only encompasses the elect, but also encompasses all of his creation.[101] Only the multi-intentioned view is able to account for both God's general and particular intentions for the atonement. These intentions are not contradictory, but instead are part of God's one plan to fully display his glory before all that he has created.

---

101. For a defense of basing one's view of the extent of the atonement on God's plan for all of his creation as it is described in the biblical narrative, see Nelson, "The Design, Nature, and Extent of the Atonement," 118–20.

CHAPTER 6

Conclusion

THE VALIDITY OF THE MULTI-INTENTIONED VIEW

THE MULTI-INTENTIONED VIEW HOLDS that God the Father, in sending his Son to die on the cross, had both particular and general intentions for the atonement. In accordance with the Father's will, the Son then paid for the sin of all people in the atonement in order to fulfill these multiple intentions. Based upon the Son's atoning death on the cross, the Spirit then works to apply the atonement in both particular and in general ways. By recognizing multiple intentions in the atonement, the multi-intentioned view makes better sense of Scripture than the traditional positions of particular redemption or unlimited atonement, both of which only focus on one intention in the atonement. Throughout this book we have demonstrated the theological and biblical validity of the multi-intentioned view by establishing its coherence, comprehensiveness, consistency, and adequacy.

Chapters 3–5 established the coherency of the multi-intentioned view by explaining how it accurately portrays the Bible's teaching on the extent of the atonement. Chapter 3 laid the foundation for the multi-intentioned view by demonstrating the biblical and theological basis for understanding the atonement as a penal substitutionary payment for the sins of all people, elect and nonelect. We found that Isaiah 53:4–6; John 1:29; 3:16–17; 4:42; 6:51; 12:46–47; 2 Corinthians 5:14–15, 18–21; 1 Timothy 2:4–6, 4:10; Titus 2:11; Hebrews 2:9; 2 Peter 2:1; 1 John 2:2; and 4:14 all teach that Christ died for the sins of all people. Interpretations of these verses that deny this truth were found to be wanting, either for linguistic, contextual, or theological reasons. These verses teach that Christ's atoning death on the cross was an objective sacrifice for all sin. Christ suffered for the sins of all people, he reconciled all people, he redeemed all people, and he propitiated the wrath of God against all people. This does not mean, however, that all people are saved. The Bible differentiates between the objective nature of Christ's atonement for all people and the subjective appropriation of Christ's atonement by those who believe. It is only the latter group of people, the elect, who experience salvation on the basis of Christ's atonement and by the Holy Spirit's particular saving work in their lives.

The Bible teaches that Christ did not pay for the sin of all people with the intention of securing the salvation of all people, but that he did so for different purposes. Chapter 4 established the biblical and theological basis for the general intentions of the atonement. The general intentions of the atonement were to make the universal gospel call possible, to make common grace (and not only salvific grace) possible, to provide additional condemnation to those who reject the gospel, to serve as the supreme revelation of God's character, and to make Christ's cosmic triumph over all sin possible. The Scriptures make it clear that each one of these intentions is accomplished only on the basis of the atonement. Furthermore, Chapter 4 established that each one of these intentions is only accomplished on the basis of an atonement that paid for all sin, strengthening the findings of Chapter 3.

The Bible not only teaches that God's general intentions are accomplished through the atonement, however, but it also teaches that God's particular, saving intentions for the elect are accomplished through the atonement. Chapter 5 established the biblical and theological basis for the particular intention of the atonement, which was securing of the salvation of the elect. That the atonement actually secured the salvation of the elect is seen in what the Bible teaches about individual election to salvation, God's sovereignty throughout salvation, the special love that God has only for the elect, and the unity of the Father and the Son in salvation. The way that Christ secured the salvation of the elect was by sending the Spirit to only apply salvation to the elect. We see this truth in how the Bible consistently presents every saving work of the Holy Spirit, from effectual calling through glorification, as done only on the basis of Christ's atonement. The multi-intentioned view coheres with Scripture in recognizing Christ's payment for the sin of all people as well as the general and particular intentions behind this payment for sin.

Chapters 3–5 also established the comprehensiveness of the multi-intentioned view by demonstrating how it takes into account everything that the Bible teaches about the extent of the atonement. Advocates of particular redemption and unlimited atonement both typically focus on one set of verses that seem to support their position and then attempt to make the other set of verses fit their view. Those who hold to particular redemption appeal to the verses that seem to restrict Christ's atonement to the elect (e.g., Matt 1:21; John 6:37–40; 10:11, 15; Acts 20:28; Rom 8:31–39; 2 Cor 5:15; Eph 5:25; and Titus 2:14) while supporters of unlimited atonement emphasize the verses of Scripture that seem to present an unlimited scope to Christ's atonement (e.g., Isa 53:6; John 3:16; Rom 5:6–8; 2 Cor 5:14–15, 19; 1 Tim 2:4–6; 4:10; 2 Pet 2:1; 3:9; 1 John 2:2; and 4:14). This practice is not necessarily wrong, as one of the cardinal rules of evangelical hermeneutics is the "analogy of faith," that Scripture is consistent and therefore doctrines fit with other doctrines. One ambiguous verse or obscure passage of Scripture cannot be allowed to overturn a clear teaching of Scripture. This rule, however, is not a license to accept unlikely interpretations of texts because they fit better with one's theological system. When it comes to the extent of the atonement, it seems that many theologians (on both sides of the issue) are so convinced of the truth of their view that they accept unlikely or even implausible interpretations of certain passages of Scripture for the sake of theological consistency (as has been demonstrated throughout our study). The multi-intentioned view, on the other hand, attempts to give equal weight to both sets of passages. According to the multi-intentioned view, not only is the atonement seen to be a general payment for all sin with general intentions for the elect and the nonelect (Chaps. 3–4), but it is also seen to have special reference to elect and to actually secure their salvation (Chap. 5). In this way, the multi-intentioned view is comprehensive because it is able to account for all of what the Bibles teaches about the extent of the atonement.

In addition to establishing the coherency and the comprehensiveness of the multi-intentioned view, Chapters 3–5 also established its consistency. The multi-intentioned view is first of all internally consistent. The particular and general intentions of God in the atonement do not contradict one another because they are both part of God's one plan for his creation. God's plan concerns the elect, but it also concerns the nonelect, angels and demons, and the creation as a whole. The Bible presents the atonement as accomplishing different things for different people and the creation. It is only when people understand the atonement as having one intention that inconsistency between God's universal and general purposes is present.

The multi-intentioned view is also externally consistent, in that it is consistent with other biblical doctrines. We can see this especially in the areas of Christology, soteriology, theology proper, Trinitarian theology, and eschatology. The multi-intentioned view fits with the nature of the atonement as primarily penal substitution, but also recognizes the *Christus Victor* and moral influence aspects of the atonement. The multi-intentioned view coheres with the Bible's teaching about salvation, as it recognizes that God has made it possible for all people, in principle, to have an opportunity to be saved, but that not all people will be saved. The view is fully consistent with the universal gospel call, the difference between salvific and common grace, unconditional election, and effectual calling. The unity and diversity of the Trinity is preserved in the multi-intentioned view, as God the Father, God the Son, and God the Holy Spirit all work together in their distinct ways to fulfill God's general and particular intentions for creation. The multi-intentioned view fits with the unity of Christ's work as prophet, priest, and king, because the atonement accomplished God's prophetic, priestly, and kingly intentions. God's character is fully consistent with the multi-intentioned view, as all the aspects of God's love, justice, wisdom, and grace are present. Finally, the multi-intentioned view is consistent with biblical eschatology, as it recognizes God's final intentions for all facets of his creation.

Our study has not only established the coherence, comprehensiveness, and consistency of the multi-intentioned view, but it has also established its adequacy. The multi-intentioned view is a better description of what the Bible teaches about the extent of the atonement than other competing views. Chapter 2 provided an overview of the history of the doctrine of the extent of the atonement. The primary positions throughout church history have been particular redemption and unlimited atonement. While explanations of particular redemption have been relatively similar throughout church history, explanations of unlimited atonement have varied according to other theological commitments, such as a Calvinist or Arminian soteriology. Theologians such as Thomas Aquinas, John Davenant, Jacob Arminius, Moïse Amyraut, Richard Baxter, John Wesley, and Lewis Sperry Chafer have all offered their own variations of unlimited atonement. Evangelicals continue to disagree over the extent of the atonement, carrying on a doctrinal debate that began in Augustine's time and has been a significant issue within the church since the ninth century. The multi-intentioned view hopes to advance the debate by demonstrating how the extent of the atonement is both universal and particular at the same time, while avoiding some of the inconsistencies that have plagued other similar attempts.

THE MULTI-INTENTIONED VIEW AND THE PREACHING OF THE WORD

Doctrines should not only be biblically coherent, consistent, comprehensive, and adequate, but they should also be practical. Paul told Timothy that the purpose of doctrinal instruction is love, a good conscience, and sincere faith (1 Tim 1:5). Paul also states that the Scriptures are profitable for all right thinking and behavior (2 Tim 3:16–17). If the multi-intentioned view makes better sense of biblical, Christian practices than its alternatives, then this helps to establish its theological validity, and it therefore helps to establish our findings. There are several practical implications of the multi intentioned view that we could explore, as one's view of the extent of the atonement has implications for worship, prayer, missions, evangelization, the relationship between believers and unbelievers, and how God relates to the world. However, we will briefly examine the relationship between the multi-intentioned view and preaching. This examination is especially appropriate because preaching is at the heart of evangelical Christianity (Rom 10:14–17; Col 1:25–29), the atonement is the ground of New Testament preaching,[1] and because God uses preaching to apply the accomplishments of the atonement. As Robert Mounce states, "Preaching is that timeless link between God's great redemptive act and man's apprehension of it. It is the medium through which God contemporizes His historic self-disclosure and offers man the opportunity to respond in faith."[2]

The multi-intentioned view makes better sense of the biblical purposes for the preaching of the Word than either particular redemption or unlimited atonement.[3] This is because God has both particular and general purposes for preaching, and these purposes correspond with his particular and general intentions for the atonement. God's particular purposes for preaching are the saving, sanctifying, and glorifying of the elect. These purposes correspond to his intention to secure the salvation of the elect in the atonement. The Holy Spirit uses the preaching of the gospel to call people to salvation (Rom 10:14–17; 1 Cor 1:21; 2 Thess 2:13–14; 1 Pet 2:22–25). He then uses the preaching of the Word to sanctify believers (2 Tim 3:16–17; 4:2), with the Spirit's inspiration of the Scriptures forming the basis for Paul's exhortation to Timothy to "preach the word" (2 Tim 4:2).[4] Finally, the

---

1. Piper, *The Supremacy of God in Preaching*, 32.
2. Mounce, *The Essential Nature*, 153.
3. I have defended this thesis in much more detail in Shultz, Jr., "God's Purposes in Preaching." The following paragraphs are a brief summarization of that paper.
4. Adam, *Speaking God's Words*, 90.

Holy Spirit uses the preaching of the Word to lead believers to the consummation of their salvation in glorification, as Colossians 1:28 states that the goal of preaching is to "present every man complete in Christ," referring to glorification.[5] God has purposed to save the elect through the preaching of the Word, and this is only possible because he has secured the salvation of the elect in the atonement.

God not only has particular purposes for preaching, however, but he also has general purposes for preaching. These general purposes for preaching correspond to God's general intentions in the atonement. God desires for all people to hear the good news of what he has done for humanity through Christ. This is evident from the universal gospel call that is meant for all of creation (Mark 16:15; cf. Matt 28:18–20; Luke 24:47; John 20:23; Acts 1:8). This purpose for preaching corresponds to God's purpose in the atonement to make the universal gospel call possible. The universal gospel call also results in an additional basis of condemnation for those who reject it, which again is based upon Christ's payment for the sin of all people. God also uses preaching to extend his common grace and to show forth his character to all people. The faithful preaching of God's Word demonstrates God's patience in judgment, which in turn shows forth God's love and justice (2 Pet 3:9). God is patient in his judgment so that preaching might have an opportunity to do its work. Even preaching that never results in salvation is used by God to delay the full display of his righteous judgment against sin. Preaching also results in God's restraining of sin and evil in his creation. The church is the pillar and support of the truth (1 Tim 3:15) because it is the body of people who are responsible for the truth, the Word of God that is Scripture (cf. Eccl 12:10; 2 Tim 3:16–17; Heb 4:12). As the body of people responsible for the truth of God in Scripture, one of the primary ways that the church stands up for the truth is through the preaching of the Word. In standing up for the truth by preaching the Word, churches affect the world around them, changing societies and cultures for the better. Finally, preaching plays an important role in Christ's cosmic triumph over all sin, as God uses it to combat the evil of Satan and his demons (Acts 26:18; Eph 6:12–17). Every time a person is saved through the preaching of the Word and rescued from Satan's clutches, a blow is dealt to Satan's kingdom (Acts 26:18), notching one small victory for God as he works toward the subjection of all things in heaven and in earth (1 Cor 15:28), which will take place when all things are reconciled to him (Col 1:20; Phil 2:9–11).

That God has both general and particular purposes in preaching, and that these purposes correspond to his multiple purposes in the atonement,

---

5. Bruce, *The Epistles to the Colossians*, 87–88.

demonstrates the practical validity of the multi-intentioned view. The multi-intentioned view provides a better theological foundation for biblical preaching than either particular redemption or unlimited atonement. Particular redemption is able to account for the particular purposes of preaching, but is forced to see the general purposes as superfluous, or at best secondary. One concrete illustration of this is the problem that advocates of particular redemption have always had with incorporating the clear truth of the universal gospel call into their theological system.[6] Likewise, if unlimited atonement was the correct understanding of Scripture, then one could expect Scripture to only present general purposes for the preaching of the Word. Unlimited atonement is able to account for the Bible's general purposes of preaching, but has no grounding for the particular purposes. One concrete example of this can be seen by the dismissal of God's particular purposes in preaching by almost all of those who hold to an unlimited atonement. Preaching is understood as presenting the opportunity for one to be saved or sanctified, not actually the means the Holy Spirit uses for accomplishing salvation or sanctification.[7] The multi-intentioned view, however, is able to account for both the particular and the general purposes of preaching because it recognizes multiple intentions in the atonement.

CONCLUSION

The goal of this book has been to present the multi-intentioned view as a valid evangelical option in the debate over the extent of the atonement. I hope that the findings of this study will help advocates of both unlimited atonement and particular redemption to recognize the weaknesses of their own position and the strengths of the opposing view. Perhaps this may help foster unity among evangelicals and within churches and denominations that continue to be divided over this issue. One does not have to choose between unlimited atonement and particular redemption when it comes to a position on the extent of the atonement. There is a consistent, biblical way to believe in both a general payment for all sin in the atonement and the sovereign grace of God throughout salvation, and that is to realize that God had multiple intentions for the atonement. Jesus Christ has paid for all sin

---

6. For evidence of this, see the discussion of several of the Reformers and how they attempted to reconcile particular redemption with the universal gospel call in Thomas, *The Extent of the Atonement*, 41–123, 224–44.

7. This is seen especially in the Arminian understanding of unlimited atonement. E.g., Hunt, *What Love is This?*, 443–44; and Miethe, "The Universal Power of the Atonement," 83–85.

and has secured the salvation of the elect. May our Lord and Savior receive all the praise, honor, and glory due his name for all that he has accomplished through the blood of his cross.

Bibliography

Adam, Peter. *Speaking God's Words: A Practical Theology of Preaching*. Leicester, England: Inter-Varsity, 1996.
Aldrich, Roy L. "The Gift of God." *Bibliotheca Sacra* 122 (1965) 248–53.
Allen, David L. "The Atonement: Limited or Universal?" In *Whosoever Will: A Biblical-Theological Critique of Five-Point Calvinism*, edited by David L. Allen and Steve W. Lemke, 61–107. Nashville: B&H Academic, 2010.
Aloisi, John. "The Paraclete's Ministry of Conviction: Another Look at John 16:8–11." *Journal of the Evangelical Theological Society* 47 (2004) 55–69.
Anselm. *Why God Became Man*. Translated by Janet Fairweather. In *Anselm of Canterbury: The Major Works*, edited by Brian Davies and G. R. Evans, 260–356. Oxford's World Classics. Oxford: Oxford University Press, 1998.
Archibald, Paul Noel. "A Comparative Study of John Calvin and Theodore Beza on the Doctrine of the Extent of the Atonement." Ph.D. diss., Westminster Theological Seminary, 1998.
Arminius, Jacob. *An Examination of a Treatise, Concerning the Order and Mode of Predestination and Amplitude of Divine Grace, by Rev. William Perkins, D. D., A Theological Writer of England*. In *The Writings of James Arminius*, translated by James Nichols and W. R. Bagnall, 3:266–555. Grand Rapids: Baker, 1956.
———. *The Writings of James Arminius*. Translated by James Nichols and W. R. Bagnall. 3 vols. Grand Rapids: Baker, 1956.
Armstrong, Brian A. *Calvinism and the Amyraut Heresy*. Madison: University of Wisconsin Press, 1969.
Augustine. *Answer to the Two Letters of the Pelagians*. In *Answer to the Pelagians II*, edited by John E. Rotelle, translated by Roland J. Teske, 116–219. The Works of Saint Augustine, pt. 1, vol. 24. Hyde Park, NY: New City, 1998.
———. *The Augustine Catechism: The Enchiridion on Faith, Hope, and Love*, edited by John E. Rotelle, translated by Bruce Harbert, with an introduction by Boniface Ramsey. Hyde Park, NY: New City, 1999.
———. *On the Gift of Perseverance*. Translated by John A. Mourant and William J. Collinge. In *Saint Augustine: Four Anti-Pelagian Writings*, with an introduction and notes by William J. Colinge, 271–337. The Fathers of the Church: A New Translation, vol. 86. Washington, DC: Catholic University of America Press, 1992.

———. *The Perfection of Human Righteousness.* In *Answer to the Pelagians*, edited by John E. Rotelle, translated by Roland J. Teske, 289–316. *The Works of Saint Augustine*, pt. 1, vol. 23. Hyde Park, NY: New City, 1997.

———. *On the Predestination of the Saints.* Translated by John A. Mourant and William J. Collinge. In *Saint Augustine: Four Anti-Pelagian Writings*, with an introduction and notes by William J. Colinge, 218–70. The Fathers of the Church: A New Translation, vol. 86. Washington, DC: Catholic University of America Press, 1992.

———. "Sermon 121—On the Words of the Gospel of John 1:10–14: 'The World Was Made Through Him, Etc.'" In *Sermons*, edited by John E. Rotelle, translated by Edmund Hill, 230–40. *The Works of St. Augustine*, pt. 3, vol. 4. Brooklyn, NY: New City, 1992.

———. "Sermon 138—On the Words of the Gospel of John 10:30: 'I and the Father are One.'" In *Sermons*, edited by John E. Rotelle, translated by Edmund Hill, 380–91. *The Works of St. Augustine*, pt. 3, vol. 4. Brooklyn, NY: New City, 1992.

———. *Ten Homilies on the First Epistle General of St. John.* Translated by John Burnaby. In *Augustine: Later Works*, edited by John Burnaby, 251–348. Library of Christian Classics, vol. 8. Philadelphia: Westminster, 1955.

Aulén, Gustav. *Christus Victor: An Historical Study of the Three Main Types of the Idea of the Atonement.* Translated by A. G. Hebert. 1931. Reprint, Eugene, OR: Wipf and Stock, 2003.

Bancroft, Emery H. *Christian Theology: Systematic and Biblical.* Edited by Ronald B. Mayers. 2nd ed. Grand Rapids: Zondervan, 1976.

Bangs, Carl. *Arminius: A Study in the Dutch Reformation.* Nashville: Abingdon, 1971.

Barnes, Tom. *Atonement Matters: A Call to Declare the Biblical View of the Atonement.* Webster, NY: Evangelical Press USA, 2008.

Barnett, Paul. *The Second Epistle to the Corinthians.* The New International Commentary on the New Testament. Grand Rapids: Eerdmans, 1997.

Bauckham, Richard. *Jude, 2 Peter.* Word Biblical Commentary, vol. 50. Waco, TX: Word, 1983.

Baugh, Steven M. "The Meaning of Foreknowledge." In *Still Sovereign: Contemporary Perspectives on Election, Foreknowledge, and Grace*, edited by Thomas R. Schreiner and Bruce A. Ware, 183–200. Grand Rapids: Baker, 2000.

———. "Savior of All People: 1 Timothy 4:10 in Context." *Westminster Journal of Theology* 54 (1992) 331–40.

Bavinck, Herman. *Reformed Dogmatics.* Vol. 2, *God and Creation*. Edited by John Bolt. Translated by John Vriend. Grand Rapids: Baker Academic, 2004.

———. *Reformed Dogmatics.* Vol. 3., *Sin and Salvation*. Edited by John Bolt. Translated by John Vriend. Grand Rapids: Baker Academic, 2006.

Baxter, Richard. *Plain Scripture Proof of Infants Church-membership and Baptism.* London: For Robert White, 1651.

———. *The Practical Works of Richard Baxter: With a Life of the Author and a Critical Examination of His Writings by William Orme.* 23 vols. London: J. Duncan, 1830–58.

———. *Universal Redemption of Mankind by the Lord Jesus Christ.* London: n.p., 1694.

Beachy, Alvin J. *The Concept of Grace in the Radical Reformation.* Neuwkoop, Netherlands: Hes and De Graff, 1977.

Beasley-Murray, George. *John.* 2nd ed. Nashville: Thomas Nelson, 1999.

Bell, M. Charles. "Calvin and the Extent of the Atonement." *Evangelical Quarterly* 55 (1983) 115–23.
Beilby, James, and Paul R. Eddy. "The Atonement: An Introduction." In *The Nature of the Atonement: Four Views*, edited by James Beilby and Paul R. Eddy, 9–21. Downers Grove, IL: Intervarsity, 2006.
Beougher, Timothy K. *Richard Baxter and Conversion: A Study of the Puritan Concept of Becoming a Christian*. Fearn, Scotland: Mentor, 2007.
Berkhof, Louis. *Systematic Theology*. Grand Rapids: Eerdmans, 1941.
Beza, Theodore. *Correspondance de Théodore De Bèze*. Edited by Hoppolyte Aubert, Fernand Aubert, and Henri Meylan. Geneva: E. Droz, 1960.
Blacketer, Raymond A. "Definite Atonement in Historical Perspective." In *The Glory of the Atonement*, edited by Charles E. Hill and Frank A. James, 304–23. Downers Grove, IL: InterVarsity, 2004.
Blocher, Henri. "*Agnus Victor*: The Atonement as Victory and Vicarious Punishment." In *What Does it Mean to be Saved? Broadening Evangelical Horizons of Salvation*, edited by John G Stackhouse, 67–91. Grand Rapids: Baker, 2002.
Bloesch, Donald G. *The Holy Spirit: Works and Gifts*. Vol. 5 of *Christian Foundations*. Downers Grove, IL: InterVarsity, 2000.
———. *Jesus Christ: Savior and Lord*. Vol. 4 of *Christian Foundations*. Downers Grove, IL: InterVarsity, 1997.
Blum, Edwin A. *2 Peter*. In vol.12 of *The Expositor's Bible Commentary*. Edited by Frank E. Gaebelein, 257–92. Grand Rapids: Zondervan, 1981.
Bock, Darrell. *Acts*. Baker Exegetical Commentary on the New Testament. Grand Rapids: Baker, 2007.
Boersma, Hans. "Calvin and the Extent of the Atonement." *Evangelical Quarterly* 64 (1992) 333–55.
———. *Violence, Hospitality, and the Cross: Reappropriating the Atonement Tradition*. Grand Rapids: Baker, 2004.
Boettner, Lorraine. *The Reformed Doctrine of Predestination*. Grand Rapids: Eerdmans, 1932.
Borchert, Gerald L. *John 1–11*. The New American Commentary, vol. 25a. Nashville: B&H, 1996.
Boyce, James A. *Abstract of Systematic Theology*. Cape Coral, FL: Founder's, 2006.
Boyd, Gregory A. "*Christus Victor* View." In *The Nature of the Atonement: Four Views*, edited by James Beilby and Paul R. Eddy, 23–49. Downers Grove, IL: InterVarsity, 2006.
Brand, Chad O. "Defining Evangelicalism." In *Reclaiming the Center: Confronting Evangelical Accommodation in Postmodern Times*, edited by Millard J. Erickson, et al., 281–304. Wheaton, IL: Crossway, 2004.
———, ed. *Perspectives on Spirit Baptism: Five Views*. Nashville: Broadman and Holman, 2004.
Bruce, F. F. *The Acts of the Apostles: The Greek Text with Introduction and Commentary*. 3rd ed. Grand Rapids: Eerdmans, 1990.
———. *The Epistle to the Galatians: A Commentary on the Greek Text*. The New International Greek Testament Commentary. Grand Rapids: Eerdmans, 1982.
———. *The Epistles of John: Introduction, Exposition, and Notes*. Grand Rapids: Eerdmans, 1970.

———. *The Epistles to the Colossians, to Philemon, and to the Ephesians.* The New International Commentary on the New Testament. Grand Rapids: Eerdmans, 1989.

———. *The Gospel of John: Introduction, Exposition, and Notes.* Grand Rapids: Eerdmans, 1983.

Bucer, Martin. *Common Places.* Edited and translated by D. F. Wright. Nashville: Abingdon, 1972.

Buswell, James Oliver. *A Systematic Theology of the Christian Religion.* 2 vols. Grand Rapids: Zondervan, 1963.

Calvin, John. *Commentaries on the Catholic Epistles.* In vol. 22 of *Calvin's Commentaries.* Translated by John Owen. Grand Rapids: Baker, 1996.

———. *Commentaries on the Epistles of Paul the Apostle to the Philippians, Colossians, and Thessalonians.* In vol. 21 of *Calvin's Commentaries.* Translated by William Pringle. Grand Rapids: Baker, 1996.

———. *Commentaries on the Epistles of Paul to the Galatians and Ephesians.* In vol. 21 of *Calvin's Commentaries.* Translated by William Pringle. Grand Rapids: Baker, 1996.

———. *Commentaries on the Epistles to Timothy, Titus, and Philemon.* In vol. 21 of *Calvin's Commentaries.* Translated by William Pringle. Grand Rapids: Baker, 1996.

———. *Commentary on the Epistle of Paul the Apostle to the Hebrews.* Translated and edited by John Owen. Grand Rapids: Eerdmans, 1948.

———. *Commentary on the Gospel of John.* In vol. 17 of *Calvin's Commentaries.* Translated by William Pringle. Grand Rapids: Baker, 1996.

———. *Commentary on a Harmony of the Evangelists, Matthew, Mark, and Luke.* In vol. 16 of *Calvin's Commentaries.* Translated by William Pringle. Grand Rapids: Baker, 1996.

———. *Concerning the Eternal Predestination of God.* Translated with an introduction by J. K. S. Reid. London: James Clark & Co., 1961.

———. *The Deity of Christ and Other Sermons.* Translated by Leroy Nixon. Grand Rapids: Eerdmans, 1950.

———. *Institutes of the Christian Religion.* Edited by John T. McNeill. Translated by Ford Lewis Battles. Library of Christian Classics, vols. 20–21. Philadelphia: Westminster, 1960.

———. *New Testament Commentaries.* Edited by David W. Torrance and Thomas F. Torrance. Various Translators. 12 vols. Grand Rapids: Eerdmans, 1959–70.

———. *Sermons on the Epistles to Timothy and Titus.* Translated by L. T. London: G. Bishop, 1579. Reprint, Edinburgh: Banner of Truth, 1983.

———. *Sermons on Isaiah's Prophecy of the Death and Passion of Christ.* Edited and translated by T. H. L. Parker. London: James Clarke & Co., 1956.

———. *Theological Treatises.* Translated by J. K. S. Reid. Library of Christian Classics, vol. 22. Philadelphia: Westminster, 1954.

———. *Tracts and Treatises on the Doctrine and Worship of the Church.* 2 vols. Translated by Henry Beveridge with notes by Thomas F. Torrance. Edinburgh: Calvin Translation Society, 1849. Reprint, Grand Rapids: Eerdmans, 1958.

Campbell, John McLeod. *The Nature of the Atonement.* Cambridge: Macmillan, 1856. Reprint, Eugene, OR: Wipf and Stock, 1996.

Carson, D. A. *The Difficult Doctrine of the Love of God.* Wheaton, IL: Crossway, 2000.

———. *The Gospel of John*. The Pillar New Testament Commentary. Grand Rapids: Eerdmans, 1991.

———. *Matthew*. In vol. 8 of *The Expositor's Bible Commentary*. Edited by Frank E. Gaebelein, 1–599. Grand Rapids: Zondervan, 1984.

———. "Reflections on Assurance." In *Still Sovereign: Contemporary Perspectives on Election, Foreknowledge, and Grace*, edited by Thomas R. Schreiner and Bruce A. Ware, 247–76. Grand Rapids: Baker, 2000

Chafer, Lewis Sperry. "For Whom Did Christ Die?" *Bibliotheca Sacra* 137 (1980) 310–26.

———. *Systematic Theology*. 8 vols. Dallas: Dallas Seminary Press, 1948.

Chang, Andrew D. "Second Peter 2:1 and the Extent of the Atonement." *Bibliotheca Sacra* 142 (1985) 52–63.

Chisholm, Robert B., Jr. "The Christological Fulfillment of Isaiah's Servant Songs." *Bibliotheca Sacra* 163 (2006) 387–404.

Clarke, F. Stuart. *The Ground of Election: Jacobus Arminius's Doctrine of the Work and Person of Christ*. Bletchley, UK: Paternoster, 2006.

Cole, Graham A. *He Who Gives Life: The Doctrine of the Holy Spirit*. Foundations of Evangelical Theology. Wheaton, IL: Crossway, 2007.

Combs, William C. "Does the Bible Teach Prevenient Grace?" *Detroit Baptist Seminary Journal* 10 (2005) 3–18.

Cottrell, Jack W. "The Classical Arminian View of Election." In *Perspectives on Election: Five Views*, edited by Chad Owen Brand, 70–134. Nashville: Broadman and Holman, 2006.

Crawford, Thomas J. *The Doctrine of the Holy Scripture Respecting the Atonement*. Grand Rapids: Baker, 1954.

Culver, Robert Duncan. *Systematic Theology: Biblical and Historical*. Fearn, Scotland: Christian Focus, 2005.

Cunningham, William. *Historical Theology*. 2 vols. 4th ed. London: Banner of Truth Trust, 1960.

Dabney, Robert Lewis. *Lectures in Systematic Theology*. Grand Rapids: Zondervan, 1972.

Daniel, Curt D. "HyperCalvinism and John Gill." Ph.D. diss., University of Edinburgh, 1983.

Davenant, John. *A Dissertation on the Death of Christ, as to its Extent and Special Benefits: Containing a Short History of Pelagianism, and Shewing the Agreement of the Doctrines of the Church of England on General Redemption, Election, and Predestination, with the Primitive Fathers of the Christian Church, and Above All with the Holy Scriptures*. Translated by Josiah Allport. In *An Exposition of the Epistle of St. Paul to the Colossians*, by John Davenant, translated by Josiah Allport, 2:313–569, 588–89. London: Hamilton, Adams, and Co., 1832.

Davids, Peter H. *The Letters of Jude and 2 Peter*. The Pillar New Testament Commentary. Grand Rapids: Eerdmans, 2006.

Delitzsch, Franz. *Biblical Commentary on the Prophecies of Isaiah*. Translated by James Martin. 2 vols. Grand Rapids: Eerdmans, 1950.

Demarest, Bruce A. *The Cross and Salvation: The Doctrine of Salvation*. Foundations of Evangelical Theology. Wheaton, IL: Crossway, 1997.

Dodd, C. H. *The Epistle of Paul to the Romans*. London: Hodder and Stoughton, 1932.

———. "Hilaskesthai: Its Cognates, Derivatives, and Synonyms in the Septuagint." *Journal of Theological Studies* 32 (1931) 352–60.

———. *The Johannine Epistles*. London: Hodder and Stoughton, 1946.

Douty, Norman F. *Did Christ Die Only For the Elect? A Treatise on the Extent of the Atonement*. Irving, TX: William & Watrous, 1978. Reprint, Eugene, OR: Wipf and Stock, 1998.

Driscoll, Mark, and Gerry Breshears. *Death by Love: Letters from the Cross*. Wheaton, IL: Crossway, 2008.

Dunham, Duane A. "The Limited Atonement Revisited." Paper presented at the Northwest regional meeting of the Evangelical Theological Society, Portland, OR, 8 April 1995.

Dunning, H. Ray. *Grace, Faith, and Holiness: A Wesleyan Systematic Theology*. Kansas City, MO: Beacon Hill, 1988.

Earle, Ralph. *1 Timothy*. In vol. 11 of *The Expositor's Bible Commentary*. Edited by Frank E. Gaebelein, 339–90. Grand Rapids: Zondervan, 1981.

Ellingworth, Paul. *The Epistle to the Hebrews: A Commentary on the Greek Text*. The New International Greek Testament Commentary. Grand Rapids: Eerdmans, 1993.

Elliott, Grant T. "A Biblical Defense of Particular Redemption." Paper presented at the Eastern regional meeting of the Evangelical Theological Society, Lancaster, PA, 4 April 2003.

Elwell, Walter A. "Atonement, Extent of." In *The Evangelical Dictionary of Theology*. Edited by Walter A. Elwell. Grand Rapids: Baker, 2001.

Erickson, Millard. *Christian Theology*. 2nd ed. Grand Rapids: Baker, 1998.

Feinberg, John S. *No One Like Him: The Doctrine of God*. Foundations of Evangelical Theology. Wheaton, IL: Crossway, 2001.

Ferguson, Sinclair B. *The Holy Spirit*. Contours of Christian Theology. Downers Grove, IL: InterVarsity, 1996.

Fesko, J. V. *Diversity within the Reformed Tradition: Supra- and Infralapsarianism in Calvin, Dort, and Westminster*. Greenville, SC: Reformed Academic, 2001.

Finney, Charles. *Finney's Lectures on Systematic Theology*. Edited by J. H. Fairchild. Grand Rapids: Eerdmans, 1953.

Forlines, F. Leroy. *The Quest for Truth*. Nashville: Randall House, 2001.

Frame, John M. *The Doctrine of God*. Phillipsburg, NJ: P&R, 2002.

Freeman, M. S. "The Doctrine of Predestination from Augustine to Peter Lombard." *Bibliotheca Sacra* 47 (1890) 645–68.

Fudge, Edward William, and Robert A. Peterson. *Two Views of Hell: A Biblical and Theological Dialogue*. Downers Grove, IL: InterVarsity, 2000.

Garland, David E. *2 Corinthians*. The New American Commentary, vol. 29. Nashville: Broadman and Holman, 1999.

Garrett, James Leo. *Systematic Theology: Biblical, Historical, and Evangelical*. 2 vols. 2nd ed. North Richland Hills, TX: Bibal, 2001.

Geisler, Norman L. *Chosen But Free*. 2nd ed. Minneapolis: Bethany House, 2001.

———. *Systematic Theology*. Vol. 3, *Sin, Salvation*. Minneapolis: Bethany House, 2004.

Gentry, Peter J. "The Atonement in Isaiah's Fourth Servant Song (Isaiah 52:13–53:12)." *The Southern Baptist Journal of Theology* 11 (2007) 20–47.

Godfrey, W. Robert. "Reformed Thought on the Extent of the Atonement to 1618." *Westminster Theological Journal* 37 (1975–76) 133–71.

———. "Tensions within International Calvinism: The Debate on the Atonement at the Synod of Dort, 1618-1619." Ph.D. diss., Stanford University, 1974.

Grounds, Vernon C. "God's Universal Salvific Grace." In *Grace Unlimited*, edited by Clark H. Pinnock, 21-30. Minneapolis: Bethany House, 1975.

Grudem, Wayne. "The Meaning of *Kephalē* ("Head"): A Response to Recent Studies." In *Recovering Biblical Manhood and Womanhood: A Response to Evangelical Feminism*, edited by John Piper and Wayne Grudem, 425-68. Wheaton, IL: Crossway, 1991.

———. *Systematic Theology*. 2nd ed. Grand Rapids: Zondervan, 2000.

Guy, Fritz. "The Universality of God's Love." In *The Grace of God and the Will of Man*, edited by Clark Pinnock, 31-49. Minneapolis: Bethany House, 1995.

Hall, Basil. "Calvin against the Calvinists." In *John Calvin*, edited by G. E. Duffield, 19-37. Nashville: Abingdon, 1966.

Hamilton, Jr., James M. *God's Indwelling Presence: The Holy Spirit in the Old and New Testaments*. Nashville: B&H, 2006.

Hammett, John. "A Multiple Intention View of the Atonement." In *Three Views on the Extent of the Atonement*, edited by Andrew Naselli and Mark Snoeberger, n. p. Nashville: B&H Academic, forthcoming.

Hansen, Colin. *Young, Restless, Reformed: A Journalist's Journey with the New Calvinists*. Wheaton, IL: Crossway, 2008.

Hansen, Wayne S. "Two Aspects in the Design of Christ's Atonement." *Journal for Baptist Theology and Ministry* 2 (2004) 85-98.

Harris, Murray J. *The Second Epistle to the Corinthians: A Commentary on the Greek Text*. The New International Greek Testament Commentary. Grand Rapids: Eerdmans, 2005.

Harris, W. Hall. "An Out-of-this-World Experience: A Look at 'Kosmos' in the Johannine Literature." Paper presented at the annual meeting of the Evangelical Theological Society, Washington, DC, 16 November 2006.

Hartog, Paul. *A Word for the World: Calvin on the Extent of the Atonement*. Schaumburg, IL: Regular Baptist Press, 2009.

Hawthorne, Gerald F. *Philippians*. Rev. ed. Revised by Ralph P. Martin. Word Biblical Commentary, vol. 43. Nashville: Thomas Nelson, 2004.

Helm, Paul. *Calvin and the Calvinists*. Edinburgh: Banner of Truth Trust, 1982.

Hicks, John Mark. "The Theology of Grace in the Thought of Jacobus Arminius and Philip van Limborch: A Study in the Development of Seventeenth-Century Dutch Arminianism." Ph.D. diss., Westminster Theological Seminary, 1985.

Hiebert, D. Edmund. "A Portrayal of False Teachers: An Exposition of 2 Peter 2:1-3." *Bibliotheca Sacra* 141 (1984) 255-65.

———. Titus. In vol. 11 of *The Expositor's Bible Commentary*. Edited by Frank E. Gaebelein, 419-449. Grand Rapids: Eerdmans, 1981.

Hill, Charles E. "Atonement in the Apocalypse of John." In *The Glory of the Atonement*, edited by Charles E. Hill and Frank A. James, 190-208. Downers Grove, IL: InterVarsity, 2004.

Hill, Charles E., and Frank A. James III, eds. *The Glory of the Atonement: Biblical, Historical, and Practical Perspectives*. Downers Grove, IL: InterVarsity, 2004.

Hodge, Archibald Alexander. *The Atonement*. Grand Rapids: Eerdmans, 1950.

———. *Outlines of Theology*. Rev. ed. New York: Robert Carter and Brothers, 1878.

Hodge, Charles. *Systematic Theology*. 3 vols. New York: Scribner's, 1872–73. Reprint, Grand Rapids: Eerdmans, 1946.
Hoekema, Anthony A. *A New Translation of the Canons of Dort*. Calvin Theological Journal 3 (1968) 133–61.
———. *Saved By Grace*. Grand Rapids: Eerdmans, 1989.
Horton, Michael. *For Calvinism*. Grand Rapids, Zondervan, 2011.
Hunt, Dave. *What Love is This? Calvinism's Misrepresentation of God*. Bend, OR: Berean Call, 2004.
Jeffery, Steve, et al. *Pierced for Our Transgressions: Rediscovering the Glory of Penal Substitution*. Wheaton, IL: Crossway, 2007.
Jewett, Paul K. *Election and Predestination*. Grand Rapids: Eerdmans, 1985.
Jinkins, Michael. "Theodore Beza: Continuity and Regression in the Reformed Tradition." *Evangelical Quarterly* 64 (1992) 131–54.
Johnson, Timothy. *Hebrews: A Commentary*. The New Testament Library. Louisville: Westminster John Knox, 2006.
Kaiser, Jr., Walter C. "The Baptism in the Holy Spirit as the Promise of the Father: A Reformed Perspective." In *Perspectives on Spirit Baptism: Five Views*, edited by Chad Owen Brand, 15–46. Nashville: Broadman and Holman, 2004.
Kärkkäinen, Veli-Matti. *Pneumatology: The Holy Spirit in Ecumenical, International, and Contextual Perspective*. Grand Rapids: Baker, 2002.
Kelly, J. N. D. *Early Christian Doctrines*. 5th ed. San Francisco: HarperCollins, 1978.
———. *The Pastoral Epistles*. Black's New Testament Commentary. Peabody, MA: Hendrickson, 1993.
Kendall, R. T. *Calvin and English Calvinism to 1649*. Oxford: Oxford University Press, 1979.
Kennard, Douglas W. "Petrine Redemption: Its Meaning and Extent." *Journal of the Evangelical Theological Society* 30 (1987) 399–405.
Kennedy, Kevin Dixon. *Union with Christ and the Extent of the Atonement in Calvin*. Studies in Biblical Literature. New York: Peter Lang, 2002.
Kent, Jr., Homer A. *Philippians*. In vol. 11 of *The Expositor's Bible Commentary*. Edited by Frank E. Gaebelein, 93–160. Grand Rapids: Zondervan, 1981.
Klein, William W. *The New Chosen People: A Corporate View of Election*. Grand Rapids: Zondervan, 1992.
Knight, George W., III. *The Pastoral Epistles: A Commentary on the Greek Text*. The New International Greek Testament Commentary. Grand Rapids: Eerdmans, 1992.
Koester, Craig R. "'The Savior of the World' (John 4:42)." *Journal of Biblical Literature* 109 (1990) 665–80.
Köstenberger, Andreas J. *John*. Baker Exegetical Commentary on the New Testament. Grand Rapids: Baker, 2004.
———. "What does it Mean to Be Filled with the Holy Spirit? A Biblical Investigation." *Journal of the Evangelical Theological Society* 40 (1997) 229–40.
Kruse, Colin. *The Letters of John*. The Pillar New Testament Commentary. Grand Rapids: Eerdmans, 2000.
———. *The Second Epistle of Paul to the Corinthians: An Introduction and Commentary*. Tyndale New Testament Commentaries. Grand Rapids: Eerdmans, 1987.
Kuiper, R. B. *For Whom Did Christ Die?* Grand Rapids: Eerdmans, 1959.
Ladd, George Eldon. *A Theology of the New Testament*. Edited by Donald A. Hagner. Rev. ed. Grand Rapids: Eerdmans, 1993.

Lake, Donald M. "He Died for All: The Universal Dimensions of the Atonement." In *Grace Unlimited*, edited by Clark H. Pinnock, 31–50. Minneapolis: Bethany House, 1975.
Lane, Anthony N. S. "The Quest for the Historical Calvin." *Evangelical Quarterly* 55 (1983) 95–113.
Lane, William. *Hebrews 1–8*. Word Biblical Commentary, vol. 47. Dallas: Word, 1991.
Langford, Thomas A. *Practical Divinity: Theology in the Wesleyan Tradition*. Nashville: Abingdon, 1983.
Lea, Thomas D., and Hayne P. Griffin, Jr. *1, 2 Timothy, Titus*. The New American Commentary, vol. 34. Nashville: Broadman, 1992.
Leahy, F. S. "Calvin and the Extent of the Atonement." *Reformed Theological Journal* 8 (1992) 54–64.
Letham, Robert. *The Work of Christ*. Contours of Christian Theology. Downers Grove, IL: InterVarsity, 1993.
Lewis, Gordon L., and Bruce A. Demarest. *Integrative Theology*. 3 vols. in 1. Grand Rapids: Zondervan, 1996.
Lightner, Robert P. *The Death Christ Died: A Biblical Case for Unlimited Atonement*. 2nd ed. Grand Rapids: Kregel, 1998.
Lincoln, Andrew T. *Ephesians*. Word Biblical Commentary, vol. 42. Waco, TX: Word, 1990.
Lints, Richard. *The Fabric of Theology: A Prolegomenon to Evangelical Theology*. Grand Rapids: Eerdmans, 1993.
Lombard, Peter. *Sententiae*. In *Cursus Completus Patrologiae*, edited by J. P. Migne. Paris, 1845.
Long, Gary D. *Definite Atonement*. 3rd ed. Frederick, MD: New Covenant Media, 2006.
Longenecker, Richard N. *Galatians*. Word Biblical Commentary, vol. 41. Waco, TX: Word, 1990.
López, René A. "Is Faith a Gift from God or a Human Exercise?" *Bibliotheca Sacra* 164 (2007) 259–76.
Luther, Martin. *Bondage of the Will*. Translated by J. I. Packer and O. R. Johnston. London: Fleming H. Revell, 1957.
———. *Luther's Works*. Edited by Jeroslav Pelikan (vols. 1–30) and Helmut T. Lehmann (vols. 31–55). Philadelphia: Muhlenberg; St. Louis: Concordia, 1955–86.
MacArthur, Jr., John F. "The Love of God for Humanity." *The Master's Seminary Journal* 7 (1996) 7–30.
Macchia, Frank D. *Baptized in the Spirit: A Global Pentecostal Theology*. Grand Rapids: Zondervan, 2006.
MacDonald, William G. "The Biblical Doctrine of Election." In *The Grace of God and the Will of Man*, edited by Clark H. Pinnock, 207–29. Minneapolis: Bethany House, 1989.
Malone, M. T. "The Doctrine of Predestination in the Thought of William Perkins and Richard Hooker." *Anglican Theological Review* 52 (1970) 103–17.
Mangum, R. Todd. "Is There a Reformed Way to Get the Benefits of the Atonement to 'Those Who have Never Heard?'" *Journal of the Evangelical Theological Society* 47 (2004) 121–36.
Marshall, I. Howard. *The Epistles of John*. The New International Commentary on the New Testament. Grand Rapids: Eerdmans, 1978.

———. "For All, for All My Savior Died." In *Semper Reformandum: Studies in Honor of Clark H. Pinnock*, edited by Stanley P. Porter and Anthony R. Cross, 322–46. Carlisle, UK: Paternoster, 2003.

———. "The Meaning of Reconciliation." In *Unity and Diversity in New Testament Theology: Essays in Honor of George E. Ladd*, edited by Robert A. Guelich, 117–32. Grand Rapids: Eerdmans, 1978.

———. "Universal Grace and Atonement in the Pastoral Epistles." In *The Grace of God and the Will of Man*, edited by Clark H. Pinnock, 51–69. Minneapolis: Bethany House, 1989.

Martin, Ralph P. *2 Corinthians*. Word Biblical Commentary, vol. 40. Waco, TX: Word, 1986.

———. *Reconciliation: A Study of Paul's Theology*. Atlanta: John Knox, 1981

McCartney, Dan G. "Atonement in James, Peter, and Jude." In *The Glory of the Atonement*, edited by Charles E. Hill and Frank A. James, 176–89. Downers Grove, IL: InterVarsity, 2004.

McDonald, H. D. *The Atonement of the Death of Christ: In Faith, Revelation, and History*. Grand Rapids: Baker, 1985.

McGonigle, Herbert Boyd. *Sufficient Saving Grace: John Wesley's Evangelical Arminianism*. Carlisle, UK: Paternoster, 2001.

Miley, John. *Systematic Theology*. 2 vols. Peabody, MA: Hendrickson, 1989.

Michaels, J. Ramsey. "Atonement in John's Gospel and Epistles." In *The Glory of the Atonement*, edited by Charles E. Hill and Frank A. James, 106–18. Downers Grove, IL: InterVarsity, 2004.

Miethe, Terry L. "The Universal Power of the Atonement." In *The Grace of God and the Will of Man*, edited by Clark Pinnock, 71–96. Minneapolis: Bethany House, 1995.

Moore, Jonathan D. *English Hypothetical Universalism: John Preston and the Softening of Reformed Theology*. Grand Rapids: Eerdmans, 2007.

Moore, Russell D. "Personal and Cosmic Eschatology." In *Theology for the Church*, edited by Daniel L. Akin, 858–926. Nashville: B&H, 2007.

Morey, Robert A. *Studies in the Atonement*. Shermans Dale, PA: Christian Scholars, 1989.

Morris, Leon. *The Apostolic Preaching of the Cross*. 3rd ed. Grand Rapids: Eerdmans, 1965.

———. *The Epistle to the Romans*. The Pillar New Testament Commentary. Grand Rapids: Eerdmans, 1988.

———. *The First Epistle of Paul to the Corinthians: An Introduction and Commentary*. Tyndale New Testament Commentary. Grand Rapids: Eerdmans, 1985.

———. *The Gospel According to John*. The New International Commentary on the New Testament. Rev. ed. Grand Rapids: Eerdmans, 1995.

———. *Hebrews*. In vol. 12 of *The Expositor's Bible Commentary*.vEdited by Frank E. Gaebelein, 3–158. Grand Rapids: Zondervan, 1981.

Mounce, Robert. *The Essential Nature of New Testament Preaching*. Grand Rapids: Eerdmans, 1960.

Mounce, William D. *Pastoral Epistles*. Word Biblical Commentary, vol. 46. Waco, TX: Word, 2000.

Mouw, Richard J. *He Shines in All That's Fair: Culture and Common Grace*. Grand Rapids: Eerdmans, 2001.

Mozley, J. B. *A Treatise on the Augustinian Doctrine of Predestination*. 2nd ed. New York: E. P. Dutton, 1878.

Muller, Richard A. *Christ and the Decree: Christology and Predestination in Reformed Theology from Calvin to Perkins*. Studies in Historical Theology 2. Durham, NC: The Labyrinth, 1986.

Mullins, Edgar Young. *The Christian Religion in its Doctrinal Expression*. Philadelphia: Judson, 1917.

Murray, John. "Calvin on the Extent of the Atonement." *Banner of Truth* 234 (1983) 20–22.

———. *Redemption Accomplished and Applied*. Grand Rapids: Eerdmans, 1955.

Naselli, Andy. "John Owen's Argument for Definite Atonement in *The Death of Death in the Death of Christ*: A Brief Summary and Evaluation. *The Southern Baptist Journal of Theology* 14 (2010) 60–82.

Nelson, David P. "The Design, Nature, and Extent of the Atonement." In *A Southern Baptist Dialogue: Calvinism*, edited by E. Ray Clendenen and Brad J. Waggoner, 115–38. Nashville: B&H, 2008.

Nettles, Thomas J. *By His Grace and for His Glory*. 2nd ed. Lake Charles, LA: Cor Meum Tibi, 2002.

Nicole, Roger. "Amyraldianism." In *The Encyclopedia of Christianity*. Edited by Edwin H. Palmer. Wilmington, DE: National Foundation for Christian Education, 1964.

———. "The Case for Definite Atonement." *Bulletin of the Evangelical Theological Society* 10 (1967) 199–207.

———. "C. H. Dodd and the Doctrine of Propitiation." *Westminster Theological Journal* 17 (1955) 117–57.

———. "Covenant, Universal Call, and Definite Atonement." *Journal of the Evangelical Theological Society* 38 (1995) 403–11.

———. "The Doctrine of Definite Atonement in the Heidelberg Catechism." *Gordon Review* 3 (1964) 138–45.

———. "John Calvin's View of the Extent of the Atonement." *Westminster Theological Journal* 47 (1985) 197–225.

———. "Particular Redemption." In *Our Savior God: Studies on Man, Christ, and the Atonement*, edited by James Montgomery Boice, 165–78. Grand Rapids: Baker, 1980.

Nineham, Dennis. E. "Gottschalk of Orbais: Reactionary or Precursor of the Reformation?" *Journal of Ecclesiastical History* 40 (1989) 1–18.

O'Brien, P. T. *Colossians, Philemon*. Word Biblical Commentary, vol. 44. Waco, TX: Word, 1982.

———. *The Letter to the Ephesians*. The Pillar New Testament Commentary. Grand Rapids: Eerdmans, 1999.

———. *The Letter to the Hebrews*. The Pillar New Testament Commentary. Grand Rapids: Eerdmans, 2010.

Oden, Thomas C. *Systematic Theology*. 3 vols. Peabody, MA: Hendrickson, 2006.

Olson, Roger E. *Against Calvinism*. Grand Rapids: Zondervan, 2011.

———. *Arminian Theology: Myths and Realities*. Downers Grove, IL: InterVarsity, 2006.

Osborne, Grant R. *The Hermeneutical Spiral: A Comprehensive Introduction to Biblical Interpretation*. Downers Grove, IL: InterVarsity, 1991.

———. *Revelation*. Baker Exegetical Commentary on the New Testament. Grand Rapids: Baker, 2002.

———. "Soteriology in the Gospel of John." In *The Grace of God and the Will of Man*, edited by Clark H. Pinnock, 243–60. Minneapolis: Bethany House, 1989.

Oswalt, John N. *The Book of Isaiah: Chapters 40–66*. The New International Commentary on the Old Testament. Grand Rapids: Eerdmans, 1998.

———. "Isaiah 52:13–53:12: Servant of All." *Calvin Theological Journal* 40 (2005) 85–94.

Outler, Albert C. *The Wesleyan Theological Heritage*. Edited by Thomas C. Oden and Leicester R. Longden. Grand Rapids: Zondervan, 1991.

Owen, John. *The Death of Death in the Death of Christ*. Carlisle, PA: Banner of Truth, 1959.

Packer, J. I. *Evangelism and the Sovereignty of God*. Downers Grove, IL: InterVarsity, 1961.

———. "Introductory Essay." In *The Death of Death in the Death of Christ*, by John Owen, 1–25. Carlisle, PA: Banner of Truth, 1959.

———. "The Love of God: Universal and Particular." In *Still Sovereign: Contemporary Perspectives on Election, Foreknowledge, and Grace*, edited by Thomas R. Schreiner and Bruce A. Ware, 277–91. Grand Rapids: Baker, 2000.

———. *The Redemption and Restoration of Man in the Thought of Richard Baxter*. Vancouver: Regent College, 2003.

———. "To All Who Will Come." In *Our Savior God: Studies on Man, Christ, and the Atonement*, edited by James Montgomery Boice, 179–89. Grand Rapids: Baker, 1980.

———. "What Did the Cross Achieve: The Logic of Penal Substitution." *Tyndale Bulletin* 25 (1974) 3–45.

Palmer, Edwin H. *The Five Points of Calvinism*. Grand Rapids: Baker, 1972.

Pelikan, Jaroslav. *The Christian Tradition: A History of the Development of Doctrine*. Vol. 1, *The Emergence of the Catholic Tradition (100–600)*. Chicago: University of Chicago Press, 1971.

———. *The Christian Tradition: A History of the Development of Doctrine*. Vol. 3, *The Growth of Medieval Theology (600–1300)*. Chicago: University of Chicago Press, 1978.

———. *The Christian Tradition: A History of the Development of Doctrine*. Vol. 4, *Reformation of Church and Dogma (1300–1700)*. Chicago: University of Chicago Press, 1984.

Peterson, Robert A. *Calvin and the Atonement*. Fearn, Scotland: Christian Focus, 1999.

———. *Election and Free Will: God's Gracious Choice and Our Responsibility*. Explorations in Biblical Theology. Phillipsburg, NJ: P&R, 2007.

Peterson, Robert A., and Michael D. Williams. *Why I Am Not an Arminian*. Downers Grove, IL: InterVarsity, 2004.

Picirilli, Robert E. *Grace, Faith, Free Will; Contrasting Views of Salvation: Calvinism and Arminianism*. Nashville: Randall House, 2002.

Pieper, Frank. *Christian Dogmatics*. St. Louis: Concordia, 1951.

Pink, Arthur W. *The Sovereignty of God*. Grand Rapids: Baker, 1979.

Pinnock, Clark H. "Divine Election as Corporate, Open, and Vocational." In *Perspectives on Election: Five Views*, edited by Chad Owen Brand, 276–314. Nashville: Broadman and Holman, 2006.

———. *The Flame of Love: A Theology of the Holy Spirit.* Downers Grove, IL: InterVarsity, 1996.

———. *A Wideness in God's Mercy: The Finality of Jesus Christ in a World of Religions.* Grand Rapids: Zondervan, 1992.

Piper, John. "Are There Two Wills in God?" n *Still Sovereign: Contemporary Perspectives on Election, Foreknowledge, and Grace*, edited by Thomas R. Schreiner and Bruce A. Ware, 107–31. Grand Rapids: Baker, 2000.

———. *Fifty Reasons Why Jesus Came to Die.* Wheaton, IL: Crossway, 2006.

———. *Let the Nations Be Glad: The Supremacy of God in Missions.* Grand Rapids: Baker, 1993.

———. *The Supremacy of God in Preaching.* Grand Rapids: Baker, 1990.

Ponter, David. "Review Essay (Part One): John Calvin on the Death of Christ and the Reformation's Forgotten Doctrine of Universal Vicarious Satisfaction: A Review and Critique of Tom Nettles' Chapter in Whomever He Wills." *Southwestern Journal of Theology* 55 (2012), 139–59.

———. "Review Essay (Part Two): John Calvin on the Death of Christ and the Reformation's Forgotten Doctrine of Universal Vicarious Satisfaction: A Review and Critique of Tom Nettles' Chapter in Whomever He Wills." *Southwestern Journal of Theology* 55 (2013), 253–71.

Pope, William Burton. *A Compendium of Christian Theology.* 2 vols. 2nd ed. New York: Phillips and Hunt, 1874.

Rainbow, Jonathan H. *The Will of God and the Cross: An Historical and Theological Study of John Calvin's Doctrine of Limited Redemption.* Allison Park, PA: Pickwick, 1990.

Ramm, Bernard. *The Witness of the Spirit: An Essay on the Contemporary Relevance of the Witness of the Holy Spirit.* Grand Rapids: Eerdmans, 1959.

Reisinger, John G. *Limited Atonement.* Frederick, MD: New Covenant Media, 2002.

Renshaw, John Rutherford. "The Atonement in the Theology of John and Charles Wesley." Th.D. diss., Boston University School of Theology, 1966.

Reymond, Robert L. "A Consistent Supralapsarian Perspective on Election." In *Perspectives on Election: Five Views*, edited by Chad O. Brand, 150–94. Nashville: B&H Academic, 2006.

———. *A New Systematic Theology of the Christian Faith.* Nashville: Thomas Nelson, 1998.

Rist, John M. "Augustine on Free Will and Predestination." *Journal of Theological Studies* 20 (1969) 420–47.

Ryrie, Charles C. *Basic Theology.* Colorado Springs, CO: Victor, 1986.

Sailer, William S. "The Nature and Extent of the Atonement: A Wesleyan View." *Bulletin of the Evangelical Theological Society* 10 (1967) 189–98.

Sanders, John. *No Other Name: An Investigation into the Destiny of the Unevangelized.* Grand Rapids: Eerdmans, 1992

Scaer, David. "The Nature and Extent of the Atonement in Lutheran Theology." *Bulletin of the Evangelical Theological Society* 10 (1967) 179–87.

Schaff, Philip. *History of the Christian Church.* 8 vols. Peabody, MA: Hendrickson, 1996.

Schreiner, Thomas R. *1, 2 Peter, Jude.* The New American Commentary, vol. 37. Nashville: Broadman and Holman, 2003.

———. "Does Romans 9 Teach Individual Election unto Salvation?" In *Still Sovereign: Contemporary Perspectives on Election, Foreknowledge, and Grace*, edited by Thomas R. Schreiner and Bruce A. Ware, 89–106. Grand Rapids: Baker, 2000.

———. "Does Scripture Teach Prevenient Grace in the Wesleyan Sense?" In *Still Sovereign: Contemporary Perspectives on Election, Foreknowledge, and Grace*, edited by Thomas R. Schreiner and Bruce A. Ware, 229–46. Grand Rapids: Baker, 2000.

———. "Penal Substitution View." In *The Nature of the Atonement: Four Views*, edited by James Beilby and Paul R. Eddy, 67–98. Downers Grove, IL: InterVarsity, 2006.

———. *Romans*. Baker Exegetical Commentary on the New Testament. Grand Rapids: Baker, 1998.

Sell, Alan F. *The Great Debate: Calvinism, Arminianism, and Salvation*. Grand Rapids: Baker, 1983.

Sharp, Larry. "The Doctrines of Grace in Calvin and Augustine." *Evangelical Quarterly* 52 (1980) 84–96.

Shedd, William G. T. *Dogmatic Theology*. 3 vols. Grand Rapids: Zondervan, 1969.

Shelton, R. Larry. "Initial Salvation: The Redemptive Grace of God in Christ." In *A Contemporary Wesleyan Theology*, edited by Charles W. Carter, 473–516. Grand Rapids: Zondervan, 1983.

Shultz, Gary L., Jr. "God's Purposes in Preaching and the Extent of the Atonement." Paper presented at the annual meeting of the Evangelical Theological Society, San Diego, CA, 15 November 2007.

———. "God's Purposes in the Atonement for the Nonelect." *Bibliotheca Sacra* 165 (2008) 145–63.

———. "The Necessity of the Gospel in the Holy Spirit's Saving Work." *Journal of Baptist Theology and Ministry* 6.1 (2009) 74–83.

———. "The Reconciliation of All Things in Christ." *Bibliotheca Sacra* 167 (2010) 442–59.

———. "Why a Genuine Universal Gospel Call Requires an Atonement that Paid for All Sin." *Evangelical Quarterly* 82 (2010) 111–23.

Skeat, T. C. "'Especially the Parchments': A Note on 2 Timothy 4:13." *Journal of Theological Studies* 30 (1979) 173–77.

Smalley, Stephen S. *1, 2, 3 John*. Word Biblical Commentary, vol. 51. Waco, TX: Word, 1984.

Smeaton, George. *The Apostle's Doctrine of the Atonement*. Grand Rapids: Zondervan, 1957.

Sproul, R. C. *The Truth of the Cross*. Orlando, FL: Reformation Trust, 2007.

Stott, John R. W. *Baptism and Fullness: The Work of the Holy Spirit* 2nd ed. Downers Grove, IL: InterVarsity, 1975.

———. *The Cross of Christ*. 2nd ed. Downers Grove, IL: InterVarsity, 2006.

Strange, Daniel. *The Possibility of Salvation among the Unevangelized: An Analysis of Inclusivism in Recent Evangelical Theology*. Carlisle, UK: Paternoster, 2002.

Strauss, James D. "God's Promise and Universal History." In *Grace Unlimited*, edited by Clark H. Pinnock, 190–208. Minneapolis: Bethany House, 1975.

Strehle, Stephen A. "The Extent of the Atonement at the Synod of Dort." *Westminster Journal of Theology* 51 (1989) 1–23.

———. "The Extent of the Atonement within the Theological Systems of the Sixteenth and Seventeenth Centuries," Th.D. diss., Dallas Theological Seminary, 1980.

Strong, Augustus H. *Systematic Theology*. Valley Forge, PA: Judson, 1907.
Summers, Thomas. *Systematic Theology: A Complete Body of Wesleyan Arminian Divinity*. 2 vols. Nashville: Methodist Episcopal Church, South, 1888.
Symington, William. *The Atonement and Intercession of Jesus Christ*. New York: Robert Carter & Brothers, 1863. Reprint, Grand Rapids: Reformation Heritage, 2006.
Tasker, R. V. G. *The Second Epistle to the Corinthians*. Tyndale New Testament Commentaries. Grand Rapids: Eerdmans, 1958.
Tenney, Merrill C. *The Gospel of John*. In vol. 9 of *The Expositor's Bible Commentary*. Edited by Frank E. Gaebelein, 3–206. Grand Rapids: Zondervan, 1981.
Thiessen, Henry C. *Lectures in Systematic Theology*. Revised by Vernon D. Doerksen. Grand Rapids: Eerdmans, 1979.
Thiselton, Anthony C. *The First Epistle to the Corinthians: A Commentary on the Greek Text*. The New International Greek Testament Commentary. Grand Rapids: Eerdmans, 2000.
Thomas Aquinas. *Summa Theologica*. Translated by Fathers of the English Dominican Province. 3 vols. New York: Benzinger Brothers, 1947–48.
Thomas, G. Michael. *The Extent of the Atonement: A Dilemma for Reformed Theology from Calvin to Consensus (1536–1675)*. Studies in Christian History and Thought. Blechtley, UK: Paternoster, 1997.
Thomas, Robert. *1 & 2 Thessalonians*. In vol.11 of *The Expositor's Bible Commentary*. Edited by Frank E. Gaebelein, 227–338. Grand Rapids: Zondervan, 1981.
Tiessen, Terrance L. *Who Can Be Saved? Reassessing Salvation in Christ and World Religions*. Downers Grove, IL: InterVarsity, 2004.
Torrance, James B. "The Incarnation and 'Limited Atonement.'" *Evangelical Quarterly* 55 (1983) 83–94.
Towner, Philip H. *The Letters to Timothy and Titus*. The New International Commentary on the New Testament. Grand Rapids: Eerdmans, 2006.
Troxel, A. Craig. "Amyraut 'at' the Assembly: The *Westminster Confession of Faith* and the Extent of the Atonement." *Presbyterion* 22 (1996) 43–55.
Turner, David L. "Paul and the Ministry of Reconciliation in 2 Cor. 5:11–6:2." *Criswell Theological Review* 4 (1989) 77–95.
Turretin, Francis. *Institutes of Elenctic Theology*. Edited by James T. Dennison, Jr. Translated by George Musgrave Giger. 3 vols. Phillipsburg, NJ: P&R, 1992–97.
———. *Turretin on the Atonement of Christ*. Board of Publication of the Reformed Protestant Dutch Church, 1859. Reprint, Grand Rapids: Baker, 1978.
Vaughan, Curtis. *Colossians*. In vol. 11 of *The Expositor's Bible Commentary*. Edited by Frank E. Gaebelein, 161–226. Grand Rapids: Zondervan, 1981.
Waggoner, Brad J., and E. Ray Clendenen, eds. *Calvinism: A Southern Baptist Dialogue* Nashville: B&H, 2008.
Waldron, Sam. "The Biblical Confirmation of Particular Redemption." In *A Southern Baptist Dialogue: Calvinism*, edited by E. Ray Clendenen and Brad J. Waggoner, 139–52. Nashville: B&H, 2008.
Walls, Jerry L., and Joseph R. Dongell. *Why I Am Not a Calvinist*. Downers Grove, IL: InterVarsity, 2004.
Walvoord, John F. *The Holy Spirit*. 3rd ed. Grand Rapids: Zondervan, 1954.
———. *Jesus Christ Our Lord*. Chicago: Moody, 1980.
———. "Reconciliation." *Bibliotheca Sacra* 120 (1963) 3–12.

Bibliography

Wardlaw, Ralph. *Discourses on the Nature and Extent of the Atonement.* Glasgow: James Maclehose, 1854.

Ware, Bruce A. "*Cur Deus Trinus*? The Relation of the Trinity to Christ's Identity as Savior and to the Efficacy of His Atoning Death." *The Southern Baptist Journal of Theology* 10 (2006): 48–56.

———. "Divine Election to Salvation: Unconditional, Individual, and Infralapsarian." In *Perspectives on Election: Five Views*, edited by Chad O. Brand, 1–58. Nashville: Broadman and Holman, 2006.

———. "Effectual Calling and Grace." In *Still Sovereign: Contemporary Perspectives on Election, Foreknowledge, and Grace*, edited by Thomas R. Schreiner and Bruce A. Ware, 203–28. Grand Rapids: Baker, 2000.

———. "Extent of the Atonement: Outline of the Issue, Positions, Key Texts, and Key Theological Arguments." Unpublished class handout. The Southern Baptist Theological Seminary, Louisville, KY, n.d.

———. *Father, Son, and Holy Spirit: Relationships, Roles, and Relevance.* Wheaton, IL: Crossway, 2005.

Warfield, Benjamin B. *The Person and Work of Christ.* Edited by Samuel G. Craig. Phillipsburg, NJ: Presbyterian and Reformed, 1950.

———. *The Plan of Salvation.* Rev. ed. Grand Rapids: Eerdmans, 1935. Reprint, Eugene, OR: Wipf and Stock, 2000.

———. *Selected Shorter Writings of Benjamin B. Warfield.* Edited by John E. Meeter. 2 vols. Nutley, NJ: Presbyterian and Reformed, 1970–73.

Watson, Richard. *Theological Institutes.* 2 vols. New York: Lane & Scott, 1851.

Wells, Paul. *Cross Words: The Biblical Doctrine of the Atonement.* Fearn, Scotland: Christian Focus, 2006.

Wells, Tom. *A Price for a People: The Meaning of Christ's Death.* Carlisle, PA: Banner of Truth Trust, 1992.

Wellum, Stephen J. "An Evaluation of the Son-Spirit Relation in Clark Pinnock's Inclusivism: An Exercise in Trinitarian Reflection." *The Southern Baptist Journal of Theology* 10 (2006) 4–23.

Wesley, John. *The Works of John Wesley.* Edited by Frank Baker. The Bicentennial ed. Nashville: Oxford, 1975–93.

———. *The Works of John Wesley* [CD-ROM]. Edited by Thomas Jackson. Franklin, TN: Providence House, 1994.

Wiley, H. Orton. *Christian Theology.* 2 vols. Kansas City, MO: Beacon Hill, 1941.

Williams, Jarvis J. *For Whom Did Christ Die? The Extent of the Atonement in Paul's Theology.* Milton Keynes, UK: Paternoster, 2012.

Wood, Arthur Skevington. "The Contribution of John Wesley to the Theology of Grace." In *Grace Unlimited*, edited by Clark H. Pinnock, 209–22. Minneapolis: Bethany Fellowship, 1975.

Yarbrough, Robert W. "Divine Election in the Gospel of John." In *Still Sovereign: Contemporary Perspectives on Election, Foreknowledge, and Grace*, edited by Thomas R. Schreiner and Bruce A. Ware, 47–62. Grand Rapids: Baker, 2000.

Name Index

Abelard, Peter, 142
Adam, Peter, 157
Allen, David, 4, 52
Ambrose, 18, 44
Amyraut, Moïse, 23, 34–39, 52–53, 156
Andreae, Jakob, 28–29
Anselm, 19, 21
Archibald, Paul, 16–18, 23–24, 26, 32
Arminius, Jacob, x, 29–31, 39, 44, 46–47, 49, 52, 156
Armstrong, Brian, 23, 27, 34–37
Arnold, Clinton, 112–13
Athanasius, 44
Augustine, 12–17, 19–20, 24–25, 44, 48–49, 52
Aulén, Gustav, 113

Bancroft, Emery, 50–51
Bangs, Carl, 31
Barnes, Tom, 49
Barnett, Paul 69–70, 94
Barth, Karl, 7, 15
Bauckham, Richard, 79–80, 83
Baugh, Steven, 72–76, 128
Bavinck, Herman, 13, 15, 54–55, 65, 67, 73, 77–78, 88, 102, 107, 111
Baxter, Richard, 36, 39–41, 52–53, 156
Beachy, Alvin, 23
Beasley-Murray, George, 136
Beilby, James, 142
Bell, M. Charles, 23, 26
Beougher, Timothy, 39–40
Berkhof, Louis, 2–3, 5, 15, 48, 54–55, 60, 66–67, 70, 73, 75, 77–78, 82–84, 92–93, 97, 102, 108, 130, 144
Beza, Theodore, ix, 2, 17, 23, 26–30, 36, 49
Blacketer, Raymond, 13, 15, 19, 24
Blocher, Henri, 117
Bloesch, Donald, 47, 108, 138–39
Blum, Edwin, 80, 82, 100–101
Bock, Darrell, 131
Boersma, Hans, 24, 55, 102
Boettner, Lorraine, 7, 48, 54, 102, 124–25
Borchert, Gerald, 118
Boyce, James, 48
Boyd, Gregory, 113
Bradwardine, Thomas, 21
Brand, Chad, 47, 147
Breshears, Gerry, 7
Brine, John 92
Bruce, F. F., 61–62, 96, 111, 116, 126–27, 130–32, 134–37, 143, 158
Bucer, Martin, 23, 26
Bullinger, Heinrich, 27, 29
Bushnell, Horace, 142
Buswell, James, 49

Calvin, John, 17, 22–27, 35, 36, 48–49, 52, 66, 75, 78, 101, 148
Cameron, John, 35, 37
Campbell, John, 50
Carson, D. A., 7, 58–61, 90, 100, 108–9, 129–30, 133–36, 143, 150
Chafer, Lewis, 6, 50–51, 53, 73, 82, 92, 96, 156
Chang, Andrew, 80–82

Name Index

Chisholm, Robert, 56
Clarke, F. Stuart, 31
Clendenen, Ray, 52
Cole, Graham, 139, 141, 146–47, 149
Combs, William, 7, 127
Cottrell, Jack, 124, 128–29
Crawford, Thomas, 96–97
Culver, Robert, 7, 105
Cunningham, William, 48

Dabney, R. L, 48
Daniel, Curt, 23, 25–26
Davenant, John, 13, 29, 33, 53, 156
Davids, Peter, 79–82, 99
Delitzsch, Franz, 57
Demarest, Bruce, 4–5, 7, 51, 71, 73, 85, 90, 108, 127–28, 133, 140, 143–44, 148, 150–51
Denck, Hans, 23
Dodd, C. H., 64
Dongell, Joseph, 50
Douty, Norman, 22–23, 51, 71, 73, 78, 92, 130, 132
Driscoll, Mark, 7
Dunham, Duane, 49
Dunning, Ray, 7, 50, 127

Earle, Ralph, 72–73
Eddy, Paul, 142
Edwards, Jonathan, 47
Ellingworth, Paul, 78
Elliott, Grant, 49
Elwell, Walter, 13
Erickson, Millard, 6–7, 51, 53, 55, 57–58, 76, 99, 124–25, 132, 144, 151

Feinberg, John, 126
Ferguson, Sinclair, 139
Fesko, J. V., 15
Finney, Charles, 49–50
Forlines, F. Leroy, 50
Frame, John, 62, 106, 110, 129
Freeman, M. S., 16–17, 19
Fudge, Edward, 117

Gaffin, Richard, 118
Garland, David, 68, 70–71
Garrett, James, 15, 51

Geisler, Norman, 15, 145
Gentry, Peter, 58
Gill, John, 2, 92
Godfrey, W. Robert, 15, 18, 24, 28–29, 32, 34
Gottschalk, 16–17, 20–21, 52
Gregory of Rimini, 18, 21
Griffin, Hayne, 73–74, 76–77
Grotius, Hugo, 39–40
Grounds, Vernon, 127
Grudem, Wayne, 2–3, 5, 49, 61, 65, 75, 84, 97, 99, 125, 130–31, 145, 149, 151
Guy, Fritz, 91, 108

Hall, Basil, 23, 27
Hamilton, James, 146
Hammett, John, 142
Hansen, Collin, 1
Hansen, G. Walter, 144
Hansen, Wayne, 7
Harris, Murray, 67–68, 70–71
Harris, Walt, 59
Hartog, Paul, 23
Hawthorne, Gerald, 119
Helm, Paul, 23–24
Hicks, John, 31
Hiebert, D. Edmund, 77, 80, 100, 143
Hill, Charles, 49, 108
Hincmar of Reims, 16–17
Hodge, A.A., 47–48
Hodge, Charles, 3, 15, 47–48, 65, 102, 104–5, 124
Hoekema, Anthony, 33–34, 128, 143–44, 148
Hoeksema, Herman, 92
Hoffman, Melchior, 23
Hopkins, Samuel, 39
Horton, Michael, 1
Hunt, Dave, 50, 108, 124, 159
Hus, John, 21

Irenaeus, 13

James, Frank, 49
Jeffery, Steve, 49, 57, 113
Jewett, Paul, 15, 128
Jinkins, Michael, 26

Name Index

Johnson, Timothy, 78–79

Kaiser, Walter, 147
Kärkkäinen, Veli-Matti, 138
Kelly, J. N. D., 13, 16, 74
Kendall, R. T., 23, 25
Kennard, Douglas, 80–81, 83
Kennedy, Kevin, 23–26
Kent, Homer, 117
Kimedoncius, Jacobus, 29
Klein, William, 124
Knight, George, 73–74, 77
Koester, Craig, 61
Köstenberger, Andreas, 61, 146
Kruse, Colin, 63, 70
Kuiper, R. B., 3, 6, 22, 48–49, 54, 62, 66–67, 70, 75, 82, 97, 102, 111, 124–25, 130

Ladd, George, 69, 115
Lake, Donald, 50, 91–92, 124
Lane, Anthony, 23
Lane, William, 78
Langford, Thomas, 7
Lea, Thomas, 73–74, 76–77
Leahy, F. S., 23–24
Lemke, Steve, 52
Letham, Robert, 2–3, 5, 15, 29, 49–50, 62–63, 65–67, 73, 85, 108, 111, 124, 138
Lewis, Gordon, 7, 51
Lightner, Robert, 4–6, 50–51, 55, 62, 71, 79. 92, 96, 98, 108, 119, 132
Lincoln, Andrew, 86, 114–15, 126, 131
Lints, Richard, 9
Lombard, Peter, 18–20, 52
Long, Gary, 3, 49, 65–66, 70, 73, 80–81, 108, 124
Longenecker, Richard, 132
López René, 145
Luther, Martin, 22–23

MacArthur, John, 62
Macchia, Frank, 147
MacDonald, William, 128–29
Malone, M. T., 30
Mangum, R. Todd, 138

Marshall, I. Howard, 4, 9, 50, 60, 64, 70–75, 77, 84–85, 92, 108, 111–12, 115, 124, 132
Martin, Ralph, 67, 70
Martinus, Matthias, 29, 33
McCartney, Dan, 82
McDonald, H. D., 30, 39, 142
McGonigle, Herbert, 39, 45–46
Michaels, J. Ramsey, 61, 64–65
Miethe, Terry, 50, 73, 92, 145, 159
Miley, John, 49–50
Moore, Jonathan, 30, 36
Moore, Russell, 99–100, 117–18
More, Thomas, 44
Morey, Robert, 49
Morris, Leon, 61, 64, 74, 79, 81, 93, 103, 130–31, 134–36
Moulin, Pierre du, 33, 35
Mounce, Robert, 157
Mounce, William, 72–74, 76–77
Mouw, Richard, 103
Mozley, J. B., 15
Muller, Richard, 24
Mullins, E. Y., 51
Murray, John, 3, 22, 24, 48, 54–55, 65–67, 78, 88, 97, 102, 130, 148
Musculus, Abraham, 29

Naselli, Andrew, 2
Nelson, David, 7, 152
Nettles, Tom, 2, 24, 51, 66, 73, 78, 81
Nicole, Roger, 2–3, 5, 24, 29, 32, 35, 47, 49–50, 54, 58–59, 64–67, 70, 73, 77–78, 82, 84, 88, 92–93, 97, 102, 108, 124–25, 132
Nineham, Dennis, 16

O'Brien, Peter, 79, 138, 144
Oden, Thomas, 50
Olevianus, Casper, 29
Olson, Roger, 1, 7, 45, 98, 108, 124, 127
Osborne, Grant, 120, 134–36
Oswalt, John, 56–58, 91
Ovey, Michael, 49, 57, 113
Owen, John 3, 6, 35, 38, 41–44, 49, 52, 58, 60, 62, 65, 67, 70, 72–73, 78, 81–82, 84, 108, 124–25

Name Index

Packer, J. I., 3, 39–41, 44, 49, 92–93, 97, 107–9, 124–25
Palmer, Edwin, 50
Pareus, David, 29, 33
Pelagius, 13
Pelikan, Jaroslav, 13, 15–17, 32
Perkins, William, 29–30
Peterson, Robert, 24, 49–50, 117, 129, 136
Picirilli, Robert, 4–5, 30, 50, 73, 85, 92, 124, 132
Pieper, Frank, 23
Pink, Arthur, 65
Pinnock, Clark, 124, 138
Piper, John, 49, 72, 90, 157
Ponter, David, 23
Pope, William, 49
Prosper of Aquitaine, 15, 44

Rainbow, Jonathan, 14–19, 22–24
Ramm, Bernard, 150
Rashdall, Hastings, 142
Reisinger, John, 49
Renshaw, John, 46
Reymond, Robert, 49–50
Rist, John, 15
Ritschl, Albrecht, 142
Ryrie, Charles, 50–51

Sach, Andrew, 49, 57, 113
Sailer, William, 6, 50, 73, 82, 132
Sanders, John, 138
Scaer, David, 23
Schaff, Philip, 17
Schilder, Klaas, 92
Schleirmacher, Friedrich, 142
Schonbergius, Eusebius, 28
Schreiner, Thomas, 7, 79–82, 101, 127–28, 131, 138, 141
Scotus, Duns, 21, 29
Sell, Alan, 39
Sharp, Larry, 15
Shedd, William, 48, 60, 66–67, 70, 78, 82, 84
Shelton, R. Larry, 50
Shultz, Gary, 6, 92, 157
Skeat, T. C., 75
Smalley, Stephen, 63–64

Smeaton, George, 48, 65, 82
Spanheim, Friedrich, 35
Sproul, R. C., 49
Stott, John, 107, 113, 138, 142, 147
Strange, Daniel, 9
Strauss, James, 128
Strehle, Stephan, 19–23, 29, 32–34, 36
Strong, Augustus, 51, 103–5, 108, 124, 143
Summers, Thomas, 49
Symington, William, 48

Tasker, R. V. G., 68
Tenney, Merrill, 130
Thiessen, Henry, 50–51
Thiselton, Anthony, 145
Thomas Aquinas, 18–21, 29, 52, 156
Thomas, G. Michael, 7, 13, 15, 19, 22–29, 32–38, 41, 159
Thomas, Robert, 104
Tiessen, Terrance, 66–67, 70, 73, 77, 82, 111, 124–25, 138
Torrance, James, 23
Tossanus, Daniel, 29
Towner, Philip, 73
Turner, David, 71
Turretin, Francis, 13, 15, 35, 38, 75

Ussher, James, 29

Vermigli, Peter, 29

Waggoner, Brad, 52
Waldron, Sam, 93
Walls, Jerry, 50
Walvoord, John 50–51, 71, 98–99, 102, 104, 139, 145–46
Ward, Samuel, 29, 33
Wardlaw, Ralph, 50
Ware, Bruce, 7, 86, 91, 123, 126–28, 131, 134, 136–37, 140–41, 144
Warfield, B. B., 47–48, 66, 111, 124–25
Watson, Richard, 49
Wiley, H. Orton, 7, 50, 124, 127
Wells, Paul, 5, 49
Wells, Tom, 49, 57–58, 65, 67, 70, 73, 78, 82–83
Wellum, Stephen, 139

Wesley, John, x, 44–47, 49, 52, 156
Whitefield, George, 45, 47
Williams, Jarvis, 13
Williams, Michael, 49–50
Williams, Stephen, 117
Wood, Arthur, 127

Wycliffe, John 18, 21–22, 52

Yarbrough, Robert, 123, 134

Zanchi, Girolamo, 29

Scripture Index

Genesis
3:15	105, 112
4:15	101, 104
9:6	104
11:1–9	104
12:1–3	123
20:6	104
41:38	146

Exodus
28:3	146
31:3	146
34:6	103
35:30–35	146

Numbers
11:17, 25	146
16:5–7	123
27:18	146

Deuteronomy
4:37–38	129
4:37	129
6:4	73
7:6–8	123
7:7–9	129
7:7–8	129
10:14–15	129
33:3	129

Judges
3:10	146
6:34	146

1 Samuel
10:9–10	146
16:13	146

1 Kings
3:8	123

Psalms
8:4–6	78
22:27	90
66:5, 7	101
73	109
89:1–4	129
104:10–11, 14–15	101
132:13	123
145:9	106
145:16–17	101, 103

Proverbs
18:22	xiii

Ecclesiastes
12:10	158

Isaiah
6:9–10	101
16:6	57
24:16	57
42:1–9	56

42:1, 4	58
42:1	123
42:6	58
42:24	57
43:3–4	129
45:21	91
45:22	90–91, 141
49–52	56
49:1–13	56
49:6	58
50:4–11	56
52:13–53:12	56
52:13–15	56–58
53	56, 58–59, 61
53:1–9	57
53:1–3	56
53:1	57
53:3–6	57
53:4–6	9, 56–57, 138, 153
53:6	3, 6, 57–58, 87, 155
53:7–9	56
53:10–12	56
53:11–12	58
53:11	58
53:12	24
54–55	56
55:1	90
64:6	103
65:2	90
65:5–6	57

Jeremiah

1:5	123
31:31–34	58

Ezekiel

33:11	106

Daniel

4:8	146
5:11–14	146
6:3	146

Hosea

11:1–4	129

Malachi

1:2–3	129

Matthew

1:21	2, 6, 129, 155
3:1–12	91
3:11–12	119
3:11	147
5:43–47	101
5:45	76, 103
10:20	92, 139
10:28	24
11:25–27	133
11:25	133
11:26	133
11:27	133
11:28–30	133
11:28	91, 133, 141
13:11–16	101
16:18	104
20:28	58
22:1–14	91
22:14	91
25:31–46	119
26:28	22
28:18–20	90–91, 158

Mark

1:3–8	91
1:8	147
10:35–40	119
10:45	58, 74
14:24	22, 24
16:15	91, 158

Luke

2:29	80
3:2–20	91
3:16	147
5:32	91
10:21–22	133
11:13	92, 139
12:47–48	100
12:49–50	119
14:16–24	91
14:23	141

22:20	58
23:34	85
24:47	91, 158

John

1:1	136, 149
1:6–8	91
1:9	15, 59, 103, 127
1:10, 29	59
1:10	60
1:12–13	144
1:14, 18	110
1:16	101
1:19–34	91
1:29, 36	130
1:29	9, 56, 59–60, 87, 91, 153
1:33	147
3:3–8	143
3:16–18	62
3:16–17	9, 14, 56, 59, 61, 153
3:16	x–xi, 3, 28, 32, 59–62, 90, 107, 129, 155
3:16a	x
3:16b	x
3:16c	x
3:18	62, 98
3:36	62
4:42	9, 56, 59–61, 63, 87, 130, 153
5:6	134
5:19–21	133–34
5:19	133–34
5:20	134
5:21	134
5:22, 26, 30	134
5:26–28	118
5:28	118
6:26–27	134
6:33, 51	59–60
6:33	59, 61
6:35	134
6:36	134
6:37ff.	130
6:37–40	2, 6, 134–35, 150, 155
6:37–38	136
6:37, 39	141
6:37	134
6:38	135, 139
6:39	135
6:40	135, 142
6:44	141
6:51	9, 56, 59–61, 153
6:65	144
7:7	59–60
7:37–39	146
7:37–38	91
7:39	139, 145
8:23	59–60
9:39	60
10:11–18	135
10:11, 14–15	129
10:11, 15	ix, 2, 6, 155
10:24–25	135
10:26–30	135
10:26	135
10:27	135
10:28–29	150
10:28	135
10:29	135
10:30	136
10:31–39	135
11:9	60
11:26	133
12:19	59
12:20–28	106
12:31	59, 112
12:32	16, 19, 22, 25, 61, 127
12:38	57
12:46–47	9, 56, 153
12:47	59, 61
13:30–32	106
14:2–3	151
14:17, 22, 27, 30	60
14:17, 19	59
14:17	146
14:22, 27, 30	59
14:26	139
14:30	112
15:4	148
15:12–14	130
15:12	130
15:13	6
15:14	130
15:16ff.	95
15:16, 19	130
15:18–16:6	95

15:18–16:4	95
15:18–19	59–60
15:19	60
15:26	139
16:7–11	95–96, 99–100
16:7	139, 146
16:8, 11, 33	59
16:8, 20, 33	60
16:8	99, 135
16:11	112
16:20	59
17	3, 85, 136
17:1–2	136
17:1	106
17:2, 6, 9, 12, 24	141
17:5	59
17:6, 9, 14	59–60
17:6	136
17:9–12	136
17:12	136
17:20	136
17:21	59
17:24	136, 142
18:36	60
20:23	158
21:24–25	59
21:25	59

Acts

1:5	147
1:8	91, 96, 158
2:1–4, 33	96
2:4	146–47
2:24	80
2:33	119, 139–40, 147
2:38–39	91
4:8	146
4:12	91
4:31	146
6:3	146
7:55	146
8:22	91
10:43	133
11:16	147
11:23	101
11:24	146
13:9–10	146
13:9, 52	146
13:48	127, 144
14:3	102
14:16–17	101
14:17	103
15:11	101
17:30–31	109
17:30	46, 106
17:32	91
18:1–17	71
20:24	101
20:28	ix, 2, 6, 131, 138, 155
26:18	158

Romans

1:7	141
1:18–3:20	86
1:18–32	95
1:20	103
1:24, 26, 28	104
2:4	106, 109
2:5	106
2:16	117
3:9–20	95, 103, 127
3:21–30	145
3:21–2, 28	141
3:22	110
3:23–26	109
3:23–25	105
3:23	105, 109
3:24–25a	105, 109
3:24	101, 109
3:25	109, 116, 138
3:25b	105
3:26, 28	145
3:26b	109
3:29–30	74
4:16	101
5	69
5:1	115–16, 141, 145
5:2	150
5:6–8	3, 155
5:8, 15	x
5:8	107, 129
5:9–10	151
5:10–11	69
5:10	3, 107, 115, 138
5:10a	115
5:10b	115

Scripture Index   187

5:11	115	1:21	157
5:12	114	1:22–24	142
5:15	24, 101	2:10–16	149
5:18	46	2:14	140
6:4–8	68	6:2	151
6:4	67	6:11	145, 148
6:23	103	6:19–20	145
8	45	6:20	81
8:5–11	150	7:23	81
8:9, 11	145	8:11	17
8:9	92, 139, 148	12–14	149
8:10	147	12:13	147
8:11	151	13:12	151
8:16	150	14:24–25	99
8:19–23	110, 114, 117	14:24	99
8:23	151	15:1–5	92–93
8:28–30	130, 141, 150	15:1–2	93
8:28–29	123	15:2	93
8:28	141	15:3–5	97
8:29	128, 149, 151	15:3–4	93
8:30	141, 145	15:3	68
8:31–39	2, 6, 130, 155	15:10	101
8:31–34	130	15:13	118
8:32	45, 130–31	15:21–22	118, 151
8:34	85	15:22	147
8:35–39	130	15:24–28	112, 118–19
8:35, 38–39	130	15:28	158
9	127	15:35–50	151
9:1–5	85, 127	15:44	151
9:6–9	128	15:45	119
9:10–16	127	15:51	151
9:10–13	128		
9:11	123	**2 Corinthians**	
10:11, 13	133	1:22	149
10:14–17	157	3:18	148
10:16	57	4:4–6	144
11:29	141	4:4	127
11:33–36	107	4:15	101
13:1–3	104	5	69
13:4	104	5:5	145, 149
13:11	150	5:11–21	66, 71
15:16	149	5:11–18	93
		5:11–12	66
1 Corinthians		5:11	94
1:2	148	5:13	66
1:9, 22–24	141	5:14–15, 18–21	9, 56, 153
1:14, 18, 21, 23	93	5:14–15, 19	3, 6
1:17–2:5	107	5:14–15	x, 66–68, 71, 79, 155

5:14	67, 94
5:15	2, 67–68, 155
5:16–17	68
5:16	68
5:17	68, 143, 148
5:18–21	68–71, 82, 87, 138
5:18–20	69, 94
5:18–19	69
5:18b–19	69
5:18	69–71
5:18a	68
5:19	14, 69–71
5:20	68, 70, 94
5:21	70–71, 138
6:1	70
12:2	148
13:5	148

Galatians

1:4	3
1:15	101
2:16	145
2:20	132, 148
3:13	3, 138
3:28	148
4:6	92, 139, 145
5:16, 25	149
5:22–23	149
6:10	75

Ephesians

1:3–14	137–38
1:3–8	xi
1:3–5	128
1:3	99, 137–38
1:4–6	106
1:4–5	129
1:4	127, 132, 137, 148
1:5	123, 137
1:7	3, 137
1:9–10	112
1:10	66, 114, 137
1:11	123, 126, 137
1:13	138, 149
1:14	139, 149
1:18	141
1:22	119
2:1–10	85
2:1–3	95, 103
2:1	86, 127, 140
2:2	86
2:3	86
2:3a	86
2:3b	86
2:8–9	101
2:8	86, 144
2:11–22	58
2:14–16	116
2:16	69
3:17	148
4:30	149
5:1–2	142
5:2	131, 138, 149
5:18–21	146
5:18	146
5:21	133
5:22–33	131
5:22–24	131
5:25–27	129
5:25	ix, 2, 6, 84, 130–31, 155
5:26–27	132
5:26	131
5:27	131–32
5:28	131
5:29–30	131
6:12–17	158

Philippians

1:19	92, 139
1:29	144
2:3–8	142
2:5–11	55
2:8–11	119–20
2:8	119
2:9–11	116–17, 158
2:9	119
2:10ff.	116
2:10	120
2:11	120
2:12–13	149
3:9	148
3:14	141
4:22	75

Colossians

1:5–6	102
1:11	151
1:15–16	111
1:19–20	6, 55, 110–11
1:20, 22	69
1:20	66, 70, 111, 114, 116–17, 119, 158
1:21–23	115–16
1:21	116
1:22	116
1:23	116
1:25–29	157
1:27	148
1:28	158
2:13–15	113–14
2:14–15	138

1 Thessalonians

1:4–5	142
1:4	129
2:12	141
3:13	151
4:16	148

2 Thessalonians

2:7	104
2:13–14	129, 157
2:13	123–24, 127, 149
2:14	91, 141, 150
2:16	101

1 Timothy

1:1	72, 76
1:5	157
2:1–8	72
2:1–7	76
2:1–2	73, 85
2:1	72–74
2:2	72–73
2:3–6	72, 75–77, 87
2:3–4	75–76
2:3	72, 76
2:4–6	3, 6, 9, 15–17, 25, 28, 56, 153, 155
2:4	4, 16, 19, 22, 72–73, 90
2:5	72–73
2:6	x, 45, 72, 74
2:7	72
2:8	72
3:15	104, 158
4:8	76
4:10	3, 6, 9, 56, 72, 75–77, 79, 153, 155
5:8, 17	75
6:1–2	80

2 Timothy

1:1	72
1:9	123, 127, 141
2:10	94–95
2:21	80
3:16–17	149, 157–58
4:2	157
4:13	75

Titus

1:1–3	74
1:1	72
1:2	127
1:3	72, 76
1:7	74
1:10	75
2:1–10	77
2:9	80
2:10	72, 76
2:11–14	77, 79
2:11	9, 56, 76–77, 101, 127, 153
2:14	2, 6, 77, 84, 138, 155
3:4	72, 76
3:5	143
3:6	143

Philemon

16	75

Hebrews

1:4–14	77
2:1–8	77
2:1–4	77
2:5–9	78

2:8	78
2:9	9, 45, 56, 77–79, 87, 101, 153
2:10–18	77–79
2:10	78, 84
2:11	78
2:12	78
2:13, 14	78
2:14	114
2:15	78, 114
2:17	78, 114, 138
3:1	141
4:12	158
7:25	85
7:26–27	138
8–10	58
9:11–15	138
9:27	24
10:29	100
12:1–3	150
12:2	142

James

1:16–17	103

1 Peter

1:1–2	128
1:3–5	151
1:5	150
1:11	92, 139, 148
1:13	101
1:18	81
2:9	123
2:13–14	104
2:18	80
2:21–25	150
2:21	142
2:22–25	157
3:18	138
5:4	150

2 Peter

1:2–7	81
1:8–11	81
1:9	81
1:10	141
1:21	79
2	99–100
2:1–3	79
2:1	3, 6, 9, 46, 56, 79–83, 87, 100–101, 138, 153, 155
2:1a	79
2:13, 15, 17	79
2:20–21	100–101
2:20	82
3:3–9	109
3:9	3–4, 46, 72, 90, 106, 109, 116, 155, 158
3:15	106

1 John

2:1–2	25, 63, 66, 79, 87
2:1	85
2:2	x, 3, 6, 9, 14, 17, 19, 21, 25, 28, 32, 45, 56, 61, 63–66, 107, 138, 153, 155
3:2	151
3:4–10	113–14
3:5	113
3:8	113
3:16	107
4:2	92, 139
4:8	107
4:9–10	107, 129
4:10	138
4:11–5:3	107
4:13	145, 148
4:14	3, 9, 56, 61, 63–64, 66, 153, 155
5:1a	144
5:11–12	99

Jude

4	80
14–15	99
15	99
24	151

Revelation

1:5	119
3:12	151

5:9	2, 81, 120, 138	20:5–7	118
5:11–14	119	20:7–15	119
6:10	80	20:7–9	117
12	113	20:10	117
12:10	85	20:11–15	117
12:11	113	20:12	99
14:3–4	81–82	21–22	117, 120
19:11–20:6	119	21:22	151
20:1–10	120	22:3	151

www.ingramcontent.com/pod-product-compliance
Lightning Source LLC
Chambersburg PA
CBHW051801230426
43670CB00012B/2381